CHILDHOOD BULLYING
A Deadly Serious Matter

DR. JEAN B. HEALEY

© 2011 – DR. JEAN B. HEALEY
All rights reserved. No portion of this book may be reproduced or transmitted in any form or by any means, electronic or mechanical – including fax, photocopy, recording, or any information storage and retrieval system – without the written permission of the author, except as granted under the following conditions:

(i) A reviewer may quote brief passages in connection with a review written for inclusion in a magazine or newspaper, with written approval from the author prior to publishing.

(ii) Opinions and statements contained in this book are the original copyright of the author, unless referenced to another.

First edition published 2011
BULLYWATCH PUBLICATIONS AND CONSULTANCY
BN21603364   ABN 39083172965

DISCLAIMER
This book is not intended to provide psychological or educational advice or to take the place of such advice and intervention from other professionals. Readers are advised to consult their own doctors or other qualified professionals regarding intervention for psychological or social issues related to bullying. The author shall not be held liable or responsible for any misunderstanding or misuse of the information contained in this book or for any loss, damage, or injury caused or alleged to be caused directly or indirectly by any treatment, action, or application of any information contained in this book. This information is not intended to diagnose, treat, cure, or prevent any actions related to bullying.

National Library of Australia Cataloguing in Publication data:
Author: Dr. Jean Healey
Title: Childhood Bullying : A Deadly Serious Matter
Edition: 1st Edition
Publisher: BULLYWATCH Publications and Consultancy
ISBN: 978-0-9808458-0-8 pbk
Notes: includes Bibliographic references and index
Subjects; Bullying; Bullying- prevention;School Violence –prevention;Children –Life skills guide
Teenagers –Life skills guide
Dewey number: 302.3

To request permission for reproduction or inquire about private consulting or speaking engagements please contact:

Dr. Jean B. Healey
B.Ed., B. Spec. Ed., M. Ed. Studies., Doctor of Education
Educational Consultancy and Training
Director, Bullywatch Publications and Consultancy
(*www.bullywatch.com.au*)
Email: support @ bullywatch.com.au

Photography courtesy
John W Toplis
Model:Ms. Isabella Harvey
Cover design: MicroArts @ Elance

Contents

FOREWORD vii
BACK IN THE PLAYGROUND BLUES ~ Adrian Mitchell (1985) ix
ACKNOWLEDGEMENTS x
PROLOGUE: THE COLUMBINE LEGACY xi
- Why and How? xiv

CHAPTER 1   CHILDHOOD BULLYING: A DEADLY SERIOUS MATTER 1
Introduction 1
VIOLENCE AND BULLYING IN SCHOOLS – THE AUSTRALASIAN CONTEXT 2
VIOLENCE AND BULLYING AS ASPECTS OF EDUCATION 14
PARAMETERS OF RESPONSIBILITY 16
- Teachers and Schools 18
- Defining School Violence 19
- Family and Community Responsibility 23

CHAPTER 2   BROADENING OUR UNDERSTANDING OF
THE PSYCHOLOGY OF PEER ABUSE 27
Introduction 27
THE CONTINUUM OF PEER ABUSE 30
- Stages of Abuse and Responses 34
THE PSYCHOLOGY OF VICTIMISATION 38
BULLYING AS A 'VALUABLE EXPERIENCE'? 42
BULLYING AS ABUSE NOT CONFLICT – A FUNDAMENTAL SHIFT 45
- Differentiating Bullying from Conflict 48
DEFINING BULLYING 50
- Definitions of Bullying 51
KEY COMPONENTS OF THE DEFINITION 52
- Repeated 53
- Intentionally harmful 53
- Abusive psychological or physical actions 54

CHAPTER 3   THE INDIVIDUAL PSYCHOLOGY OF BULLIES AND VICTIMS........ 62
Introduction 62
CHARACTERISTICS OF BULLIES 63
WHAT WE KNOW ABOUT BULLIES..70
GROOMING FOR SUPPORT..71
THE GANG MENTALITY 81
- So, what is a gang?.. 83
- Factors Differentiating Gangs, Teams and Groups 86

WHAT WE KNOW ABOUT VICTIMS OF BULLYING...89
- Victims of Bullying 91

NEW PSYCHOLOGICAL PERSPECTIVES 93

CHAPTER 4   PEER ABUSE AS CHILD ABUSE 97
Introduction 97
PEER ABUSE AS CHILD ABUSE – HOW ARE THEY THE SAME? 99
- Comparing the Data.. 102

APPLYING CHILD PROTECTION LEGISLATION TO PEER ABUSE 105

CHAPTER 5   RESILIENCY – A CRITICAL FACTOR IN RESISTING BULLYING 116
Introduction 116
RESILIENCY DEFINED 117
- Differences in Resiliency Responses 121
- What Relevant Theory Underpins Resilience?....................................... 122

CHAPTER 6   PEER ADVOCACY© AS A KEY STRATEGY IN
**   BULLYING INTERVENTION 128**
Introduction 128
BACKGROUND TO THE PRACTICE OF ADVOCACY 129
Peer Advocacy© AS AN APPROACH TO BULLYING... 130
PEER PARTNERSHIP PROGRAMS... 132
SOCIAL RESPONSIBILITY... 133

CHAPTER 7   CHALLENGING THE EFFECTS OF MEDIA INFLUENCES 136
Introduction 136
VIOLENCE VIEWING AS AN INFLUENCE ON BEHAVIOUR 137
THE REALITY FACTOR 139
MODELLING AGGRESSION 142
IMPACT OF REAL VIOLENCE 147
SO, HOW IS VIOLENT BEHAVIOUR DEVELOPED? 150
DESENSITISATION 154
BUT ADVERTISING WORKS, DOESN'T IT? 155
SUMMARY 157

CHAPTER 8   CYBERBULLYING – IMPACT AND MANAGEMENT 160
Introduction 160
DEFINITIONS 162
IMPACT AND OUTCOMES 164
INTERVENTIONS 166
THE 'FREEDOM OF SPEECH' ARGUMENT 168

CHAPTER 9   THEORIES OF INTERVENTION 172
Introduction 172
IMPLICATIONS OF CONFLICT-BASED INTERVENTION 174
PREVIOUS INTERVENTIONS 183
PREVENTATIVE RESPONSES TO INTERVENTION 187
EDUCATION AS A RESPONSE TO INTERVENTION 191
- Evaluation of Programs 192

SUMMARY 192

CHAPTER 10   GETTING SERIOUS ABOUT BULLYING 194
Introduction 194
BULLYWATCH PROGRAM OF INTERVENTION 197
- Generic Interventions 197
- Individual Intervention 198

EPILOGUE 203
REFERENCES 208

List of Figures

Figure 1: CONTINUUM DIAGRAM 37
Figure 2: CHARACTERISTICS OF BULLIES 65
Figure 3: OBSERVERS' MATRIX 76
Figure 4: FACTORS DIFFERENTIATING GANGS 85

List of Tables

Table 3: Child Abuse Statistics AIHW 102
Table 4: Peer Abuse Data 103

Appendices

Table 1: Low or Very Low Gun Ownership and Rate of Gun Homicides 225
Table 2: High or Very High Gun Ownership and Rate of Gun Homicides 226
Figure5: BULLYWATCH MODEL COMPREHENSIVE INTERVENTION 227
Permissions 228

Foreword

'Three years ago I would have described myself as an outgoing, confident, fun loving teenager with a zest for life. My life changed in many ways the day I was cowardly attacked by a group of older girls on my way to drama class. Drama was my passion, the stage was where I wanted to be when I grew up. I had performed in many productions. Since my brutal beating I haven't been able to continue with my passion .Until recently I suffered from horrendous nightmares, I would wake up lost for breath because I dreamt I had been beaten or even stabbed. I cannot go back to school as I cannot be around people who look similar to my attackers. This has had a huge impact on my life. Most teenagers are spending their time with friends, at shopping centres or at the movie theatre, as for me I would rather be at home as I cannot even trust people sitting behind me. For a while I blamed myself for the attack but today 3 years later, I know that I was a victim of mean bullying. People I thought would support me asked me what I had done to deserve it, and this made it all the worse. Today I have moved on with my life and have now been successful in completing a course of study. But I will never forget the bullying.'

Victoria, 2011

'My daughter Victoria was severely beaten at the age of thirteen by a group of older girls, whilst walking between classes at school. Our lives changed forever that day. Victoria went to school a confident, outgoing teenager, full of life, trusting everyone. I miss that girl and grieve for her and who she was destined to become. My girl was taken from me on that day. Her confidence has been replaced with anxiety and self doubt, her love of life and people is now a life filled with depression and mistrust. That day was three years ago. The bullying continued and escalated. Victoria was unable to leave the house, the group of girls got bigger and more threatening. The school refused to intervene. Those girls made my daughters life hell. There was no decision to be made, we could no longer live in that town. I gave up a well paid job that I really enjoyed. When we moved, the only job that I could get was a low paid, casual job that was physically very demanding. We went from being financially comfortable to sometimes having to depend on charity.

My daughter was emotionally unable to attend school and has since completed a certificate 3 in her chosen field and is currently continuing studies at home. I have recently been employed full time in a job that I enjoy. It has taken 3 hard years to get back to something that resembles the life that we had, but life will never be the same, the carefree girl I knew has gone forever.

Please, when you see or hear a story about bullying at school, don't say, "oh well that's just a school yard scrap, it's nothing". It's so much more. That child and his or her family's lives will never be the same.

My beautiful daughter, your strength, courage, wisdom and inner beauty, makes me smile everyday.'

Sandra, 2011

Three years ago this author was approached by Victoria's mother for help with the bullying Victoria was enduring at her high school. The school response had been to organise a meeting with the abusers and Victoria in the principal's office. This is a very common but misdirected response. The abusers did not take the meeting seriously and their attitude further offended and threatened Victoria. This family was forced to move far away from their friends and familiar surroundings in order to find some peace from the abuse. Their circumstances changed for the worst but their courage was not diminished. Victoria and her mum are now much better off psychologically and socially, to their own credit.

This story illustrates the long term and devastating impact of the effects of peer abuse.

I'm sorry I couldn't be more helpful, but I am grateful for their honesty and sincerity and for allowing me to include their story in this book.

Jean Healey, 2011

Back in the Playground Blues

Dreamed I was in a school playground, I was about four feet high.
Yes, I dreamed I was back in the playground
    and standing about four feet high
The playground was three miles long
    and the playground was five miles wide

It was broken black tarmac with a fence all around
Broken black dusty tarmac with a high fence running all around
And it had a special name to it; they called it The Killing Ground

Got a mother and a father, they're a thousand miles away
The Rulers of the Killing Ground are coming out to play
Everyone thinking, who they going to play with to-day?

    You get it for being Jewish
    Get it for being black
    Get it for being chicken
    Get it for fighting back
    You get it for being big and fat
    Get it for being small
    O those who get it get it and get it
    For any damn thing at all

Sometimes they take a beetle, tear off its six legs one by one
Beetle on its black back rocking in the lunchtime sun
But a beetle can't beg for mercy, a beetle's not half the fun

Heard a deep voice talking, it had that iceberg sound:
"It prepares them for life" – but I never found
Any place in my life that's worse than The Killing Ground

~ Adrian Mitchell, 1985

Acknowledgements

I have been privileged to share the experiences and pain of a number of bullied and hurt adults, children, young people, and their concerned families. It's too little and too late and I am sorry not to have been able to prevent the hurt, but your honest and brave accounts have helped shape this work, and others will hopefully now be safeguarded because of your courage.

I am strangely grateful to the individuals who systematically bullied me for various periods of time during my adult life. You helped crystallise my understanding of many aspects of the bullying experience. I think I've won.

I wish to acknowledge the interest and concern of a number of media representatives who have consistently attempted to ensure that bullying is kept in the public consciousness and that young lives have not been sacrificed in vain. Among these are those listed as giving permission for their work to be included in this text and in particular Mr. Bruce McDougall, and the editorial and journalist team of the Today program Channel 9, among others.

Many thanks and much love to my multi-talented husband, Dr. John Toplis, for his gifted photography included in this text.

Finally and most sincerely, I wish to acknowledge the tremendous efforts of teachers, schools, young people and families who have accepted that bullying is a deadly serious matter and are constantly trying to protect our kids.

My thanks to all of you

Dr. Jean Healey

Prologue

THE COLUMBINE LEGACY

One of the most devastating events to occur within the parameters of education in recent times was the massacre on April 20th, 1999 between 11.17 am and 12.05 pm (Jefferson County Sheriff's Report, 2000) at Columbine State High School in Colorado, USA, when thirteen students and staff were murdered and a further twenty-four people were wounded. Eric Harris and Dylan Klebold – reputedly bullied over a long period-that day became responsible for the worst mass killings of school children in America's history.

One needs to ask: Is peer murder the ultimate manifestation of bullying? Is suicide the most extreme outcome of peer abuse? What will it take to ensure that society now begins a formal process of determining the shared parameters of responsibility and commit seriously to the eradication of childhood bullying? In relation to abusive behaviours towards peers, the actions of these young murderers are without question, the most extreme ever recorded. Harris and Klebold were seeking revenge and power and enjoying the domination their weapons afforded them as they gunned down their school mates, with a total lack of empathy for their plight. All the indicators were there – that this was a grotesque manifestation of peer abuse at its impossible worst.

The plan was simple and lethal. On the morning of the massacre, the pair placed two 9-kilogram gas bottles – the type usually attached to a substantial Australian barbeque – in the crowded school cafeteria, wired to detonate at 11.17 am. Amazingly or coincidentally or quite deliberately this procedure was undertaken during the seven minutes the janitor took to change the video-tape in the security camera in the cafeteria. The bombs, inside duffle bags, were not on the previous tape but were visible at the start of the tape for April 20th.

One student later recounted how she had tried to move one of the bags aside with her foot but being unable to budge it stepped over it instead. They then returned to their vehicles, parked apart from each other, yet strategically located opposite the cafeteria exits to ensure their gun blasts would kill any students who survived the bombs and who came running out of the cafeteria. Both cars were also wired with explosives as a suicidal precaution. They were in possession of nearly one hundred pipe and other bombs inside their school bags, as well as a substantial cache of firearms including an automatic Tech 9 which holds thirty bullets. However, the cafeteria bombs did not detonate as planned.

The massacre had begun badly. They must have communicated the need to change their plans by mobile phone as they both left their cars and headed for the school entrance at about 11.20. Here Harris removed and discarded his trench coat revealing his assault rifle and both began their short careers as multiple murderers. Rachel Scott was killed as she ate her lunch on the lawn with Richard Castaldo, who became a paraplegic on that day. Several bullets remain in his body even now. A Columbine legacy. Five more students were shot outside the cafeteria exit and Daniel Rohrbough was killed at close range by Klebold before the murderers entered the school to continue their deliberate and calculated onslaught. They stalked their victims through the school corridors and cafeteria.

At 11.30 they entered the school library where fifty-six students and four staff including two teachers were located and attempting to protect themselves and each other from the killers they knew were coming up the hall. School libraries are traditionally the safest places in any school and the place where victims of bullying and rejection often seek and find refuge. But not today. During their seven-and-a-half minutes of slaughter in the library, Harris and Klebold stalked, uncovered hiding under desks and behind furniture and deliberately killed ten of their school mates as they begged for their lives. They were shot at point blank range after being asked if they wanted to die. They seriously wounded a further twelve students.

A wounded teacher managed to hide under the checkout desk and maintain an open phone connection to 911 so that all events in the library were recorded. Harris and Klebold left the library briefly but returned at 12.05 when each ended his own life by a gunshot wound to the head in a final act of awful partnership. At post-mortem, neither was found to have any history or evidence of illegal drugs use, so it must be assumed that their actions were undertaken in a clear and focused state of mind. The term often used for this is 'cold blooded'.

The rampage appeared random until investigations uncovered the extent of planning and deliberation that had been undertaken over at least a twelve month period. In that time their school mates, teachers and parents had ample opportunity to discover their conspiracy and perhaps initiate intervention if they had only heeded the many clues and warning signs. The problem of identification of their intent was evidently masked by their apparent 'normalcy' in attending school, participating, staying out of trouble there, planning for college and any number of other expected indicators of an unremarkable life plan. So what indicators were there that were missed or disregarded which could have pointed to what was about to unfold?

Both young men had expressed their hatred for peers because of being bullied and excluded from 'so many fun things'. They were able to articulate their hatred and their passion for destruction using the contemporary medium of video. Five videos were produced in the basement of Harris' home in the early hours of the morning in the weeks just prior to the massacre. These were skills they learned at school. Their video teacher, of course, was never aware of the use to which his excellent teaching was to be put. These young men were not school dropouts or school failures. They did not present as having special educational needs, nor did they challenge and defy teachers in class as one might expect of such troubled and disturbed young men. In all probability they continued to attend school because it was, on the whole, a positive experience even given the peer rejection they refer to in their diaries. They needed to belong even though this status was, at best, marginal. They were apparently seen as members of a loosely-affiliated group – by no means a 'gang' – called by observers 'the Trench Coat Mafia' because of their penchant for wearing full-length trench coats to school. They took part in school productions, did their homework and in Klebold's case planned to go to college. They also attended the senior prom after-party together with school mates they were planning to kill.

Were Eric Harris and Dylan Klebold insane murderers, or misguided youths searching for identity? Did each inherit a genetic legacy that meant their fate was sealed at birth? Or did the taunting by peers fuel their anger and instil a sense of deprivation which they directed into violence?

Both were senior students who had completed their high school education and were three weeks from graduation. They had both undertaken the whole of their secondary education at Columbine High School. This meant there had been six years of contact with teachers and school mates; six years of relatively unremarkable existence and achievement, but also six years of being seen as 'weird'; six years of rejection by peers and six years during which to develop grudges against almost everybody there. By all accounts they attended regularly, engaged in subjects they seemed to enjoy and developed reasonable academic skills. Harris even quoted Shakespeare in his diary – "Good wombs hath borne bad sons", discovered after his suicide[1]. For those left behind these questions will never be fully answered. For those of us responsible for the future in education, they must.

Why and How?

So what is the legacy Columbine has left us? What have we learned from this tragic event which can guide our future practice in intervention with violent and abusive young people here in Australia?

These were high school students who were able to plan and execute the awful proceedings while in constant contact with dedicated teachers, normal peers, devoted parents and as members of a society which has much previous experience with school massacres.

We also have several incidents described later which demonstrate that students here can and do plan assaults and abusive activities while at school. What were the clues and the indicators in Columbine? They were there, they were obvious but they were overlooked, misinterpreted and not followed up. Nobody expected them – not their teachers, not their school mates and not their parents, even in a country such as America, with a notorious reputation for killings on school premises. Could it be that the indicators of pending violence would be missed here? How can young people develop such violent dispositions and deadly intentions towards their peers without anyone in daily contact with them realising their plans? Access to means and access to victims, both critical elements in such incidents are available to Australian school students in the same measure

---

[1] Information and facts provided here from the Jefferson County Police report, 2000 and the Columbine Review Commission report 2000

as at Columbine. Our schools are open to the community and allow generally free access and movement by students, teachers and the community inside school grounds, as we expect in a free society.

The possession of multiple weapons and bombs went largely undetected and unnoticed. The Columbine Review Commission Report handed down two years later (CRC, May2001) identified the lack of action of the part of the local sheriff as a key contributing factor in the event, since so many clues and indicators were ignored. The discovery of a pipe bomb at Harris' home and directions how to make them found on his computer, should have precipitated a search of his home where numerous other such bombs would have been detected. Instead they were taken to the school that day. Threats against other students made on Harris' website and their reputation for having 'violent and suicidal tendencies' did not apparently alert police or anyone else to the need for vigilance. Their previous encounters with police were never followed up. The need for increased supervision and a requirement for them to meet specific directives were never established. It begs the question, what exactly would it take for those in authority to become seriously alarmed and initiate intervention?

The event requires an examination of a number of salient psychological, social and educational factors, which establishes relevance to our culture.

The sociopathic mental states of these young men appear to have been undetected. Whose responsibility was it to monitor their mental health and provide therapeutic intervention? By some reports Eric was the leader and Dylan the half-hearted follower on the day (Cullen ,2009).These individuals were apparently obsessed with firearms and bomb-making, but despite bombs being shared with friends and discovered by Harris' father no intervention was put in place. Could any level of supervision have interrupted the secretive collection of an expensive and lethal cache of legal and illegal weapons and bombs over a year long period?

What level of supervision did the parents feel the need to provide in any case to near-adult sons whom they did not see as challenging or resistant or very much trouble? Parents, Wayne and Cathy Harris and Tom and Susan Klebold have had to live with the unspeakable nightmare of their sons' actions for over ten years now. In that time, no doubt, they have questioned their own level of responsibility for supervision, vigilance, authority and connectedness in the family lives of these young men. It is a relationship which came under scrutiny after the discovery of the weapons purchases, bomb-making equipment at their homes and threatening videos made in their basements.

We now know that the weapons were purchased with the aid of older friends or from older acquaintances with money both boys earned undertaking legitimate work at a pizza parlour. (Kass,2009) Prosecution for any measure of responsibility was not applied to the family members who were closest to, yet so far removed from the lives of these young men. Was nobody anywhere paying attention? Preventive strategies could possibly have been put in place at the home, school, community, state or federal levels to deter their actions had anybody seen the need as a result of their, at times, overtly aggressive and threatening behaviour. How does tolerance for such behaviour develop in a community? Why didn't anyone see the need for protective intervention? The National Rifle Club of America, as well as many other US citizens, seem to believe people like Harris and Klebold have the social, legal and moral right to own the weapons used to destroy their community on that day. How does the collective moral attitude of a society reach such conclusions and ignore the obvious results?

At the school level, the appearance and demeanour of the murderers as members of a strangely attired group seemingly went unnoticed or unchallenged by school authorities. Is this level of tolerance for individuality acceptable given the clearly threatening message such attire is meant to give? It is unthinkable that such attire would be tolerated in the Australian school system, or that such an appearance in a local school yard here would be left unchallenged. So what indicators would we need to identify similarly disturbed individuals? Both students complained of being victimised and an examination of the processes and procedures in place to deal with reports of bullying or peer abuse may indicate the level of commitment of the school to intervention. Was their experience of bullying given adequate attention and were they really victims as well as perpetrators? Could the school have intervened when Klebold wrote an essay describing a similar siege, in the months prior to the attack?

The school was criticised by the Columbine Commission for failing to act on the essay, on reports of bullying and on the 'code of silence' which students maintained in defiance of teachers. Is this what sustains bullying and abuse in Australian schools? Individual intervention with each at the school may have uncovered their distorted thinking and terrorist plan, but they apparently did not fit the profile or meet the established criteria for such an educational intervention. How do we assess those needs?

The moral, psychological, and social significance of this event precipitated an unprecedented national and international response, and resulted in a critical re-evaluation of social values, rights and responsibilities in the USA and beyond. The Columbine Review Commission was assembled to produce a report which would recommend policy changes to prevent the recurrence of such a tragedy. A dozen shootings in schools around the country in recent years must also have provided information on which to base intervention. Gun ownership laws have even been re-assessed in some local counties across America. The author personally witnessed the permanent dismantling of a Walmart gun and ammunition counter display in Michigan State on August 1st 2006, in direct response to public demands. It is interesting to note, however, that Australia has one of the highest levels of gun ownership in the world (see tables in appendix[2]) yet also one of the lowest rates of homicide by gunshot. Actual gun ownership, then, may not be the critical factor.

Columbine is not isolated from the rest of the world. American cities like this one are on our screens everyday. While there are certainly cultural idiosyncrasies in American society which are baffling by our estimation, we cannot adopt a self-satisfied attitude which resists the possibility that such events could happen here. Columbine has provided an important body of evidence by which to analyse and scrutinise our own preparedness for unanticipated violence and to assess the parameters and limitations of educational intervention in extreme peer abuse in Australasia.

The Columbine legacy demands vigilance of us all. It indicates a desperate need for assuming and sustaining responsibility in dealing with troubled young people. It directs us to pay greater attention to detail, and to have the courage to challenge, intercept and prevent major events which may be indicated by

---

[2] Tables derived from data in Greenwood, C. (2000).Data based on information provided in the report by the Economic and Social Council, Commission on Crime Prevention and Criminal Justice, presented to the Secretary General of the United Nations, 1999

suspicious behaviours. Currently, our practices in the management of peer abusive behaviours although well-meaning, are disjointed and uncoordinated. How can we reconcile this given the extreme nature of this event? Could peer abuse escalate to peer murder here? Are the suicides which occur as an outcome of peer abuse now merely a precursor to more violent incidents? Australia cannot isolate itself from the rest of the world in this regard.

All the evidence points to an urgent need to start taking bullying for what it really is – *A DEADLY SERIOUS MATTER.*

1 A Deadly Serious Matter

Introduction

In order to understand the complex social, psychological and educational implications of serious childhood bullying it is important to firstly understand the young people for whom it has become a lifetime challenge, the environments in which it secretly and dangerously occurs and the major motivations of the abusers. This text examines a broad range of factors seen to have a major impact on sustaining peer abusive behaviour, neglecting victims and continuing to underestimate the possible deadly consequences of what was formerly seen as merely a childhood nuisance. The text examines the broader social context, the psychology of peer abuse, the motivations of bullies and the responses of their victims. There is an introduction to several new perspectives and theories which assist in establishing bullying as the greatest challenge to child safety of this era. This presents a firm foundation for the introduction to a comprehensive approach to intervention which is discussed in detail in the BULLYWATCH Program text (www.bullywatch.com.au).

The purpose of the discussion in this text is to clarify, explain and elaborate on current understandings about bullying, but to also challenge and reject certain accepted notions and offer newer interpretations which can move us forward in our quest to overcome the awful toll now rising steadily, of young people for whom the abuse became too much. All of the work here is underpinned by a program of research and review over many years, as well as the practical application of intervention for schools and teachers and a close working bond with severely effected victims of bullying and their families.

Intervention in bullying must be comprehensive, evolutionary and transformative. No individual involved in such intervention should emerge unchanged for the better. That is the focus and mission of the BULLYWATCH

Initiative and if one young life is saved as an outcome of supportive intervention or one abuser reformed by the remedial emphasis, then the mission is accomplished.

VIOLENCE AND BULLYING IN SCHOOLS — THE AUSTRALASIAN CONTEXT

The level of violence currently evident in schools in Australasia in no way approaches the death and injury toll in other places worldwide and probably never will. However, we need to understand why and what maintains our relatively secure educational environment so that currently effective management and organisational structures and processes can be identified and strengthened. The level of bullying, however, is on a par with other countries and remains the greatest challenge currently for contemporary educators. We need to examine the full spectrum from individual to systems approaches to establish a comprehensive response to the problem. There is a diminishing feeling of security and events currently occurring indicate a need for urgent analysis and intervention.

Several case-studies serve to illustrate aspects of the phenomena of violence and bullying in Australasian schools, as many questions remain unanswered with regard to responsibility and effective responses. The article by *Kara Lawrence (2008)*, demonstrates the type of invasive attack now being experienced in schools which demand a serious community response. Teachers are not trained to manage these events and the gaps in their professional preparation are becoming more evident as such incidents continue to be reported.

The article by *Elder and Krien (2004)* expresses an opinion that attempts to diminish the violence of the 'schoolyard' as insignificant, while explaining that these major events-'youth battles' – including the amputation of limbs, actually have very insignificant origins, relative to the outcomes. The journalists are right to stress the seriousness of the outcomes, but 'schoolyard spats' are a common element in the most severe forms of peer violence today. It is valuable to highlight these events and ensure the community is aware and responsive.

Chapter 1 — A Deadly Serious Matter

The Daily Telegraph – *April 12, 2009, 12:00*

By Kara Lawrence

IT was the start of a typical school week at Merrylands High School on Monday morning with the school community gathering for assembly. About 750 students and their teachers were in the school quadrangle.

While the school has security fencing, the gates were open for students who were running late. But at 8.50am, chaos erupted when five boys aged 14 to 16 dressed in jeans and hooded jumpers stormed the assembly, making threats with baseball bats, machetes and a samurai sword.

School principal Liliana Mularczyk yelled out "lock-down" – and the teachers quickly ushered their students inside classrooms. The gang of boys pursued them, searching for a student over a perceived slight said to be about one of their cousins. Using their weapons, they smashed their way through glass windows to gain access to the classrooms. Two teachers and seven students – three of them female – were injured after being assaulted and cut by flying glass.

And when police stormed the school six minutes after the original attack, the attackers – four of whom were of Pacific Islander background and one of Middle Eastern origin – showed no fear. The youths, who are associated with a Guildford-based gang known as Gee40, laughed while in police custody and claimed there was more to come in their reign of terror.

The Sunday Age, Melbourne – *April 18, 2004*

Reporters John Elder and Anna Krien

The truth behind youth battles

Most gang fights are basically overblown schoolyard spats,

When it came off and flew into the grass, nobody knew it was a hand, except perhaps the young man who'd lost it.

It was chaos in the Fitzroy Gardens at that moment: everybody screaming and chopping and slashing, all of them out of their minds with fear, and with desperation to not get hit by the blades.

And then they noticed the man sitting in the grass with his back to the madness, nursing his arm. Then they saw him running off into the night. Soon after, his boys followed him, throwing their weapons at the enemy as they departed.

And so came another headline story about Asian gangs going at it with swords and machetes (and steel bars pulled from supermarket trolleys), the word being it was all about some kind of "payback". And once again the wild doings of ethnic youth seemed so mysterious and threatening to society at large.

The pathetic truth, as told to *The Sunday Age* by participants of various battles around town, is that most of the fights are basically overblown schoolyard spats. A wild brawl between African and Asian teenagers in Richmond three years ago was over a girl. About the same time, a series of armed battles between East Europeans and Africans in the western suburbs - including school and home invasions of spectacular violence - were in part over teenage love rivalry, wounded pride and street pecking order.

The article by Saffron Howden refers to high school bullying, and the fate of Alex is described. He was a high school student surrounded by peers, teachers and others who, if asked, would probably be able to quote the school's anti-bullying policy and mission. *It didn't work for Alex.* Stated policy in and of itself is worthless as either an indicator of commitment or of safety in a school. This is one of the sad but gradually dawning realities of the world of peer abuse. As with problems in society as a whole, simply stating an intention to reject bullying behaviour or activity does nothing to prevent or interrupt its commission. Policy needs to be part of a comprehensive intervention as described further in this text, but is possibly the least effective element of all prescribed components.

Alex was failed by his community and finally, 'when no hope was left inside' (*Don McLean, 1971*) took his own life in what can be called 'precipitated retaliation' (see *Figure 1*, page 49), whereby a violent response is the only avenue the victim can see as a solution to the problem. What risk assessment strategies are available to schools and parents to determine the stage of despair the abused individual has reached, assuming they are aware of the situation? What resources can be put in place to ensure Alex's lonely end does not happen to another child or young person?

Sydney Morning Herald

High-school bullying drove teen to suicide
SAFFRON HOWDEN

Tragic death of bullied boy Alex

14-year-old Alex Wildman took his own life after being failed by an education system that couldn't protect him for bullies.

A fortnight before his mother found him dead in the family garage on a damp winter's morning in 2008, Alex Wildman confided to a school friend: "It's getting too much. I want to commit suicide."

He was 14 years old.

For at least four months at Kadina High School in Lismore, Alex was physically and verbally bullied, threatened with violence via online social networking sites and taunted and ostracised by his peers. During a 10-day inquest at Ballina in October, the court heard he was called a "mono nut", a "faggot", a "dickhead", and a "cheeky c---". The findings were handed down at the Coroner's Court in Glebe yesterday.

One student wrote on MySpace: "He's such a dickhead and I hope he dies in a hole." Seven days before Alex died, another wrote: "I'm only gonna keep bashing him till he learns hey [sic] . . . so let Romeo know that he better watch out."Alex was "bashed" three times in the week before he committed suicide – the final time on school grounds in full view of a group of students.

The assault was recorded on a spectator's mobile phone for distribution designed to "humiliate" Alex. But it was deleted by Kadina's then-deputy principal, Bradd Farrell, before it could be shown to police, or Alex's parents.

Less than 48 hours later, on July 25, he was dead.

These experiences played a "significant role" in the boy's decision to end his life, Deputy State Coroner Malcolm MacPherson said yesterday.

Policies designed to protect students from bullying at Kadina "failed" in Alex's case, he said.

Until shortly before his death, apparently not one teacher had any idea it was happening until [two days before his suicide]," Mr. MacPherson said.

The coroner said Kadina's "confusing and unclear" posters outlining anti-bullying procedures reflected "a more general problem in NSW schools".

Among his nine recommendations, Mr. MacPherson said the Education Department should employ a full-time counsellor at schools with 500 or more pupils. He said the department should also provide clear advice about police involvement in the event of harassment by students.

Alex's mother, Justine Kelly, and his stepfather, Bill Kelly, sat quietly in court yesterday.

The article by Margaret Burin (below) highlights the activities of the bereaved parents of Allem Halkic and suggests a number of useful interventions which could contribute to the safety of abused individuals. Holding an awareness day, acting as a support group, raising awareness and concerns about cyber bullying and looking to the community for more responsibility could all contribute to addressing the issue of serious bullying.

The Werribee Banner – *4 March, 2009, 3:00am*

BY MARGARET BURIN

Death highlights trauma of cyber bullying

THE parents of an Altona Meadows teenager who took his life last month have held an emotional suicide awareness day at West Gate Park. About 200 people attended the meeting on Saturday to tackle two key issues that Allem Halkic's parents say resulted in his death - cyber bullying and the lack of public safety barriers on the West Gate Bridge.

"We as parents thought, even though our son is gone, we have to help other families in terms of the bullying and the West Gate Bridge," Allem's mother, Dina Halkic, said.

"We need to do something so we can save other kids that are in the same situation, and bullies themselves can hear what they can do, because they're going t o have to carry this for the rest of their lives."

Mrs Halkic said networking sites such as *MySpace* should advertise Helplines for young people who were being abused online.

The article by Sue Bramwell and Deidre Mussen in the *Auckland Star* highlights the awful impact of secretive text bullying on a very vulnerable young person. In the early hours of a rainy morning on February 18th 2003 a 16 year old youth in Auckland, New Zealand stepped off a cliff into the Oamaru Harbour. He had been the victim of continuous text-messaging taunts over an extended period of time and decided his life would never be normal. He had congenital neurofibromatosis which was gradually disfiguring his face and this was the main focus of the taunts and abuse he endured from peers, to which he eventually succumbed that night. Use of private and personal phone messaging is becoming a high impact and devastating means of bullying for young people, and for victims it seems almost impossible to escape its impact

We need to consider:

- What restrictions or legislative interventions can or are being put in place to deter this form of bullying and whose responsibility is it to monitor and intervene in such acts? Does this form of bullying occur within school hours and environments and if so, is the school responsible for deterring the activities? If not, what are the true parameters of school responsibility? When does such an incident become a community concern and responsibility? Even more importantly, what level of responsibility can internet and communications providers be expected to accept when serious harm is being perpetrated by their products?

- Can empathy be taught to young people? Can resiliency be taught? Can young people be encouraged and trained to advocate for each other rather than contribute to the destruction of their peers? The utter tragedy of the suicide of Daniel, described above, highlights the extreme impact of peer abusive behaviour and the lethal outcome for those forced to endure cruel and vicious taunts from unthinking peers whose only concern seems to have been to raise their own status within their peer group.

We must ensure:

- Young people are educated about their responsibilities to others in terms of interpersonal interactions. We can no longer insist on a 'no blame'ideal whilst we attempt to teach young people to behave appropriately and with responsibility. By the teenage years empathy, tolerance and responsibility should already be embedded in interpersonal relationships but for young people whose behaviour can lead to such tragic outcomes, there is an urgent need for intensive behaviour training. It is too late after the event to notice that some young people do not understand *the impact of their behaviour and communications.* As teachers and parents it is a serious responsibility to ensure that behaviours indicative of this level of cruelty, disconnectedness and rejection are identified and addressed in a comprehensive manner before more tragedies occur.

Why are teachers and parents so reluctant to name bullying for what it is? Why are we so concerned for the 'reputation' of the violent or abusive individual at the expense of the victim? Is it that we really do think that victims ought to be able to 'get on with it' and 'get over it' with no supportive intervention? We need to seriously evaluate what it is we see as the parameters of our responsibility and contribution to the development of appropriate socialisation of young people.

> **ANOTHER CASE** in recent years in Australia involved an adolescent whose experiences of bullying had led to hospitalisation from school on three separate occasions.
>
> His principal offered to lock to him in a classroom as a means of 'protection' when he was asked to intervene.
>
> This young man came across his tormenters as he entered a busy shopping mall. While inside the complex he bought a set of kitchen knives, ostensibly to give to a friend who was an apprentice chef, but in all probability to also provide himself with some protection from an anticipated attack. As he was approached by the bullies outside the mall he used one of the knives to stab and seriously wound the leading tormenter, whose taunts he had endured over many years. He ultimately received a conviction and a suspended sentence.
>
> Not long thereafter he successfully undertook litigation against the state Department of Education authorities for failing to provide a safe place in which to undertake his education since he had been forced to leave high school before completing his education as a direct result of the abuse he endured.[3]

We need to know:

- What are the likely long-term effects of his abusive experiences and his violent retribution?
- What support and counselling could have been provided to ensure he had protective structures in place to avoid further victimisation?
- What more could parents do to ensure the safety of their son at school, other than notify and continue to notify authorities that the abuse was occurring?

---

[3] The facts of this case were made available to the author by the barrister acting for the victim in order that the author could provide an expert witness report for litigation ;access to the Police Report (1998) and other documentary evidence was made available.

- What evidence is there that he demonstrated resilient and resistant behaviours which were ignored or not supported at the school level?
- Why were his tormenters allowed to have continuous access to this young man, despite severely beating him on a number of occasions?
- Does the duty of care embedded in the child protection legislation under which teachers are widely mandated to report all forms of abuse, apply to peer abuse or bullying?
- What could the school, the teachers and his peers have done to alleviate the victimisation of this young man, assuming they were motivated to do so?
- What level of intervention in bullying in schools will provide the best protection for all community members?

> **ON MONDAY** 21st of October, 2002 two students were shot and killed and a further five students and staff were wounded by another student, Huan Yun Xiang, in their tutorial room at a university in Australia.
>
> He was stressed at having to give an oral presentation, aware his English language skills were inadequate, so this reportedly frustrated loner decided that violence and death were the only answer to his problems.
>
> This incident represented the first recorded deaths in an Australian institution of education at the hands of a solitary gunman.
>
> In terms of the educational context, however, it is difficult to determine clear and unequivocal indicators that such violent urges were developing and a procedure by which the risks could be adequately assessed and addressed.

We need to ask:

- How skilled are educators at detecting such indicators and should their training include basic risk assessment competencies?
- What level of responsibility can educators reasonably be asked to assume for monitoring the mental health of their students, assuming indicators are present?
- What authority does an educator have to recommend or require mental health intervention should they detect or suspect the need in a student?
- What supportive interventions can and are provided for struggling and failing students, and what is their impact in terms of prevention of such events?
- How resilient is such an individual and how could he be assisted? Is murder the most extreme manifestation of bullying?

> ON APRIL 3, 2003 a jilted male secondary student used a crossbow at point blank range to critically wound his ex-girlfriend and another student in an incident in a northern New South Wales high school ("Cross-bow Tragedy," 2003).
>
> He had allegedly been rejected by her and brought his crossbow into the school to inflict a cautionary wound, though not to kill her. The bow entered her back and exited her chest, lodging in the legs of another student nearby. He also threw a Molotov cocktail against a wall to reinforce his point, but the victims survived both attacks.
>
> In his defence, he claimed to have been severely bullied over a long period of time, though not by his victim. He was sentenced to nine years in prison.
>
> In analysing such an event, consideration must be given to the question of what it is that convinces a young person that the answer to his problems lies in the destruction of another person, physically and psychologically.

We need to be informed:

- What was the state of the mental health of this young man that he would decide to undertake this act, and why didn't anybody notice his disturbed state?
- The crossbow had been purchased over the internet at a cost of over $1000. How does an adolescent procure such weapons?
- What sanctions are in place to restrict access to the purchase of weapons by young people and how does a young person procure the funds?
- How can such access be unsupervised or unnoticed by family and friends?
- How was this student able to carry such a weapon into the school without being challenged or detected?
- Why was he able to produce the weapon and use it in the school yard without the intervention of peers or a supervising teacher?
- What protocols were in place at the school to respond to the event in a timely and effective manner?
- Was the alleged bullying a cause of the incident or merely his excuse?

The suggestion that violence of this magnitude could ever occur in our education systems has often been met with derision and disbelief. Nevertheless, Australia has now joined the USA, Great Britain and Germany as societies in which the sanctity of the school as a safe haven for learning has been breached forever. What factors do such events have in common? Is it possible to prepare for, or to prevent further such episodes in our schools? What precipitating factors within the individual or the community result in such destructive forces and deadly acts? Is it possible to determine the origins, the parameters and effective interventions for violence and bullying in our schools?

VIOLENCE AND BULLYING AS ASPECTS OF EDUCATION

The World Report on Violence and Health (World Health Organisation, 2002) clearly demonstrates the pervasive significance of this issue and notes a number of alarming statistics. Each year over 1.6 million people world-wide lose their lives to violence and young people, aged 10 to 19 years old, are at the greatest risk of a violent death in modern society, and are most at risk from each other. Furthermore, young men are twice as likely (14% of their deaths) as young women (7% of their deaths) to meet a violent end and are implicated in 90% of violent incidents in this age group.

Nevertheless, placing violence in the context of education seems at first to be a contradictory notion. Traditionally, places of learning have been viewed as safe and inviolate, notwithstanding the equally familiar tradition of the school bully. It is reassuring that schools are still comparatively secure environments where most students on a daily basis, arrive safely and experience no aggression. Yet in recent times these previously polarised concepts are more frequently discussed in the same context. Violence, in the form of mass murder of students and staff in schools, has been increasingly reported, particularly in the USA, and in the past decade, addressing school bullying has become a priority for researchers and policymakers throughout the world.

The occurrence of violent events both in Australian and in international educational contexts serves as an impetus to many researchers to continue to develop proactive solutions to the psychological and physical violence which apparently is ever present in schools. Violence and abuse is increasingly being conceptualised as a component of the learning environment and education providers have begun to noticeably extend their efforts to include methodologies, practices and policies to address these issues. Given the contemporary significance of this issue the purpose of this discussion is to attempt to contribute to international efforts to develop practical strategies to address school violence and bullying as an education issue of immediate concern.

Students manifesting a range of problematic behaviours, linked to psychological and intellectual disorders in mainstream and specialist classrooms within a range of education systems serve as the motivation to create empathetic and realistic interventions. The presence of aggressive behaviours that may characterize the conditions of emotional and conduct disorders, childhood and adolescent psychiatric illnesses, sociopathic conditions and juvenile criminology are all manifested in formal educational settings, not as the norm of behavioural interaction, but certainly with great enough frequency to challenge teachers and educational authorities. Every mass murderer has at some point been a member of an educational community. Many teachers have worked in close proximity to such individuals and have provided possibly the only positive and rewarding experiences in the lives of individuals who could quite reasonably be described as social misfits. Education may have the power to change, and to influence, the life outcomes of such people. Resolving violence and bullying through education is the key mission of contemporary intervention.

Childhood bullying, by definition, occurs during the early years of life from five to eighteen when most children and young people are in school. The focus here, therefore, in discussing childhood bullying will necessarily relate to experiences both in and out of school, the relationship between the two environments and the possibility of collaboration between families and school personnel.

Despite the shared connections between bullies and victims, their teachers and families however, collaborative intervention is not always possible. All participants in the bullying phenomenon have both shared and individual responses and their partnerships are more socially constructed than selected. Nevertheless, the players are united in the drama by destructive forces and guidance and support is needed by each. Current understandings of the bullying phenomenon need close examination before prospective interventions can be considered.

PARAMETERS OF RESPONSIBILITY

Management of abusive peer behaviour amongst children and young people is a shared responsibility for parents, schools and teachers and the community, at the most fundamental level. Governments must also take their share of responsibility for providing the resources, structures and processes necessary to support the combined efforts of concerned individuals at all levels of society. Bullying, as has been firmly established, is a major social safety issue affecting the most vulnerable members of the community whose wellbeing is often seriously compromised. It is clear that firm parameters of responsibility need to be established for each sector and stakeholder in order for collaborative and co-operative intervention to be facilitated.

Responsibility for serious peer abuse is based in the actions, intentions, beliefs, attitudes, directives and responses of:

- The primary abuser
- The family of the primary abuser
- The peers and other people who engage with the primary abuser
- The educational environment within which the primary abuser usually engages in the behaviour
- The social environment or community within which the primary abuser operates
- The macro-system environment including government policy and legislation

Clearly, the initial responsibility for abusive behaviour rests within the individual. Abusive behaviour is a preferred and selected form of interaction which is reinforced, condoned, ignored and even admired by various sections of the community. Given that their deviant behaviours are exhibited within a whole of society framework, however, the level of responsibility can be apportioned across a range of culpable sectors.

The parameters of responsibility are therefore widely spread, and it comes as no surprise that some are more willing than others to accept and address their own responsibility for the continuation of the problem. Least likely to accept responsibility are the primary perpetrators, and most likely are teachers and schools. It is suggested here that the parameters of responsibility for serious and sustained peer abuse need to be carefully defined, documented and accepted for each sector, if interventions are to be effective. An examination of some of these contributory factors will assist our understanding of why bullying is sustained and escalates over time.

Teachers and Schools

Abusive student behaviour in schools has been an issue of concern to varying degrees over the past decade or longer. In more recent times the emphasis has shifted to bullying as the key behaviour of concern, and much academic and educational time and effort has been expended attempting to devise and apply appropriate interventions for management.

The behaviours of concern discussed in this text represent the extreme end of the bullying and abuse continuum (see *Figure 1*, Continuum of Peer Abuse, Healey, 2010). The discussion articulates concerns for the extreme outcomes of the abusive behaviours which are not currently given adequate consideration in the community. Teachers know their own limitations; schools are limited by resourcing and time constraints in relation to implementation of interventions. It is time to extend the parameters of responsibility to a much greater and more practical extent to include the broader community and government to ensure the security of schools.

While it had previously been argued that it is not possible to separate the responsibilities of the school from those of the wider community, it was successfully posited in formulating the following definition that it is imperative for the health, safety and welfare of teachers and students that precisely such a distinction is made. This definition was an attempt to acknowledge the limitations of authority, liability and expertise of school personnel in managing violence of any kind and more specifically to formalise the parameters of their involvement in intervention. In this way schools could define the parameters of their responsibility in relation to school violence and abuse and ensure the wider community accepts that they, and not teachers alone, are required to provide safe and secure environments for students and school personnel.

Defining school violence

Violence in schools was defined in the 1994 Commonwealth Government inquiry into school violence report titled 'Sticks and Stones', as follows:

> 'violence in schools refers to violent, assaultive or aggressive acts resulting from the interaction of teachers, students or school community members with each other, or with school property, which occur within normally accepted school hours and school boundaries and situations.' (JENKIN SUBMISSION, 1993).

In light of the Columbine massacre, this definition may be inadequate to describe the most serious of all abusive and violent situations, murder by a member or members of the school community. Nevertheless, what it does is define the parameters within which school violence can be examined. This is important since it confines consideration to *'within normally accepted school hours and school boundaries and situations'* and thereby eliminates community incidents which involve school students.

These distinctions were seen as necessary and resulted in setting limits confining the operational definition to within–school episodes rather than incorporating all incidents occurring on schools grounds as well as community –based or invasion incidents, as had previously been the case, for example in the Commonwealth 'Schools Australia' report 1992. Under that definition, the incidents mentioned above would qualify as violence in schools, whereas, for example, the Beslan incident in September, 2004 in Russia, whereby a terrorist gang invaded the school from outside and perpetrated mass murder within the school setting, would not.

There are reports of schools being invaded by groups or gangs from the community who have no close affiliation with the school, but who may have a target individual inside the school who they wish to assault. Attacks in school playgrounds, entry into classrooms for the forcible removal of student targets and abusive behaviour towards teachers by these gangs are not uncommon events in schools in Australia. They are rarely reported in the media. Such incidents are the responsibility of law enforcement agencies and the community must accept their responsibility for intervention.

The distinction made in the definition, therefore, is important as it devolves responsibility for prevention and protection beyond the school gate and requires the community to ensure that schools are safe locations. The protection of schools and their occupants from violence which originates and is resourced within the wider community, goes well beyond the parameters of responsibility of teachers and school administrators, and this distinction may need to be more definitively articulated as incidents occur and schools become more reliant on the protective services available within the community. Schools are not capable of managing, nor can they be expected to manage, individuals who plan and initiate major incidents which originate outside the school. Indeed, they must also be supported in their efforts to contain incidents that do fall within the above definition, and must have a school plan for such occurrences.

The incident reported (see next page) is an example of a situation which is within the community domain and is therefore within the parameters of responsibility of parents, students and other community members who may have been aware of or witnessed the incident. The incident is linked to the school by means of the headline which seems to suggest that this fight and others were organised by the school, not just by students of the school. Journalism plays a crucial role in the dissemination of factual information and keeping the community informed about current issues. It can have a positive influence on the opinions of the community if it accurately depicts situations. Bruce McDougall attempts in this article to alert the community to a phenomenon which is occurring in schools with tragic consequences. Unfortunately, the general community will often misinterpret the information and, as in this case, seek to lay blame where none is due.

Clearly, the school had no part in organising this 'brawl' and teachers have no official jurisdiction in the park. The only measure of responsibility that could be levelled at the school is if somebody there with authority knew about the arrangements and failed to act, which is obviously not the case. Indeed the use of the term 'school' is irrelevant to the reporting of this incident, which is a fight between two boys in their own time and selected location. Utterly tragic though the incident turned out to be, the school was not participant, nor culpable. This is a clear example of failure to establish, recognise or endorse the parameters of responsibility of the community rather than the school.

Crisis management plans have been developed within schools over at least the past fifteen years, but it may well now be the time to review such plans and to incorporate a wider range of responsive and preventative measures available within the broader community to ensure student and personnel safety. These would include a review and recording of access to police (federal and state), anti-terrorist squads, negotiators and specialist defence personnel in order to upgrade protective measures. It would also require an increased expectation of responsibility on the part of community members for supervision, vigilance and reporting of suspect activities within the community which may be targeted at the school or at members of the school community.

Teachers are not responsible for supervising students outside school grounds and hours except in specific designated circumstances. It must be considered possible that had members of the community taken greater measures of responsibility before the Columbine massacre, when 13 students and staff lost their lives, Klebold and Harris would not have been able to assemble an arsenal of weapons and explosive materials to use at the school.

Violence per se, in the form of physical and personal assaults has again been in the news recently as reports emerged of yet another massacre in an American education institution, this time in Virginia Tech. in April 2007. Recent reports of rising incidents of violence in schools in Australia, surprisingly now, often including violence perpetrated by females, is once again beginning to raise awareness and concern amongst educators.

The 'causes' or origins of the violence have been sought in violent video materials, lack of discipline and supervision in the home, and other social factors, but a more pragmatic analysis would consider other issues as relevant to the management and reduction of these incidents. These would include the trend towards teacher education courses in many universities being reduced to one year and behaviour management strategies and training being diminished or disregarded in favour of more curriculum-based content. Teachers are not well enough prepared, therefore, for managing challenging behaviours in school, or for predicting behaviours in order to intervene in a timely fashion. Some levels of student violence and abuse, not involving weapons, can and must be managed by teachers given appropriate management training. The violent and abusive behaviour of students towards each other and towards their teachers must now be prioritised for protective intervention approaches, particularly at the pre-service level.

The true parameters of responsibility then, for teachers and schools, resides in their responses to abusive activities perpetrated within the normal bounds of school attendance, of which they have been notified. These would of course include bullying behaviours, resulting in harm and distress, and would require a systematic and effective intervention. This is the area that now requires a comprehensive overhaul in most schools.

Family and Community Responsibility

The contribution made by family and close relatives and friends to recovery from bullying cannot be underestimated. When family members support and protect victims of peer abuse, sometimes to the extent of having to hide them from bullies and remove them from school or schools, the prognosis is much more positive. Nevertheless, some attitudes are entrenched in society and a range of views can be expressed which are unhelpful for the victim. Family members may find themselves in a position of having to defend their abused relative from unsupportive and sometimes dangerous advice given. In particular, the issue of 'fighting back' and 'sticking up for yourself' are grossly misunderstood by many who try to advise the victim. Attitudes towards peer abuse commonly diminish the seriousness of the matter. The chapter on resiliency covers this issue in more detail.

The notion that 'it takes a village to raise a child' reinforces the importance of the need for a shared, supportive approach to safety.

The principle of maintaining a fair and equitable society, at least in terms of opportunities for success and survival, must be extended as a right to all members of the society. A community which is failing to protect children and young people against abusive behaviours negates this right and is an indictment of those with the authority to intervene and establish protective interventions.

Defining the parameters of community is a first step towards defining the parameters of responsibility. Close community can be defined for the purposes of this discussion to include the immediate location, the school and neighbourhood as well as local government boundaries, and the people within those confines. It is essential that some level of community responsibility for the protection of children and young people be established formally to ensure their safety while out in the community. This particularly refers to the issues of bullying in the community. The safety of all children is the responsibility of all community members in a morally sound society.

Currently, unaccompanied children and young people may find themselves being bullied in shopping centres, parks, on public transport, public toilets, sporting venues and many other locations, with no responsible adult or organisation willing to accept responsibility for their immediate welfare. Responsibility need not be onerous and it may simply be a matter of establishing safety guidelines for distribution across a community to inform observers of bullying where and how to intervene and report their concerns to a central authority. Children and young people need to also be assured that their request for intervention and protection will not be denied as it is when community members refuse to accept responsibility.

This is never more apparent than when peer abuse occurs outside school grounds and school hours. Violence between school children, bullying and victimisation, witnessed in the community, needs to be seen as a community responsibility even when students are in school uniform. Currently, however, such incidents witnessed out in the community inevitably lead to reports to the school with the expectation that they will accept responsibility and address the issue.

Social responsibility for the impact and outcomes of serious bullying needs to be confronted and appropriate interventions established. The article by Bruce McDougall below illustrates the level of community responsibility that may well result from unprotected individuals who resort to attempted suicide in a bid to end the abuse and misery. Dakoda –Lee is now a fully dependent invalid as a direct outcome of the lack of intervention available to protect him from abusive peers. The cost to his family and the community to provide such care is far greater than any anti-bullying intervention.

There are some key elements in this commentary which have been suggested on a number of occasions in the literature (Healey, 2004) including reporting officially and providing an email address in schools to which reports can be forwarded with some measure of security for the victim.

This is not a difficult strategy to implement and therefore should be readily available in schools and notified to all students. Of course, such reports must be monitored and follow up offered to ensure student s will continue to see the service as protective and effective for managing bullying.

Bullied to suicide bid

Bruce McDougall
Education Reporter, Daily Telegraph, June 21st 2010

Brain-damaged teenager is facing life in a wheelchair

EXTREME bullying has left a teenage boy in a wheelchair unable to speak or walk and taking food and liquids through a tube to his stomach. Dakoda-Lee Stainer, 14, suffered brain damage when deprived of oxygen for more than 20 minutes after attempting to take his own life. The teen, now under around-the-clock care in priority disability housing, endured months of relentless attacks by bullies before reaching the point of despair. Friends said Dakoda had rocks thrown at him and was admitted to hospital for a head injury as the cruel bullying turned physical. On the day he tried to end it all he had been accosted by the same gang of youths on the school bus. The teen, who attended Melville High School at Kempsey, on the North Coast of NSW, was found in a bedroom at home on September 4 last year — about 13 months after another 14-year-old, Alex Wildman, killed himself at Lismore because of violent run-ins with schoolmates. Dakoda's family and friends agreed to speak about his plight in a bid to get authorities to take bullying more seriously and prevent further tragedies.

In the wake of the Wildman case, the Department of Education and Training said it would review the way in which counsellors were allocated to schools and trial a new email address in selected schools inviting people to report bullying. Dakoda's mum Theresa said yesterday: "I can't imagine what those kids [bullies] would have put him through to get him to that state. I don't know how these mongrels ate away at my boy's strength." Theresa, said her son was making progress, communicating with his eyes and by shaking. He was attempting to move his arms and legs. **"He** lost oxygen to the brain for at least 22 or 23 minutes," she said.

"When we got to hospital it took them 12 minutes to restart his heart."

Society and the close community need to accept their responsibility to intervene or accept the responsibility to rehabilitate and support such victims. Peers have a supportive role in securing the assistance of the wider community and relevant adults in intervening to protect young people from bullying, while in the community. Local government authorities may need to establish guidelines for distribution to commercial premises and other community locations such as railway stations and bus terminals. This would notify community members there of the possibility of abusive interactions between children and young people, and their responsibility to report such incidents to relevant listed authorities including the police, and to offer sanctuary to children seeking refuge from attacks.

2   Broadening our Understanding of the Psychology of Peer Abuse

Introduction

Bullying research and intervention has grown steadily over the past decade as more stories of suicides, serious physical harm and long term psychological trauma are reported in the media and online. For some years, the focus of research was to determine the extent of bullying and the personal and social characteristics of the main participants in terms of gender, age, personality, culture and location, with particular emphasis on school bullying.

Research then focussed primarily on defining the parameters of peer abuse and describing the experiences, attitudes and perceptions of the individuals involved. Who are these individuals who bully others? Are boys or girls more likely to be bullied? At what age does it commence or decline? Is there really a cultural or racist component to the behaviour? Where is bullying most likely to occur? The nature of bullying in terms of frequency, types of behaviours and the characteristics of bullies and victims have been thoroughly explored and reported. We can also describe the impact of the behaviours.

It has been established that bullying is endemic in schools in Australia and overseas with up to 20% of all students reporting bullying (Healey, 2004; Rigby, 1996). Up to 25% of boys in primary schools report being frequently bullied and 27% have engaged in physically, psychologically or verbally bullying behaviour on three or more occasions (Alsaker & Brunner, 1999; de Almeida, 1999). A surprising degree of consistency is evident in the international literature relating to bullying in high schools with an overall 12 to 18% of students reporting involvement as either a bully or victim. Bullying is reported to peak during the early years of high school, and gradually diminish as students develop a more mature sense of empathy and a willingness to support those being victimised. Furthermore, cultural, gender and age differences can be demonstrated (*Morita, Soeda, Soeda & Taki, 1999*). Most recently, research has focussed on the extended reach of bullying into the homes and lives of victims as internet and mobile phone access allow abuse to occur despite the former safety of distance and the family home. Today there is no escape from the abuse for some victims.

We now have the answers to most questions related to the behavioural parameters of bullying and the evidence is so internationally and consistently similar that the focus must turn to determining the key psychological indicators and the most effective response strategies. What have not been fully addressed in recent times are the critical psychological components of childhood bullying, and the most effective strategies for protection, remediation and comprehensive intervention.

It is timely to attempt to extend our understanding of peer abuse beyond descriptive analyses to a deeper knowledge of the psychological influences and impact of phenomenon using new explanations supported by innovative interpretations and reflection. Fundamentally, these analyses indicate the need for a new horizon of understanding in the psychology of peer abuse and paradigm shifts to accommodate new perspectives. Analysis of the behaviours and beliefs of both perpetrators and victims of childhood bullying will inform the development of new solutions for intervention.

For too long bullying has been examined within the framework of conflict instead of abuse. This critical distinction has meant that many interventions are misdirected towards dispute resolution, rather than protection and support. The focus of this work is on the abuse paradigm and appropriate interventions to address the implications of long term and high impact abuse of children by their peers, and this forms the basis of all discussion.

Additionally, the professional work of the author as a teacher and experience with the development of a broad range of specialised education programs to address the needs of young people has influenced both theory and practice in this discussion. This includes work with students having emotional and behavioural disorders in schools, psychiatric facilities, juvenile detention and high security units, as well as work undertaken with young people for whom murder, rape and attempted suicide had been elements of their recent life experience. Being in daily contact with the most difficult and destructive behaviours has informed the development of new perspectives and interventions and provided first-hand knowledge of the limitations of traditional approaches. It has also provided an impetus to discover new methods to inform successful intervention for those involved in violence and bullying in the pre-adult years.

Students professionally assisted include a young man who committed one of the most high profile and shocking rape-murders in Australia in recent times. Currently serving a life sentence with no hope of either rehabilitation or freedom, the author witnessed his behaviour in juvenile detention classrooms where his powerful and intimidating personality dominated fellow inmates and sustained his status even while still a juvenile. Observing the evolution of his bullying persona in this challenging environment was a critical source of information for the development of interventions described here.

Most recently the parents of several girls and young women have reported personally to the author the destructive and physically devastating effects of bullying at the high school level. One student, consistently bullied by peers, yet left unprotected at school, eventually ceased attending. Nevertheless her tormenters located her at a party outside school hours and used a full bottle of liquor to beat her about the head. She sustained brain damage and is currently in litigation against her former school. This raises the issue of the parameters of responsibility for protective intervention. The efforts of the school to intervene in her defence and protection will no doubt come under close scrutiny.

Another child recently brought to the attention of the author in order to secure support, was afraid to cross the school playground each morning because of the bullying to which she was subjected. The school refused to allow the mother to accompany the child to her classroom and eventually took legal action to prevent the mother entering school grounds! The child was removed to a safer environment.

These and many more examples of critical incidents and serious outcomes of the bullying experience underpin the pragmatic approaches described here. The focus of intervention is education, therapeutic and remedial programs of behavioural instruction for both bullies and their victims and includes a consideration of suitable and effective deterrents. There can be no doubt that individual interventions, such as those used in special education intervention, can be valuable in addressing the individual behavioural needs of both bullies and their victims.

Fundamentally, this text deals with serious peer abuse, its consequences and high impact for victims. The term 'peer abuse 'is often used in preference to 'bullying' since this latter term does not seem to adequately describe the real destructive process that is occurring. 'Bullies' are legitimately referred to as 'perpetrators', just as they are in other forms of abuse, and their destructive behaviours are clearly identified. The term 'victims' of peer abuse is used in preference to 'survivors' since 'survival' implies that the individual has experienced trauma and emerged from it, sometimes stronger[4]. This is often not the case with victims of peer abuse who may well carry the hurt and harm with them into adulthood, and too many of whom now, do not survive at all.

---

[4] Research undertaken by the author underpins most of this work and reference to relevant published documents can be found in the references section and throughout the text

THE CONTINUUM OF PEER ABUSE

Peer abuse differs along a continuum of severity and therefore victim responses correspondingly differ in terms of levels of distress, hurt, and eventually fear and anxiety.

The diagram in *Figure 1* illustrates the progressive severity of peer abusive behaviours, their impact on victims and the obvious need for varied levels of intervention necessary to secure the safety and psychological wellbeing of the victim. The diagram displays peer abusive behaviours along a continuum of stages of severity from milder to moderate to severe and extreme. The continuum uses accepted psychological designations of severity. The classifications 'mild', 'moderate' and 'severe' are used in the DSM IV(TR)(4th Edition,2010) to specify the level of social impairment related to psychological responses in the disturbed individual. In this analysis the designations refer both to the abusive behaviour and the responses they elicit.

MILD	refers to 'no more than minor impairment in social ... functioning'
MODERATE	refers to 'functional impairment between mild and severe'
SEVERE	refers to 'symptoms that are particularly severe ... marked impairment in social ... functioning' (*DSM –IV, 2010, page 2*)

In terms of frequency, most incidents of bullying occur in the milder region, but these nevertheless cause distress and harm to the victim. Prior to this stage there may well be unreported bullying. The implementation of a whole school or class anti-bullying intervention has been shown to precipitate reporting as the victim is assured of support, gains confidence and is able to identify and report the behaviours.

The typical types of behaviours engaged by the bully are noted at each stage, which also illustrates the range of harmful psychological and physical activities along the continuum. These include psychologically distressing communications from derogatory verbal comments then more abusive verbal insults and abuse through to sustained harassment and public denigration. The use of abusive texting to mobile phones, emails to the private email address of the victim and the use of social networking sites to publically denigrate the victim also occur along a continuum of severity and harm. Graffiti, rumours and exclusionary behaviour all contribute to the abuse.

As well, a range of increasingly destructive physical behaviours escalate from verbal threats to safety and often posturing or simulated attacks to physical intimidation such as fists held to the face, actual physical abuse such as pushing, kicking, punching and other violent actions along the continuum to beatings causing severe harm, use of weapons and as has been clearly documented, the most extreme violence towards peers. These and many other behaviours are used to intimidate and terrify the victim, and may eventually lead to the most serious consequences.

The continuum illustrates the location of the most serious incidents of peer abuse including the Columbine murders and the murder of James Bulger by older peers in the UK in February 1993.

Along the continuum of responses engaged by the victim, the correspondence to the level of victimisation is clear. The victim may initially respond with confusion and hurt feelings as they try to understand why the abuse if happening to them in particular. They may begin to resist the behaviour asking for it to cease and may reject the bully. However they will continue to attend school and demonstrate some resiliency by making a verbal report to the teacher or parent. As the bullying becomes more severe the psychological equilibrium of the victim may shift from resistant and resilient towards higher levels of anxiety, school refusal and even dropping out of school. As can be documented, however there are many victims now who simply find that all hope is gone and suicide is the only option for relief from the torment.

The victim is encouraged and trained at every stage to seek help and support and to report the incidents formally in the BULLYWATCH program, however this does not guarantee protective intervention and the bullying may well persist. For victims the most serious consequence is identified as the victim response: 'precipitated retaliation'. This occurs when the abused individual finally reaches the end of their capacity for endurance and turns on themselves or the abuser.

Suicide and murder are the most extreme possible outcomes of this mental state, as are attacks on abusers and severe withdrawal and depression. There are, as yet, no known or reported cases of victims murdering their abusers in this age group, unless the Columbine massacre is included as a response to reported bullying. There are, however, many recorded cases of precipitated retaliation incidents including attempted murder of the bully (see incident discussed page 30), numerous suicide attempts and well-documented suicide completions as an outcome of extreme peer abuse.

Although the development of severe bullying is self evident from this analysis, there is still no guarantee that the process will be recognised, accepted or acted upon within the school framework of responses. It is still very common for school principals to deny that bullying exists and to reject victim reports and distress.

Further, the continuum illustrates the escalating emotional and psychological responses that are evident in victims of peer abuse. While initially they may cope, once the abuse escalates from threats to actual harm, for example, the fear, distress and avoidance responses of the victim correspondingly escalate. This figure illustrates the increasing severity of bullying along a series of stages leading to increasing distress and impact for the victim. It must be noted, however, that the beginning point of the abuse may be far from the mild phase and bullies may well begin their abuse using more serious behaviours at the start.

Consequently, the responses of the victim may be extreme early in the interaction as they attempt to cope with the situation. The diagram indicates progressively more damaging abuse but also enables the abusive behaviour to be located if initiated at more severe levels. However, in later stages, if their resilience, reporting and expressions of distress have been ignored or dismissed, they may well begin to refuse to attend school. The most extreme response is 'precipitated retaliation' when victims respond by attacking their abuser, attempting suicide or worse.

A recent report to the author (August 2010) concerned a 13-year-old high school student, very tall for her age, being abused with graffiti, abusive texts, public denigration and rumours. She was already considering a change of school and refusing to attend school at the time of the consultation. Her bullying was initiated at the severe level, giving her no time to develop or practice resiliency. The school principal refused to accept her complaints, stating that there was no evidence of bullying at his school. She was un-supported, isolated and rejected and intervention would need to be immediate and protective to sustain her attendance at this school and provide for her mental health and wellbeing. In this case she may well be better off changing schools and starting a new education program at a more receptive location.

Stages of Abuse and Responses

STAGE 1: MILD ABUSE/RESPONSES

Most abusive peer behaviour remains in the milder portion of the spectrum in terms of intensity and comprises the frequently reported behaviours listed. Most reported incidents of bullying are milder in both intensity and frequency. The anticipated responses of victims are both psychological/emotional and functional. The psychological responses will include some distress, hurt and confusion, and the victim may attempt to resist and reject the behaviours, but they may still attend school and behave in a resilient manner. They may also make a formal verbal report to a teacher or parent about the bullying. At this stage the victim usually still expects to be supported and assisted with the problem by friends, family and school authorities.

STAGE 2: MODERATE ABUSE/RESPONSES

Many incidents of bullying are in the moderate range of severity and include the behaviours listed, which may begin to escalate from threats to safety to physical intimidation, for example showing fists, weapons etc to the victim. The bullying may initiate at this level or may have escalated from milder forms of abuse. In this case the victim is likely to respond with greater fear and distress, begin to attempt to avoid the bully, seek help from friends, family and school personnel, all of which are resilient behaviours to be encouraged and reinforced. They may also begin to take absences from school and they may report again to authorities, but if the bullying is escalating it is highly likely that these reports are falling on deaf ears and the victim remains unsupported.

STAGE 3: SEVERE ABUSE/RESPONSES

Severe abuse includes physical assault, cyber-bullying / cyberassment, public denigration through graffiti and other sustained harassment through emails, texts and verbal abuse. While there are fewer incidents at this level of intensity, the outcomes for the victim are far more serious and require intensive intervention. Victims of this level of peer abuse will become withdrawn and depressed, particularly if they believe their reports and attempts to gain protection and support are being ignored or rejected. Often, resilient victims of bullying who are assertive in reporting the abuse and seeking help are seen as dependent, inadequate and passive and the responses of those with the authority to intervene are often unsupportive and rejecting. For this reason, victims of bullying become withdrawn and depressed, refuse to attend school because of concerns for their own safety, they may request a change of school or drop out as a result of the severity of the abuse.

STAGE 4: EXTREME ABUSE/RESPONSES

Extreme incidents of peer abuse are well documented and always shock those who hear about the suicide or death of young people as a result of incidents of bullying. Nevertheless they do occur and must be considered along the spectrum of peer abuse. While these incidents are rare, they are increasing in frequency and pose a genuine threat to the sanctity of childhood and education settings. The abuser engages in extreme behaviours including beatings, spreading of rumours and private information on social network sites, stalking victims and exposing them to public humiliation. At this level of sustained abuse the victim is in severe distress, feels and possibly is, unsupported and unprotected, and may well encounter a situation whereby they feel it necessary to defend their safety by attacking their abuser, a response labelled 'precipitated retaliation' in this approach. This may or may not be a pre-meditated decision. If the abuser is encountered in a situation whereby the victim feels an immediate threat, the attack may occur spontaneously. This, of course, alters the entire abuse paradigm and places the victim in the position of perpetrator, despite the provocation they have endured. Documented incidents of attacks by abused individuals, as often occurs also in adult abusive relationships, may be termed 'precipitated retaliation' since they occur abruptly and as a response to fear. Precipitated retaliation occurs when the victim reaches the full extent of their capacity to cope with the abuse and turns on themselves or their abuser, often with tragic consequences.

A thorough description and discussion of the components of intervention in this model is continued in the publication *BULLYWATCH Programs and Resources for Dealing with Bullying* (Healey, 2010, at www.bullywatch.com.au)

Chapter 2 —Broadening our Understanding

PEER ABUSIVE BEHAVIOURS:	INCREASING SEVERITY →		SUSTAINED ABUSE
UNREPORTED BULLYING			
• Insulting verbal comments • Exclusion • Property damage • Theft • Abusive texts • Threats to safety	• Abusive verbal comments • 'Ganging up' • Extortion • Cyberbullying • Abusive emails/texts • Physical intimidation	• Sustained harassment • Graffiti • Threats in emails/texts • Cyberassment • Physical abuse	• Social network sites used • Rumours • Stalking • Public emails/texts • Public denigration • Beatings • Weapons used • Murder (Columbine; Bulger)
STAGE 1	STAGE 2	STAGE 3	STAGE 4
INTENSITY MILD	MODERATE	SEVERE	EXTREME
FREQUENCY MOST INCIDENTS	MANY INCIDENTS	FEWER INCIDENTS	RARE/INCREASING INCIDENTS

VICTIM RESPONSES:	INCREASING DISTRESS →		CUMULATIVE IMPACT
Emotional/Psychological			
• Distress • Hurt • Confusion • Resist/Reject behaviour • Attend school • Resiliency	• Fear • High distress • Report • Avoid • Seek help • School absences • Isolation	• Withdrawal • Depression • School refusal • Change school/Dropout	PRECIPITATED RETALIATION • Attack bully • Suicide • Murder • Attempted suicide • Attempted murder
Formal REPORT 1 (Verbal)	REPORT 2	REPORT 3	REPORT 4
INTENSITY MILD	MODERATE	SEVERE	EXTREME

©Healey, 2010

FIGURE 1: CONTINUUM OF SEVERITY OF PEER ABUSE and VICTIM RESPONSES

THE PSYCHOLOGY OF VICTIMISATION

Paramount to an understanding of the nature of victimisation in bullying is an understanding of the social forces which appear to reinforce, condone and encourage bullying while ignoring victims' protestations and cries for help (McCarthy, Sheehan and Wilkie, 1996). The characteristics of bullies and their victims seem to contribute to this situation and in a contradictory way may operate in favour of the bully and lead to the abandonment of the victim.

There is a continuum of characteristics exhibited by victims of bullying and while the personal interaction and response style of a victim may be deemed passive, ineffectual and lacking resilience, they can just as often be assertive and resistant in response to the bullying behaviour. Victims are not necessarily, as is popularly believed, all weak and vulnerable individuals incapable of defending themselves against the aggressive demands of the bully. A critical component of the victimisation is the lack of support, assistance and empathy evident in their peers and others throughout their ordeal. While some victims may be selected on the basis of their perceived passivity and social ineptitude, it is often the socialisation which precedes, and social processes and responses encountered following victimisation which incapacitate the victim.

Numerous cases of victimisation are reported in the literature and the popular press which serve to illustrate the social forces contributing to the victimisation of those individuals targeted by bullies. While reports are often seen of passive individuals badgered into suicide by the aggressive bully, other stories describe victims who seek assistance, report incidents, and practice avoidance and confrontation in an effort to deter the bully, only to find they are ignored, rejected and disbelieved by those to whom they turn. The social conspiracy of inactivity to which they also fall victim seems to subscribe to the belief that the often charismatic, powerful and dominant behaviours which epitomise the bully's style either cannot or should not be challenged nor can they be called to account for their activities. Bullies flourish in environments from early childhood to executive suites where these principles are reinforced.

Bullies are not necessarily viewed as aggressive individuals whose pattern of interaction is based on demanding, selfish and destructive behaviours designed to maintain their self-esteem at the expense of others'. Society seems to view bullies often as successful 'leaders' in a competitive environment where aggression is a justifiable means to a lucrative and indulged future. It is the very characteristics which society so values, and which bullies are so skilled at emulating, which places bullies in a position to wield such destructive influence over their victims. Less attractive, less popular, less flamboyant and far less socially impressive victims cannot muster support for their complaints against such charismatic beings. Couple this with the bully's capacity for deviance and secretive abusive behaviours which leave the victim with no evidence of the destructive events and it becomes clear that the victim is unlikely to be able to overcome the social bias as well as the victimisation and it is little wonder they often abandon the effort.

Victims are often dismayed at the trivialization of their ordeal and at the superficial advice offered to avoid the bully or worse still to make sure the bully gets whatever it is he requires, in order to prevent further victimisation. Contact with the bully is often unavoidable and socially engineered such as in age-based classrooms, sporting groups, social activities and travel arrangements and victims are therefore in no position to protect themselves from the encounters. The Peer Advocacy© program described later provides a means by which the case for the victim can be put to supportive and committed authority figures who have the power to intervene and change the circumstances whereby bullies have unlimited access to their victims. Without the establishment of such a structured process, however, victims remain at the mercy of bullies and cannot rely on the judgement of adults who may be deceived by the bully's demeanour.

Another factor in the continuation of victimisation is an essentially Australian pre-occupation with creating individuals who will not be "dobbers"– an undeniable pre-cursor to the creation of victims of bullying. There is little opportunity afforded young Australians to develop an understanding of the difference between legitimate reporting of incidents which require adult intervention to avoid harm to others and themselves, and "dobbing" which is essentially the reporting of insignificant or harmless activities for the purpose of getting others into trouble.

Young people are discouraged from seeking assistance from those in authority by the responses they receive which clearly indicate that their complaints are not viewed as significant and indeed which may be viewed as unwelcome, unnecessary and despicable. It may be a misinterpretation of the intent of adults who are concerned with both the individual's welfare and the preparation of them for the challenges of the future, but the net result is the development, over time, of passive individuals who may not seek assistance even when it is genuinely needed. This reinforces bullies and creates the unprotected environments in which they flourish. Peer Advocacy© training addresses this issue by providing sanctioned processes for the recording and reporting of harmful and prohibited behaviours.

Victimisation, then, is not the just the *result* of bullying but the *process* of bullying. The response of the individual to the bullying, whether resilient or not, does not reduce the level of victimisation. We need to ask, is the individual who resists bullying and seeks assistance to halt the process less victimized than the individual who succumbs emotionally and without resistance to the behaviour? By measuring the impact of the behaviour in terms of the responses of the victims, we may well minimize the responsibility of the bully and the degree of bullying occurring for which intervention is essential.

The true measure of the level of victimisation is not the degree of distress evident but the extent of the behaviours perpetrated against the target individual irrespective of their impact. Fortunately, some victims will respond in a resilient manner which affords them some protection, (*Healey 2000; Kampulainien, et al, 1998*) but this does not reduce the level of responsibility of the bully. In this regard, the role of the Peer Advocate©, described later, is more, or less, representative depending upon the capacities of the victim, but the level of victimisation should not be assessed on the basis of the assertiveness or otherwise of the response.

If we do consider victimisation to be based upon the competency of the individual to respond in a self-protective manner, we are possibly engaging in a process of re-victimisation of the more competent individual. If there is the possibility that intervention will be withheld because of the perception that the victim is 'coping' there may be a consequent failure to ensure that bullies are accountable for their behaviour. Should the bully of the most passive victim be held differently accountable to the bully of the more assertive victim? Does the level of competence of the victim responding in a help-seeking and effective manner prescribe a less vigorous intervention than that instituted for the more passive victim? There is a real risk that the latter reinforces a passive and dependent response, when an assertive response is preferable in terms of long-term protective behaviours

To expand further on a concept discussed later in this text, "resilience" is often described inappropriately in the context of bullying intervention when it is suggested that the behaviours endured by victims may have positive outcomes by contributing to the development of a strong and resilient character and skills for future social struggles. While there is value in the acquisition of resilience through life experiences, this is not at all the same as suffering in silence from the harassment and aggression meted out by bullies

Being the victim of aggression and harmful psychological interactions is not a good preparation for adjustment to life, and indeed provides the foundation for later psychological distress and inadequacy, rather than strength. It is clear that adults who are well adjusted, assertive and resilient individuals would not tolerate the behaviours young victims of bullying are expected to endure, and it is the appropriate development and demonstration of both resilience and assertiveness which victims need in order to counteract the effects of bullying.

It should be noted that bullies need assertiveness training in order to differentiate this legitimate behaviour from the aggressive interactions they generally prefer. They do not require resilience training as they are usually quite adequately able to ignore the viewpoints of others which may be critical of them. Bullies do not require social skills training as they already generally enjoy high social status and levels of competency. However, empathy, tolerance and responsibility are attributes that would contribute substantially to improvement in the bully's life trajectory.

BULLYING AS A 'VALUABLE EXPERIENCE"?

A continuing theme in discussions of bullying is that it somehow assists the growth of 'character', 'manliness' and 'toughness' for future experiences. This notion is usually only applied to bullying of vulnerable children and young people, however, and it is rarely suggested that adults could benefit in the same way from bullying in their personal or work relationships. It is important to consider that irrespective of the degree of resiliency demonstrated by the victim, the emotional impact of bullying is likely to remain substantial. Resilient behaviours are demonstrated despite the distress experienced not as an alternative response to it.

Some individuals will couple the emotional pain with overtly effective behavioural responses called resiliency while others will respond in an ineffective, non-resilient manner along with the distress. The level of resilience evident in their responses however, does not indicate the level of emotional impact and this is a critical factor in intervention in bullying. Victims of bullying who respond in a more pro-active and self-protective manner should not be viewed as less damaged than those who are incapable of demonstrating effective help-seeking responses. Resilient behaviours do not preclude emotional damage and depression (Luthar, 1997), and the danger is that apparently resilient individuals will be less well-supported and indeed may be excluded from, or denied intervention to halt the abuse on the basis of their more competent social responses. This can increase the emotional impact and lead to re-victimisation through the withholding or restriction of support and intervention.

For young people who are not resilient, that is, who do not have the capacity to recover spontaneously from adverse experiences, the notion that exposure to physical and emotional abuse whether through bullying or another source somehow has the potential for a positive outcome, is clearly questionable. The literature is replete with research which indicates that repeated exposure to maltreatment results in negative psychological and social outcomes for most abused individuals (Spatz-Widom, 1995).

The popular contention, therefore, that bullying prepares young people psychologically for 'real world' challenges involves a fundamental corruption of the notion of resilience. While young people do need to develop self-protective attitudes and behaviours in order to cope with life's disappointments and challenges, to apply a philosophy of tolerance for abuse to the issue of bullying is no more acceptable for young people than it would be if directed to adults in abusive situations. It is rarely suggested that adults in abusive relationships should take the opportunity to develop inner strength and psychological fortitude, nor that they will emerge from the situation having experienced personal growth. Although it is a popular view, in relation to peer abuse, this notion needs to be reviewed if young people are to secure the protection needed to avoid bullying.

While there are specific defining features of the behaviour described as bullying it is now routinely discussed as abusive and traumatic and is perceived as having as great psychological impact as other forms of abuse (Healey, 2006; Finkelhor and Dziuba-Leatherman, 1994,). Discussion throughout this document is premised on the status of bullying in this capacity.

Further, if violence is seen as intentional behaviour, chosen *'as a tactic associated with attempts to control and dominate'* then ...

> *'defining violence as intentional leads to a discourse identifying perpetrators as responsible and accountable for their act.'*
> *(Dobash & Dobash, 1992)*

Discussions of the 'value 'of bullying are often directed more towards males than towards females. Males are evidently much more likely to 'gain' by abuse in this analysis. Discourse which compares an essentially masculine dominance in the perpetration of violence to the apparent increase in girls' aggression through bullying (Chesney-Lind, 2003; Espelage, 2003; Stein, 2003) indicates that although girls appear now to be more inclined towards bullying, serious violence is still the domain of the masculine gender. Indeed, some researchers have defined gender as causal rather than correlational (Egger, 1995; Braithwaite and Daly, 1995) state categorically that:

> *'Violence is gendered: it is in considerable measure a problem and consequence of masculinity.'* *(Page 221)*

Indeed, most societal violence is perpetrated by males and using neutral language which refers to violent 'people' does not accurately describe the true composition of the problem, nor assist intervention. In relation to bullying, the research indicates that males are bullied to a greater extent than females, and they are bullied by other males. Nevertheless, the Daily Telegraph reported (3/09/07) that female students 'punched and spat at' their teacher, as a response to what the school later termed 'provocation' by the teacher as she had requested they be removed from her class for disruptive behaviour. This teacher was obviously within her parameters of responsibility seeking to protect herself and possibly other students from the abusive behaviour of these students. No charges were laid, however, even though the teacher required hospital treatment.

The Australian Education Union in recent research reported in the Adelaide Advertiser (03/09/07) found that 90% of teachers surveyed were struggling under the extra workload generated by having to teach children with difficult behaviours. Further, reports from the NSW Bureau of Crime Statistics and Research indicate a remarkable increase in violent incidents in schools reported to police, where female students were responsible. In both government and private schools, of 1242 reported incidents, 373 or approximately 33% were perpetrated by females. However, in the final analysis it matters not whether the attacker is male or female, the concern for Australian teachers is the rise in the risk of being physically assaulted while at work. Approaches which identify specific behaviours as problematic, and which address the need for behaviour training of individuals who engage in those behaviours will be more appropriate and ultimately more effective.

BULLYING AS ABUSE, NOT CONFLICT — A FUNDAMENTAL SHIFT

Today, views about bullying are shifting as more evidence becomes available about the serious impact of the behaviour. The broader community is beginning to question previously held notions that bullying is a mild form of annoyance and to examine reported suicides and school responses for evidence of effective interventions. We are beginning to reflect on definitions of bullying which indicate that bullying is best viewed as abuse, in rejection of many earlier views that it is evidence of conflict. It is important to note that no currently accepted definition of bullying refers to 'conflict' as an element. As bullying episodes clearly lead to extreme psychological distress and suicides are recorded daily as a tragic response to peer abuse, it may well now be time for this theory to find its rightful place in the analysis of peer abuse. Of major concern are the implications for intervention.

As noted, bullying is very often confused in the eye of the beholder with peer 'fighting' or conflict. Teachers, in particular can often assume that all altercations between children are the result of mutual aggression and conflict. In the case cited earlier, despite the victim being hospitalised several times from school, the events were classified in critical incident reports as 'fighting' when in fact he was the victim of systematic abuse. The fact was that school reports indicated that he was identified as a withdrawn and passive individual overall, not prone to 'fighting'.

Fundamentally, bullying is readily distinguished from 'fighting', 'conflict' and 'play' by the presence of reciprocity between participants. In fighting, two antagonists engage in often physical aggressive interactions in order to establish dominance of one over the other and both participants are psychologically focussed on resisting the dominance of the other while establishing their own status. Similarly with conflict situations two or more individuals have opposing desires and conflict arises when each party attempts to assert their wishes at the cost of the others'.

Conversely in a 'play' situation the participants are mutually enjoying a shared activity to which all have consented. It can be readily seen therefore that none of these explanations adequately describe the interactions of the bully and victim primarily because of the lack of reciprocity. Even though bullies will often describe their behaviour as 'play' and 'fighting', astute observers, in particular teachers should be able to differentiate the unhappy and resistant demeanour of the victim from the triumphant behaviour of the bully. A key factor here is to know the characteristics of the participants well enough to be able to determine the likelihood that a normally passive, co-operative and compliant student is likely to be engaged in aggressive behaviours or fighting.

Accounts of bullying are often described by teachers and other witnesses as 'fights' when clearly there is usually one person left significantly worse off than the others. Despite the fact that the altercation is between well-known aggressive individuals and equally well-known non-aggressive individuals, adults responsible for managing such situations fail to interpret the interaction as bullying. Teachers have a particular level of exposure since they are with children and young people constantly and develop professional intuition for appropriate behaviour. Nevertheless, given the amount of abuse which is not addressed or challenged, the accepted notions may need some adjustment and teachers may need to be provided with professional development to incorporate peer abuse identification as a new professional skill.

Teachers must be professionally prepared to enable them to use their intimate knowledge of the participants to make more reasonable assessments of the aggressive interaction they have witnessed. They should then be able to confidently dispute the bully's description of the event as 'play' or 'fighting' when clearly one individual is more recipient than participant. The picture below, an illustration from the cover of the *Casdagli, et al (1990)* book 'Only Playing Miss', clearly depicts the fear of the victim and the intent of the bully, but may well still be interpreted as a 'play' situation by teachers or observers.

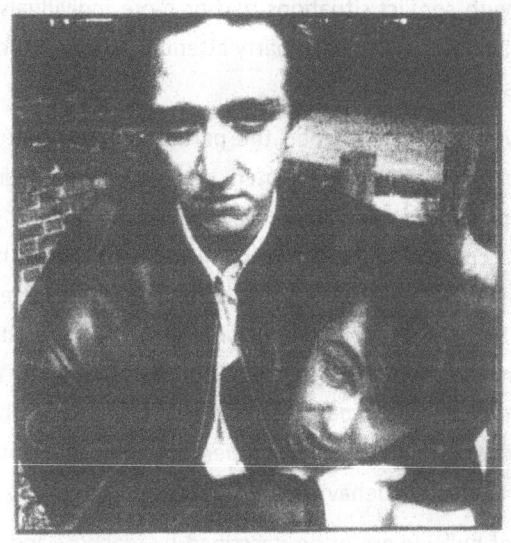

Differentiating Bullying from 'Conflict' / Fighting

Conflict: *'clash or be in opposition or at variance'* (Macquarie dictionary)

'Conflict ' generally involves the following:

- an aggressive event or incident
- participants are threatening to each other
- there is mutual aggression/disagreement
- there may be no power difference between the participants
- it occurs between two individuals in dispute
- each has their own goal to 'win'
- each may have supporters
- there is reciprocal abuse and fighting
- both or neither are hurt
- there are accusations from both aggressors

This is very different to the characteristics of a bullying event, which generally involves the following:

- repeated aggressive behaviour against an individual
- intimidation of an individual
- intentional hurt /harm
- actual harm or hurt to an individual
- difference in power, based on social or physical factors
- often more than one aggressor
- peer support for bully
- not reciprocal-the victim does not 'fight back'
- denial response from bully
- accusations from victim

Given the obvious imbalance of power in abusive relationships and the abuser's capacity to control and intimidate victims, it is simply not possible to enter into a situation whereby the respective needs of the participants are 'negotiated'. As *Stubbs (1996)* points out,

> 'it cannot be assumed that a (victim) who has been subjected to violence and abuse will be willing or able to talk about that abuse in a conference, and indeed it may be unsafe for them to do so.'

Just as conflict resolution would not be deemed an appropriate response in abusive spousal relationships, nor can it be seen as appropriate for dealing with the abuse of young people by their dominant peers. Interventions for domestic violence and abuse caution that the expectation that the abused individual should participate in conjoint programs:

> 'Implies that the problem is mutual and that, as a contributor, the (victim) is expected to change; and that the focus will be on saving the relationship rather than addressing the violence and coercive control exercised by the perpetrator.' (Lipchik, Sirles & Kubicki, 1997).

Abusive individuals do not have the right to be heard in respect of their motives for abusive behaviour. There is no conflict in the sense of each party having legitimate needs to be met in co-operation with another, rather bullying represents an abuse of one individual. There is no legitimacy in the need to abuse others. While conflict and dispute resolution programs teach valuable skills for resolving differences of opinion, it is suggested here that such interventions are inappropriate and could well be damaging when applied to abuse situations. Peer abuse requires protective intervention which supports the victim while calling the abusive individual to account for their behaviour.

DEFINING BULLYING

For further clarification, an examination of the criteria which define bullying demonstrates that the key indicators of lack of reciprocity intention to harm, frequency of the attacks and misuse of social or psychological power (Jenkin, 1999; Pikas, 1989) all indicate an absence of conflict and the unmistakable presence of victimisation. Conflict resolution will not assist victims of bullying who have no wish to engage with the bully particularly in an aggressive and adversarial way, and indeed this approach may re-victimise the victim if it appears an attempt is being made to equalise responsibility for the inappropriate interactions, as often happens in school-based interventions.

DEFINING BULLYING

Whilst various definitions of what constitutes bullying abound, such definitions generally incorporate similar components, including:

- *the repetitive nature of the abuse;*
- *the range of behaviours, including psychological, physical and verbal abuse;*
- *the intention to inflict harm on the victim;*
- *harmful outcomes for victims;*
- *power differences.*

All of these components relate to abusive interactions. It is interesting to note that no current definitions of 'bullying' refer in any way to 'conflict'. It is baffling therefore that the preferred intervention priority is usually conflict resolution. This supports the contention made here that 'abuse' theory must be the definitive factor in intervention.

Bullying behaviour has been shown in a broad range of literature and research to consistently include a predictable set of parameters. The repetitive nature of bullying has resulted in definitions that characterise childhood bullying as more than one event, often occurring as a pattern of hurtful behaviour over a period of time, which differentiates it from episodic violence or assault (Olweus, 1993; Jenkin, 1999). Childhood bullying has been distinguished from other anti-social behaviours by being characterised as repeated exposure to the negative actions of a peer or group of abusive peers, resulting in harm to another individual.

Columbine occurred after a reportedly long history of peer abuse and illustrates the element of precipitation which is often a consequence of sustained bullying. Victims are encouraged to 'fight back' and to 'stick up' for themselves, and in some cases this has tragic outcomes. They may retaliate against the bully, changing the dynamic from abuse to fighting, or they may turn on themselves. What is certain is that at present there is no process in place to establish when, and if, the problem is likely to lead to an escalation of events. This is a critical element for consideration in a comprehensive intervention such as that proposed here. The continuum model described earlier illustrates the progressive nature of bullying behaviour and victim distress, and these need to be addressed to secure the safety of the victim. Accessing suicide prevention literature and other legal and medical advice can be a valuable inclusion in intervention.

Over time, definitions of what constitutes childhood bullying have become more refined, and a number of critical dimensions now differentiate bullying behaviour from violence, fighting, play and general conflict. New perspectives have evolved that contribute to developing a more focussed definition that acknowledges particular psychological elements which are commonly evident.

Specific groups or individuals may be targeted and bullies often focus attention on salient features of the victim to ensure the greatest impact of their victimisation. Importantly, the social costs of long-term bullying are now readily apparent with suicide (Olweus, 1999), murder (Burnage, 1989), attempted murder (Healey, 2001) and serious psychological problems documented internationally as resultant consequences of violent and bullying behaviour. Despite consistent research findings pointing to the pervasiveness of childhood bullying, *Harachi et al. (1999)* contend that "there appears to be no one standard definition of bullying in the popular or research literature" (p.298). Definitions which have been adopted and formed the basis of current research have ranged from the simple to the complex, including those of the following researchers:

DEFINITIONS OF BULLYING

- *'Bullying involves the repeated, intentionally harmful, abusive psychological or physical actions of one or more socially powerful individuals against an individual who cannot effectively resist and who does not reciprocate the actions' (Healey, 2004.)*

- *A student is being bullied or victimised when he or she is exposed repeatedly over time to negative actions on the part of one or more other students. (Olweus, 1993)*

- *Bullying is repeated aggression, verbal, psychological or physical conducted by an individual or group against others. (Byrne, 1993)*

- *Bullying is repeated aggression, psychological or physical, of a less powerful person by a more powerful person or group of persons. (Rigby, 1996)*

- *Bullying is a behaviour which can be defined as the repeated attack – physical, psychological, social or verbal by those in a position of power which is formally or situationally defined on those who are powerless to resist with the intention of causing distress for their own gain or gratification. (Besag, 1994)*

KEY COMPONENTS OF THE DEFINITION

If we examine the first definition it can be seen that it incorporates all key indicators for what constitutes bullying, as well as some new parameters which refine its application.

- 'Bullying involves the repeated, intentionally harmful, abusive psychological or physical actions of one or more socially powerful individuals against an individual who cannot effectively resist and who does not reciprocate the actions' (Healey, 2004.)

Let's deconstruct the definition and discuss the elements in greater detail:

- **'Bullying involves repeated, intentionally harmful, abusive psychological or physical actions'**

In order to differentiate bullying from other negative interactions between peers, the definition incorporates the following components:

Repeated

The abuse occurs repeatedly and cannot therefore be assumed to be an unintentional or episodic 'attack'. Research indicates that bullying can occur on a daily or more frequent basis and a key defining feature is that it is not 'occasional' or spasmodic. The repetitive and predictable nature of the abuse is a key underlying cause of the trauma suffered by the victim as they await the next anticipated abusive event.

Intentionally Harmful

Bullying is not a behaviour that can be misinterpreted as playing, 'mucking around' or 'fun' as the bully will often claim. Behaviours which are mildly tormenting and which cause no real or reported harm or hurt to the recipient are not the behaviours of concern when attempts are being made to identify bullying. A critical component of the behaviour is the intention to harm and the actual harm resulting for the victim.

Bullying is distinguished from other behaviour based upon intentionality. The specific purpose of bullying is to harm the recipient and as such there is a conscious choice or intention (Smith, 1994). Intentionality must be examined despite the claimed intention of the bully, who often denies or diminishes the purpose of the behaviour. The evident intention to harm, together with the actual impact on the victim and the congruence of the two must be examined together (Quine, 1999). Bullies who claim to be 'playing' or 'fighting' with their victims need to be challenged to show how their behaviours can be distinguished from abuse. Indeed the semantics of the discourse surrounding bullying is one of the greatest challenges facing interventionists. Undoubtedly during fighting episodes the intention is to hurt or harm the other party. The difference of course in bullying interactions is that the intention is only on the part of the bully. It is not reciprocated by the victim during the event. Bullying does not represent a mutually aggressive engagement when both parties intend to harm the other either physically or emotionally. Bullying involves abusive behaviour on the part of the bully intended to harm the victim alone.

Abusive Psychological or Physical Actions

Bullying has also been defined as constituting specific types of behaviour. These behaviours are described as both overt and covert, psychological and physical (*Bjorkqvist & Osterman, 1999*), which can all be classified as abusive (*Olweus, 1999*). Such behaviours may include psychological, physical or verbal threats or actions which impact on the wellbeing and self-esteem of the victim. Bullying is often misinterpreted, ignored, denied or results in punishment for the victim as the same standard of culpability is applied. Victims of bullying are often judged to be complicit in their own demise or the damage they endure is seen as the expected result of their fighting' with peers. This is a critical factor in the psychological harm experienced by victims of bullying.

Furthermore, unfortunately, when applied to the bullying of children and young people milder and less specific terminology is often used which diminishes the nature and impact of the behaviour. Consider descriptions of these behaviours, researched extensively with both primary and secondary students and selected as representative behaviours typical of the bullying spectrum:

BEING TEASED AND CALLED NAMES
Alternative descriptor: *taunting/harassment/abuse*

If adults are 'teased' it generally indicates a playful, often consensual act which is not meant to be harmful but to sustain friendly relationships. 'Teasing' is a mild descriptor for mild and generally inoffensive behaviour which may well indicate friendly or even intimate terms between the two participants. Adults are well able to differentiate between offensive and abusive verbal interactions and 'teasing'.

Children however are less resilient and less experienced. What they experience under this category of behaviour is neither mild nor inoffensive, nor is it meant to be. However, the term continues to be used to describe the highly offensive and abusive verbal taunting used by bullies to frighten and upset their targets. If we were to be honest and accurate in describing this method of bullying we would describe it as the behaviour it really is: 'taunting' 'harassment' and 'abuse'.

The impact of this behaviour is not at all the same as that of 'teasing' and the diminutive term deprives the victim of the degree of protection they need to avoid the bullying. Furthermore, expecting bullied individuals to respond to such abuse as if it were playful and harmless supports the bully and sustains the abuse. It may well be time to replace this term with the more accurate alternative to indicate the true nature of the interaction. Children consistently report that the taunting remarks of their peers are some of the worst examples of bullying they experience.

RECEIVING OFFENSIVE OR THREATENING TEXTS OR EMAILS
Alternative descriptor: *cyberbullying, internet bullying, cyberassment*

This category of abuse has grown to be the most readily accessible and effective means of bullying in recent times. Cyber bullying involves the use of the internet via blogs, Face book and other social network sites and emails and text messages to spread rumours, denigrate and generally harass peers. Internet access and communication technology skills are prevalent amongst young people and afford continuous opportunities to send abusive, embarrassing and threatening messages and pictures. The recent review of cyber-safety research (*Dooley, Cross, Hearn and Treyvaud, 2009*) indicates that rates of cyber bullying are comparatively low in Australia at < 10%, whereas international rates are up to 52% and that 82% of victims know the identity of the perpetrator (page 59).

In cyber bullying, one of the issues for the victim is not-knowing how many others are privy to their embarrassment and abuse, since it is not possible to gauge accurately the spread of the messages, taunts and sometimes photos used in the abuse. These 'observers' of the abuse are nevertheless culpable if they also spread the messages or do not attempt to assist the victim or disapprove of the bully. There are some factors which could mitigate the impact of the abuse, such as the distance between the abuser and the victim ('cyber distance'), which means they do not have 'face' their abuser and the technology itself provides a barrier to the abuse which could be used to buffer the impact. However, the evidence is clear that this type of abuse has long term and deep impact on the victim. Cyber bullying is often implicated in completed suicides in young people.

Also, it would seem that a simple solution lies in the ability of the receiver to identify the sender prior to opening the offensive material. In a similar manner to avoiding the bully when they are seen approaching, the recipient of these messages can be trained to take responsibility for their own protection by not opening the offensive material and/or forwarding it to a third party who can provide protective intervention, such as a parent or school personnel.

However, this is generally not what happens and as the example cited earlier indicates, the consistent access of the bully via these electronic means can prove to be the most highly destructive of all. Supportive strategies within the home and school such as limiting access to mobile phones and supervised computer time, can offer protection. Allowing unlimited access to mobile phones and computers without monitoring the content is the equivalent of locking a child in their room with their abuser and this is an inadequate response.

Schools may well need to assess their responsibility for access by abusers if they have no designated policy for mobile use within school hours. Adults are, in the end, responsible for the protection of children and young people and some restrictions to access must be considered if bullying is an issue. Mobile phones and the web are often described as the young person's 'lifeline' to social contact. However for the unfortunate few, they have now become a death line.

BEING LEFT OUT OR EXCLUDED ON PURPOSE
Alternative descriptor: *isolating, rejecting, spurning*

While children cannot expect to be included in all activities offered or proposed within their social world, the acts of rejection and isolating involved in bullying go well beyond the occasional missed party invitation. Children who are systematically excluded from any and all social interaction by the collective spurning behaviours of their peers may be seriously psychologically affected. This is a behaviour that bullied children find difficult to document and explain as teachers and others to whom they try to express their concerns often refuse to take them seriously. Children are aware that they cannot be 'included' in every activity on offer, but they are also aware that they are entitled to some inclusion and interaction with peers, however, their efforts to sustain these contacts require a good measure of resiliency. Many bullied individuals do not have the resiliency to resist this harmful behaviour. If adults find themselves excluded from activities which impact their work or social status they are fully protected in seeking recourse and reinstatement. Similar protection and support needs to be applied in the case of children.

BEING VERBALLY THREATENED WITH HARM
Alternative descriptor: *harassment, abuse, threats of violence, terrorizing, intimidation*

When children are threatened with physical harm to themselves, their family or pets they generally take the threats seriously and believe that they will happen. Often they will take extreme measures to protect themselves or others without seeking help, since they are also often threatened with worse harm if they 'tell' anyone else. In the adult world such behaviour and experiences would be quickly reported to police and the culprit at least cautioned for their intimidating activities. In the world of the bullied child however all hope is lost as they are neither aware nor made aware of the protective intervention adults can offer in these circumstances. Differentiating the commonly used term 'dobbing' which refers to the reporting of insignificant and harmless activities, from 'notifying ' or 'reporting' of behaviours which are harmful and destructive, is a critical area for teaching skills for dealing with peer abuse and intimidation.

> **BEING PHYSICALLY HIT, PUNCHED OR KICKED**
> Alternative descriptor: *assault, bashing, violence*

Even when children are able to show the physical signs of the often brutal attacks they endure at the hands of bullies, they are disappointed at the response they receive from teachers and parents. Inevitably they are accused of 'fighting' or 'conflict' and cautioned about such behaviour. Adults who experience physical harm at the hands of another individual are fully protected by the law and are able to bring assault charges for the damage to their person. We still do not offer children this fundamental protection. We still question their motives and the 'real' source of the harm and continue to offer punitive or conflict resolution strategies as remediation. We must now offer the same protections under the law to children who are assaulted as we offer to adult members of society, and these protections may need to be delegated to advocates for the child to ensure their protection.

Examples of extreme physically assault reported to be inflicted by bullies include: stuffing garbage into the mouth of the victim; holding the victim's head under water or in a flushing toilet for a period of time; headlocks and strangulation; pushing, tripping, and physically barging into victims, the use of implements to beat victims and more frequently reported, punches, kicks and slaps.

> **BEING FORCED TO GIVE MONEY OR BELONGINGS**
> Alternative descriptor: *extortion, robbery, theft*

Quite simply, demands for money for any purpose other than legitimate exchange for goods or services, as with adult business exchanges, is illegal extortion. Children who are subject daily to having their lunch money stolen are no less victims of mugging than adults whose wallets are stolen or demanded by criminals. Children who are consistently deprived of needed funds are robbed to the same extent as adults whose money is systematically stolen through threats and demands. Reporting stolen money or goods or demands for these is a relatively straightforward procedure for adults, however many children in this situation find themselves being questioned about their own capacity to take care of their belongings and money. Clearly, some form of intervention to protect their property is necessary if children are to be treated justly under the law.

COURTESY OF **Sydney Morning Herald**

BY ALEX McDONALD

Bullying Almost to Death

JYE HOWELL was first bullied in kindergarten, at the age of four. Constant teasing, shoving and bruising have dogged the 11-year-old since then, forcing his parents to send him to five schools. His mother, Barbie Howell, has become fed up with the abuse and the inability of Jye's teachers to stop it. A heart-wrenching conversation with her son last year prompted Mrs. Howell to go public with her family's torment. "That was the day Jye said he'd rather die than go back to school," Mrs. Howell said.

Donna Cross, a professor of adolescent health at Edith Cowan University, said aggression could be seen in children as young as two. "It happens in girls first," she said. "We think girls' social intelligence develops faster."

Jye is one of six Howell children but is their only child who has been bullied. Statistically, the family is not unusual. It is estimated that one in six Australian children is bullied each week.

The Howells lived in Sydney for 20 years before moving to Darwin in 2001. Jye would often come home covered in bruises but was reluctant to speak out. "Jye has a learning difficulty," Mrs. Howell said. "Nobody can pinpoint what's wrong with him. Jye's also got a problem with his legs." The family moved from Darwin to Ipswich in 2005. Yet the bullying continued, with Jye attending his third primary school in as many years.

Mrs. Howell said: "I had one principal say to Jye, 'This doesn't happen to anyone else; it must be you.'"

Receiving comments about their family, country of birth or religion
Alternative descriptor: *racial or cultural abuse, discrimination*

Children who are singled out because of their cultural background, religious beliefs or customs are the victims of racism. Australia is a multicultural society which offers a culturally diverse environment for general education and enjoyment.

However, cultural diversity which identifies individuals through clothing or food or religious practices is often used by bullies as an excuse for discriminatory abuse.

Care must be taken to accept that the comments are offensive and hurtful and indicative of the need for a comprehensive education program to address tolerance. Educators believe they are teaching inclusivity in their classroom programs, but the message may be only superficially noted by individuals who bully by exclusion and discrimination. Behaviour is the final determinant of true inclusivity and this may need to be carefully monitored in abusive individuals.

Receiving comments on their personal appearance
Alternative descriptor: *demeaning, insulting, derogatory personal remarks*

Children are well aware that the opinions of their peer group with regard to their personal presentation in terms of clothing, hair style, cleanliness, required uniform etc is crucial to their social acceptance. Even when they are suitably attired, however, abusive peers may well make derogatory comments about their appearance. Adults would not accept this in their workplace or home environment, but children are often left to suffer the 'slings and barbs' and the whole experience may well be trivialised if reported. It is the psychological impact of such comments which is the crucial determining factor in bullying, not the accuracy of the comment. Developing resiliency to these behaviours through training and supportive intervention may offer the victim of bullying some psychological protection. However the fact remains that serious abusive comments are often not treated as such by the adults in their lives.

DELIBERATE DAMAGE TO THEIR PERSONAL PROPERTY
Alternative descriptor: *criminal damage, destruction or property stealing*

Children may have their school bags, books, clothing and other belongings stolen or destroyed in a bullying incident, or systematically over a period of time. Various explanations for the disappearance of or damage to these items may be offered to parents and teachers, but it is the consistent occurrence of the losses which should alert adults to the possibility of bullying. Often, however the child is accused of not taking care of, or of giving away their belongings in a distorted adult view of the carefree days of childhood.

STALKING
Alternative descriptor: *stalking with intent*

Criminal proceedings can be taken against stalkers who terrorise adults by following them home, making appearances at their work, events and locations where the victim is known to be in attendance, watching at a distance or intruding into a range of everyday activities (Stalking Intervention Orders Act, Victoria, 2008.). The intention of the stalker to frighten and intimidate the victim is not questioned and once the stalking behaviour is established, apprehended violence orders and other protective legal processes may be instigated for the protection of the adult victim. Why is it that such protections are not offered children in similar circumstances? Why is it so difficult to establish the sinister intent of the abusive child stalker, when specific indicators can be applied to identify adult stalkers? A good deal more work needs to be undertaken to provide children with the same level of protection and support as adult victims of stalking.

The remainder of the analysis of the definition of bullying continues in the next chapter.

3 The Individual Psychology of Bullies and Victims

Introduction

The personality and character traits of individuals involved in the bullying paradigm cannot be overlooked if the participants are to be understood and intervention be successfully implemented. Personality traits are:

> 'enduring patterns of perceiving, relating to and thinking about the environment and oneself that are exhibited in a wide range of social and personal contexts' (DSM IV, 2010, Pg 686).

Variations in personality, evident in the manner in which individuals interact with their fellow human beings and in social and functional situations, have always been accepted as evidence of individuality. To a large extent such variations are accepted and approved and provide endless variety in our daily interpersonal interactions. We all have some eccentric friends or acquaintances who add further variation by responding in unexpected or unique ways to social situations and traditions. It is only when such responses deviate so far from the norm that they cause distress or concern to others or violate socially acceptable standards, that we feel the need to apply some preventative action or intervention.

There is a strong body of literature supporting the view that the presence of different personality traits is expressed in the range of personality types and that a range of types can be substantiated. Individuals evidently interact and respond according to type and differently to each other. Individuals display preferences in their behaviours and this capacity is very relevant to the interpretation and analysis of bullying as a behavioural interaction.

The way in which bullies relate to their peers and their victims is likely to reflect their main personality orientation, and the ways in which victims respond will also. Personality 'typing' has been criticised as overly simplistic, however many people can relate the characteristic descriptors to their observations of others in their family, at school or in the world generally. Personality typing is helpful in differentiating the behaviours evident in bullying episodes which impact on the welfare of others. Initially it is useful to examine some characteristics of bullies and their victims to gain an overview of their personality traits and responses. Relevant factors are:

- The key motivations and fears of the bully
- Their aggressive attitude
- The negative intent of their behaviour
- The types of abusive behaviours
- Response to authority
- Their source of support
- Their response to accusations of bullying
- Apparent strengths and weakness
- How they impact on teachers and parents

CHARACTERISTICS OF BULLIES

The personality characteristics of bullies may be examined in relation to accepted and familiar personality types often used to identify valuable traits and behaviours in human resources development. *The Myers Briggs Personality Inventory* (*1962*) meets accepted psychometric standards for reliability and validity and has been used for nearly sixty years to analyse the interaction and performance behaviours of people of all ages. This assessment tool was derived from the work of Carl Jung whose treatise 'Personality Types' (*1921*) introduced the concept. These types were originally based on the four 'humours 'described by Hippocrates in 400 BC when it was, in reality, simply a naïve interpretation used to explain the various types of personality evident, even then, in interpersonal interactions.

Chapter 3 — The Individual Psychology of Bullies and Victims

The 'humours' and types referred to were:

CHOLERIC (Bile)	A dominant and impatient type
MELANCHOLY (Black Bile)	A depressive and rejecting type
SANGUINE (Blood)	A cheerful and egocentric type
PHLEGMATIC (Phlegm)	A calm and undemonstrative type

These descriptors are still in use today and assist in clarifying the different and confusing behaviours and characteristics of bullies, as identified by their victims. Acknowledging the possibility of a range of motivations and intentions in the bullying behaviours observed enables the victim and those offering support to recognise key underlying factors to address in interventions. The key motivations identified in behaviour literature and personality analysis can be classified as dominance, attention-seeking, revenge and approval.

What is of grave concern in the analysis of bullying behaviour is the prognosis for progressively more severe anti-social behaviour as the bully develops into maturity and refines his abusive interaction 'skills'. Indeed, if reference is made to the *APA Diagnostic Manual of Mental Disorders* (TR) (*2010 Edition*) it becomes apparent that young people who exhibit the types of behaviours described as bullying or peer abuse, may well be presenting with a specific mental disorder such as 'Conduct Disorder'. This disorder is characterised as,

> *'a repetitive and persistent pattern of behaviour in which the basic rights of others or major age-appropriate social norms are violated' (page 93)*

The list of behaviours provided by this highly respected manual, used world-wide for the diagnosis of mental disorders, includes many of those we now associate with peer abusive behaviours including:

> *'bullying, threatening or intimidating behaviour; initiating aggression; use of weapons; physical cruelty ; extortion; (page 94)*

It is clear that such serious and evidence-based criteria must be acknowledged in assessments of the social and mental competency of some who engage in severe bullying. For this reason, intervention must be premised upon individual indicators. The long term prognosis for individuals exhibiting conduct disorder in childhood or adolescence is the likelihood for further deterioration in social competency and a possible adult diagnosis of Anti-Social personality disorder. When bullying becomes an internalised interaction behaviour, reinforced by social benefits and devoid of social sanctions or consequences, the stage is set for a lifetime of abuse and a trail of damaged individuals in the wake of the abuser.

As a means of describing variations in bullying behaviour, *Figure 2* suggests that the behaviours observed could be likened to those of certain canines! This is not to disparage our four legged friends, but to suggest a likeness to characteristics which may clarify the differences between the types of bully, their selected approaches and motivations and their possible impact on victims. Each canine type reflects certain relevant negative traits only, in relation to the discussion. The negative intention of each motivating factor assists in understanding why the bully selects particular behaviours to secure their preferred response. It is distressing to consider that these negative interactions are engaged simply to satisfy individual and self-focussed negative goals for the abuser.

MOTIVATION:	DOMINANCE	ATTENTION	REVENGE	APPROVAL
ATTITUDE:	'ROTTWEILER'	'TERRIER'	'PITBULL'	'DINGO'
NEGATIVE INTENTION:	BE IN CONTROL	GET NOTICED	HURT OR HARM	DON'T GET CAUGHT
TYPICAL BEHAVIOURS:	■ Intimidation ■ Dominance ■ Posturing ■ Gives 'orders' ■ Makes demands ■ Challenges victim ■ Uses temper to intimidate ■ Disobeys directives / rules	■ Attention Seeking ■ Makes 'jokes' about victim ■ Texts / Shares 'jokes' / Insults ■ Annoying / irritating ■ Shows off to peers ■ Public comments ■ Persistent insults ■ Targets 'defects'	■ Threatening ■ Vicious verbal attacks ■ Texts threats of harm ■ Cruel / Physical ■ Dangerous / Mean ■ Violent actions ■ Insults and taunts ■ Real harm / hurt	■ Pretend to be friend ■ Sneaky acts ■ Blames others ■ Texts pretend offers friendship / withdraw ■ Graffiti (anon) ■ Cyberbully / Rumours ■ 'Nice' to peers ■ Exclusion of victim ■ Provocative 'victim'
RESPONSE TO AUTHORITY:	■ Rejects authority	■ Ignores authority ■ Jokes / Charms	■ Challenges authority	■ Feigns obedience to authority
SUPPORT:	■ Gets support by dominance / power	■ Gets support through 'humour'	■ Gets support through fear	■ Gets support by being 'nice'
RESPONSE TO ACCUSATION:	■ Denies intention to hurt – 'Just mucking around'	■ Laughs off harm – 'Just playing'	■ Admits wanting to harm – 'He / She deserves it'	■ Denies all activities / Acts innocent – 'Wasn't me'
PERSONAL STRENGTH:	■ Charismatic	■ Entertaining	■ Exciting	■ 'Best friend'
WEAKNESS:	■ Alienates peers	■ Exhibitionist	■ Frightening	■ Unreliable
GREATEST FEAR:	■ Losing control	■ Being ignored	■ 'Disrespect'	■ Being found out
HOW DO YOU FEEL? Teacher / Parent	■ Overwhelmed ■ Defeated	■ Annoyed / Angry	■ Afraid / Threatened	■ Confused
PERSONALITY TYPE	CHOLERIC	SANGUINE	CHOLERIC / MELANCHOLY	PHLEGMATIC

©Healey, 2010

FIGURE 2: CHARACTERISTICS OF BULLIES

The negative intention of each motivating factor assists in understanding why the bully selects particular behaviours to secure their preferred response. It is distressing to consider that these negative interactions are engaged simply to satisfy individual and self-focussed negative goals for the abuser. These designations are used further to describe workplace bullies in a forthcoming text by this author (in press).

The 'Rottweiler' Attitude

Power-seeking bullies have a major goal of remaining in control–of situations, of peers and of their status in their social environment. Their behaviours in interactions with others are intimidating and dominant; they are likely to reject directives and rules whether social or educational, and to reject authority; they gain peer support through dominance and they make demands and give orders to both their peer affiliates and their victims. This bully type can be quite charismatic and hence is able to gain the admiration of peers and those in authority. They manage to do this because of their goal-oriented behaviour and ability to deliver promised outcomes. If challenged by teachers or parents trying to intervene they will deny trying to hurt the victim and claim to be just 'mucking around'. Over time, their dominant behaviours may well alienate them from peers but many remain 'faithful' in response to the intimidation. Their greatest fear is to lose control over any situation and therefore this is the best method for teachers and parents to use to manage the bullying-remove all opportunity for the choleric bully to make decisions and take charge in abusive encounters; restrict their access and isolate them from their supportive peers; this type of bully may well make the teacher or parent feel overwhelmed and defeated because of their ability to demand and dominate in interactions with adults as well as peers. *Choleric personality type*.

The "Terrier' Attitude

The attention-seeking bully engages in abusive and offensive behaviour towards their victim as a means of gaining attention and 'entertaining' their friends, however, this does not diminish the impact as harmful and destructive to the self-esteem of victims. The key motivating factor for this type of bully is attention at all costs, so they may stop their behaviours briefly when challenged or disciplined, but are highly likely to restart once their celebrity is reduced. They may use 'humour' to attack their victim, posting and spreading 'jokes' about the target individual ; they are likely to ignore the directives of authority except momentarily, and will claim to be 'playing' if challenged; they maintain peer support through 'humour' and entertainment and will not take any accusation of harm seriously. Their greatest fear is to be ignored and therefore isolation and removal from the reinforcement of peers is an effective method for management. This type of bully may make the teacher or parent feel annoyed and angry as they refuse to accept responsibility or show empathy and persist in the behaviour despite frequent warnings and directives. *Sanguine personality type.*

The 'Pit-bull' Attitude

This type of bully is the scariest of all; this personality type rejects social mores and values and operates entirely independently of laws and rules. Their major focus is to cause harm and to hurt their victim; their abusive behaviours are selected and preferred as they enjoy the reinforcement of fear and distress in their victims; they will engage in vicious attacks, threat of harm and actual physical damage. They will challenge authority if confronted about their behaviour and will claim their attacks are justified (usually because the victim is such a 'loser' and they 'deserve it'). They may make the teacher or parent feel afraid, threatened and anxious as they seem difficult to 'control' and are not afraid of any threatened punishment, nor are they prepared to consider the feelings of the victim. Their main concern is to be 'respected', so again removal from the supportive peer group who help maintain their image of power and control is an essential response to the situation. *Melancholy with Choleric personality type.*

The 'Dingo' Attitude

The passive-aggressive type needs approval so they attempt to appear as a 'goody-two-shoes' despite their abusive and harmful behaviours. They are mainly concerned with maintaining their respectable image and are afraid of getting caught out engaging in bullying behaviour; the likeness to the dingo is in relation to their cautious behaviours which allow them to go undetected and unobserved while they engage in prohibited activities (in the case of real dingoes, only stealing food!). This type of bully will use anonymous rumours, graffiti and whispers to denigrate their victim; they may send text messages which purport to be friendly, may invite the victim to attend an event or activity only to withdraw or cancel at the last minute; they will manufacture exclusionary situations to upset the victim; the 'dingo' type will behave as a provocative victim, claiming to have been harmed if their behaviour is challenged. They secure peer support by grooming them with 'nice' interactions such as invitations and goods. This type does not challenge authority but will nevertheless disobey rules while they pretend to be compliant and this causes confusion to teachers and parents because it is hard to pinpoint their deviant activities. Their main concern is to be seen as approved and 'good', therefore a reasonable intervention will include a requirement for public apology and withdrawal of approval until the behaviour ceases. *Phlegmatic personality type.*

The purpose of such a whimsical analysis is to facilitate an understanding of the individual psychology of bullies. It is important to have some relevant and simple reference points to enable an initial assessment to be made and some indicators for intervention to be discovered.

If we examine further the definition on page 51 we can analyse the behaviour of bullies in a variety of ways.

WHAT WE KNOW ABOUT BULLIES

■ *Bullying involves one or more socially powerful individuals*

Bullying is characterised as involving an unmistakable power differential between the bully and victim, which does not always correlate with the size, age or formal social status of the bully or the victim. Children, for example, can bully adults. Effective bullies may be smaller, younger or apparently less socially powerful than the victim – their power is based in their propensity or preference for engaging in threatening anti-social behaviour, their fearlessness in the face of authority, and the vicarious appeal of this to their peers. Other researchers refer to the reinforcement of self concept for bullies as an outcome of their behaviour at the expense of the self regard of their victims (*Marsh, Parada, Yeung & Healey, 2001*).

The social status and popularity of abusive individuals during adolescence is becoming a key focus of research. For example, *Espelage and Mebane (2003)* showed that students in the USA manoeuvred for social position in terms of establishing their popularity from a very young age. Being popular appears to put children in a powerful social position from which to enact harmful behaviours with immunity. In addition, the apparent Code of Silence (*Brinkley, Saarnio & Christy, 2003*) used by peers to protect aggressive individuals from detection, while at the same time ensuring personal protection from retaliation, is a focus of recent research.

We know that:

■ *Bullies are described as 'popular', 'attractive', 'sporty' leaders*

The research used to develop perspectives and interventions in this text included questionnaire responses from participants regarding both bullies and victims. Overwhelmingly, descriptors of bullies provided by students responding to the questionnaires referred in positive terms to the bully as being popular, attractive, sporty, having lots of friends, leading school sports teams and being in positions of social and educational status with regard to their achievements and personalities(Healey,2004). This does not mean that bullies are universally 'popular' people, but rather that their overall success underpins their capacity to bully others with impunity. As with other forms of abuse, the high social status of bullies and abusers provides immunity as victims struggle to convince others of the misuse of power they endure.

■ *Bullies are socially competent/ have high social and group status*

GROOMING FOR SUPPORT

The concept of 'grooming' is more often used to refer to adults who abuse children and who 'groom 'their victims for a period of time prior to abusing them. They do so by coercing them and their families with desirable activities, goods and attention. These abusers also ensure they are seen as 'child friendly', 'great with kids' and other descriptors as they insinuate themselves into the lives of their selected target. This behaviour is well–documented and a recognised factor in child abuse by adults. However, the term can also be used broadly to describe the processes used by abusers to ensure their power base is secure and their status well established before they begin to engage in inappropriate behaviour. They also 'groom' their colleagues, family and friends to believe in their socially-acceptable persona as a means of gaining support for themselves and access to their victims. Their reputation may well serve to protect them from detection and responsibility. Adult abusers are often well-respected in their communities and workplaces and maintain this image as a resource to enable them to engage in the offensive behaviours. Their colleagues and neighbours cannot believe such a 'pillar of the community' could be an abuser and as a consequence, many are never brought to justice for their acts, since their victims are never believed.

Bullies similarly engage in typical abuser behaviour as they use 'grooming' to establish a network of supporters as well as victims. They may 'groom' their supporters, including adults who misinterpret their behaviours, by engaging in socially acceptable, admired and preferred behaviours such as adherence to social and school regulations, assisting and supporting less able individuals and being available for additional responsibilities. They establish authorised status through these means, and this permits access to their victim. This activity can be termed 'pre-emptive grooming'. It is a preliminary activity undertaken prior to the abuse and involves the abuser soliciting the support and loyalty of others and establishing or using their social power base to ensure their behaviour will not be readily detected or interpreted as offensive or inappropriate. Bullies use both their 'nice', socially acceptable behaviours, and their threatening, aggressive behaviours to establish their position as 'overlords' in relation to their peers. Bullies also groom their peers to become 'underbullies' by reinforcing their loyalty, or withholding intimidation.

Some researchers insist that bullies engage in abusive behaviour because of their lack of social competency or self-esteem. This may be the case for some peer abusers but has not been borne out in the research that underpins this document. *Sutton, Smith and Swettenham (1999)* believe that the notion that bullies lack social skills is undermined by their obvious ability to direct and convince others to engage in anti-social acts. Teaching social skills to bullies is not a valuable exercise since most are already socially adept and in fact have often hold high social status as a result of their dominant behaviours. *Ozkan and Cifei (2009)* agree that although traditionally bullies were thought to have low self-esteem and poor social skills more recent research identifies high social competency as a critical factor in sustaining peer abusive behaviour.

In order for bullies to command the misguided 'respect' that they do enjoy, and their social status as 'popular' they need to be socially competent and indeed capable of directing others to do their bidding. They demonstrate social competency by discovering which triggers their followers will respond to, and manipulating them through flattery and apparent 'friendships'. Bullies make sure they have followers who are reliant upon them for some form of favourable treatment or status, such as membership on a team or in a group, and therefore hold some power over their quality of life. The evidence is certainly there to demonstrate that bullies engage in behaviours towards their followers that sustains loyalty and indeed their own status, often through their favourite means –intimidation.

A relevant film to watch which demonstrates this very clearly is 'Lord of the

Flies' (1990) which illustrates two groups of boys in an isolated situation, one led by a true 'leader' who uses democracy and fairness to lead his group and the other a despotic bully who uses intimidation to keep 'control' over his less powerful peers. There should be no doubt about the intentions and processes bullies will employ to ensure their social status is maintained. Not only that, young bullies are often able to manipulate the opinions of adults and those in authority because they are generally well thought of and socially competent in other areas of their lives. The challenge for teachers and parents is to teach alternative behaviours which are equally rewarding and this can be a very difficult task given the consistent reinforcement bullying provides.

It is also important to note that bullies do not bully everyone in their social environment. They are extremely selective and engage in abusive behaviour secretively while playing the part of a model student and friend and this is the reason their abusive persona is so difficult to expose. They are able to assemble an array of faithful individuals whom they have nurtured and assisted in various ways, and who will attest to this and seem to validate their claims that they could not possibly engage in such abuse. This is a recognised pattern of behaviour for abusive adults as well as young abusers as they lay the foundation for an impeccable character while in reality they are creating a defence for their actions.

If applied to the identification of other types of criminal activity such as stealing, it would seem ridiculous to have the defence offer the rationale for example, that since his client did not steal from everyone he came in contact with, he could not possibly be accused of stealing from the accusing individual. Nevertheless, this is the argument offered and often accepted by parents, teachers and others in the community when the issue of bullying or other forms of abuse, is raised. The status of the bully will often be their alibi. Streams of non-victims will be produced to prove that the bully does not engage in bullying of them, and therefore is unlikely to have abused another individual.

■ Bullies develop a range of bullying behaviours

Broadly defined, bullying comprises a range of harmful behaviours as described earlier, including in particular psychological abuse, physical assaults and exclusion. Often it is the secretive nature of the behaviour which causes most distress as it is least likely to be detected. When bullies manage to get their victim alone they are able to threaten them, their families and even pets with harm, in an environment where no protection is afforded the victim. Threats of harm, abusive and derogatory verbal statements, whether delivered privately or publically, form one of the most destructive types of behaviour endured by victims of bullying. Changing the type of abusive behaviour frequently, and being able to encourage others to engage in the behaviours, spreads the distress across all facets of the victim's life and relationships.

Further, because they change their practices frequently, reports of bullying vary and very often are not believed because the recipient of the report cannot accept such a range of inappropriate behaviour and actions, on the part of the nominated bully. Victims of bullying are frustrated when their claims of harassment are rejected because the bully or their followers change their modus operandi to avoid detection.

■ Bullies are powerful and confident individuals

Power is a socially defined attribute. 'Power' is:

> *'A great or marked ability to do or act; strength; might; force'.*
> *Also 'the possession of control or command over others; authority;' (Macquarie dictionary)*

Power does not necessarily reside in the size of the individual, but is more closely aligned with their use of psychological dominance. It is clear, for example that children can bully adults despite the physical power difference. As described further in this document, the power of bullying evolves as an outcome of rejection of standard principles of behaviour and the adoption of self-selected behaviours that intimidate and terrorize the target individual. Such power is highly reinforcing and develops the confidence of the bully to continue. Nor is 'authority' formally defined in this circumstance as bullies adopt 'authority' by directing others to engage in particular acts and ensuring a negative consequence if their demands are not met. This includes the victim and followers of the bully. In all situations, the behaviours are selected for impact and are deliberate in their intention to cause harm.

- **Bullies are dominant, but not 'leaders'**
- **Bullies are trusted /admired by supporters**

Dominance is often misinterpreted as 'leadership'.

> 'Dominance' refers to the ego involvement of the dominant personality, and is anchored in notions of control and tyranny; 'leadership' means to show the way, to guide or direct towards success and achievement.' (Macquarie dictionary)

Unfortunately, the teachers and parents of bullies often do not differentiate the two concepts resulting in the abusive individual being inadvertently supported by those in authority.

Bullies may be allocated 'leadership' roles to which they are entitled due to their superior performance, for example in a sport. While they behave as a guide and director of their teams they are entitled to maintain the position. However, sometimes the effect of having this role results in the individual developing and engaging in the types of behaviours described here as bullying as the bully forces their requirements for compliance or loyalty on team members. They may well for example, threaten and carry out adjustments to team roles in order to secure, not victory for their team but obedience to their demands. They may clearly give preferential treatment to some, often as a reward for undertaking a particular directive, but also simply for the sense of power the gratitude of the recipient gives, or to build their own reputation. This is how bullying is differentiated from leadership. It is really the ego or 'self' factor that changes the encounter.

The same rules apply in other leadership roles when the designated leader, often quite legitimately placed, adopts behaviours which in no way relate to the successful performance of others or the team but only to personal gain, power and status. Leaders must be allowed to 'lead' but bullies cannot be allowed to dominate and destroy others.

■ *Bullies have peer support*

Peer support sustains bullies and bullying. There can be no doubt that bullies operate within a supportive environment of peers who are either afraid to defy them or who simply admire the bully for the gains they seem to be able to acquire as a result of their behaviour. Often bullying incidents involve a number of participants but usually there is a dominant individual who issues orders for particular acts of abuse to be carried out, or who initiates them expecting others to follow. Peers of bullies are, of course, also often the peers of victims. They engage in group or gang behaviours in company but may well assert their loyalty to the victim at other times. This is confusing for victims of bullying and they express some concern about being able to understand friendships. Can a friend who engages in bullying truly be a friend when it is all over? Further discussion of this is included in the Self Guard ™ plan intervention which is part of the *Bullywatch* program for young victims of bullying. For older victims Peer Advocacy© is another intervention discussed further in this book which assists by providing a trained peer to advocate on their behalf and support their reporting of incidents. This turns the tables on bullies as they do not expect their victims to respond in a resilient manner nor to have sustained support.

Peer support for bullies is a critical sustaining factor in the maintenance of the behaviour, although this support is often not overtly offered. The matrix on p.90 (*Figure 3*) describes both passive and active, harmful and helpful responses to bullying by observers or supporters of the behaviour. There can be no longer any doubt that active support or selective ignoring of bullying behaviour contributes substantially to the impact of the behaviour, and that peers who engage in these behaviours may well be equally culpable with the bully.

FIGURE 3: MATRIX OF OBSERVER RESPONSES IN WITNESSING BULLYING (Healey, 2004)

OBSERVER BEHAVIOUR:	POSITIVE / HELPFUL	NEGATIVE / HARMFUL
ACTIVE:	■ Verbal or physical assistance to victim ■ Reporting to authorities ■ Expressed disapproval of bullying behaviour ■ Texting for help, mobile phone photos of incident	■ Verbal support for bully ■ Prevention of protective intervention of others ■ Expressed approval of bullying behaviour ■ Denying the incident ■ Refusing to be a witness
PASSIVE:	■ Remaining in vicinity of victim ■ Mentally noting names of bullies and details of events for later reporting ■ Withholding participation	■ Turning away ■ Leaving the vicinity ■ Failing to report ■ Failing to offer verbal or physical assistance ■ Withholding information ■ Ignoring bullying

The impact on observers of watching bullying has, to date been discussed in terms of concern for their emotional responses, however it is suggested in this discussion that 'bystanders' be replaced with a paradigm which places observers of bullying within the following matrix. It is clear that observers of bullying incidents are involved to some extent whatever their selected responses. 'Bystander' is a term that implies no involvement, but these individuals cannot be neutral bystanders of abusive behaviour towards others. They are impacted and must respond in some way to the incidents observed and the matrix suggests that these responses can be positive or negative in their impact as well as active or passive in their execution.

Doing 'nothing' is nevertheless responding in a manner which impacts the victim. This could include turning away, leaving the vicinity of the incident and failing to report. This is therefore a passive and negative response to witnessing bullying. Observers who are' passive' in the sense of not actively engaging in overt behaviour can nevertheless contribute positively by remaining nearby and perhaps mentally noting the details of the incident. Observers, who actively support the bully or prevent protective intervention by others, are engaging in negative and harmful behaviours akin to victimisation. The most effective and collaborative role for the observer of bullying is to engage in positive and helpful behaviours such as reporting, offering assistance, expressing disapproval to bullies and help-seeking.

The Peer Advocacy© program described further aims to develop courage and a sense of responsibility in those who witness bullying incidents. This requires training in perspective-taking as well as specific help-seeking skills.

Observers of bullying are therefore suitable candidates for the Peer Advocacy© program. The lyrics to the Kate Miller-Heidke song 'Caught in the Crowd', illustrate in a very sensitive way, the benefit of maturity and hindsight in the matter of peer abuse. This story exposes the long term negative effects on peers which may develop as they consider the impact of their behaviour in not responding with assistance to the pleas for help from a peer being abused. Understanding through more mature eyes the emotional plight of the victim, and accepting some responsibility for their distress, can be a haunting and guilty experience for their non-abusive peers.

Young people are aware of bullying behaviours, are willing to report them to teachers and others in authority and are willing to help those they see being victimised (Healey, 2003). Nevertheless, they also express negative views of the competency of victims and positive views about the personal attributes of bullies. Victims on the other hand are seen as largely responsible for their own fate due to their lack of social acceptability or standing (Olweus, 1999). This evidence establishes the need for a training program and confirms the need for the development and implementation of a response to establish more responsible and committed attitudes towards those who are victims of peer abuse. Significant differences are shown in the willingness of bullied individuals and others to report bullying to a teacher and this further indicates a need for intervention (Healey, 2004).

The same research shows significant differences between schools in terms of their perceived capacity to maintain student self-esteem. It is apparent that for some schools there is a significant difference in student perceptions about the capacity of the school to offer support and that intervention a particular school would not necessarily be useful in another location.

Further evidence of the necessity for comprehensive intervention is provided in the responses regarding the willingness of students to assist others they saw being bullied. While bullied students are almost equally willing to help others, some students feel less inclined to offer assistance and this could be related to their perception of the amount of support available within the school. Overall the impact of peer responses to bullying behaviour cannot be underestimated in the design of intervention.

Teachers in particular need to receive training in order to recognise and address bullied students' concerns about the seriousness of the problem even though the majority of students surveyed in research did not view the problem as serious, evidently since they were not personally effected. The legitimate concerns of bullied individuals obviously need to be addressed to ensure protection from victimisation.

THE GANG MENTALITY

In Australian schools we do not have the same level of formal 'gang' membership and consequent illegal activity by gangs as there is, for example in the United States. We do not see much of the colours and signs, the graffiti and tattoos which differentiate gangs elsewhere. However, there is no question that ethnic-based groups form into gangs and that community–based gangs of differing memberships invade schools. Gang activity can be clearly identified as *White (2003)* states:

> *'For many young people, gangs serve to provide a sense of social inclusion, support and security. They can also provide opportunities for status, group identity and excitement.'*

Olweus was responsible for the initial interest and focus on gang activity in relation to bullying, which he termed 'mobbning' and he instigated the preliminary research in Sweden in 1970 (*Olweus,1999*). Other contributors included *Dueholm* in Denmark who examined the school 'mobbe' (*Dueholm, 1999*) as well as *Bjorkvist, Osterman* and *Lagerspetz* who replicated *Olweus*' research from Sweden in Finland (1982). These researchers focussed specifically on the peer gang or mob who targeted vulnerable individuals and worked together to intimidate and harm.

Frequently, bullies will assemble with their peers into threatening groups which cruise around schools and districts causing trouble and singling out individuals for torment and worse. The *Thompson and Stolz* article in *The Courier-Mail* (*2008*) describes 'swarming' and indicates the level of violence such gangs engage in within the community. If challenged such groups will defend their 'right' to assembly by claiming to be just good friends who are out for 'fun'. For teachers in particular it is crucial that such gangs be clearly differentiated from teams or genuine friendship groups and that their activities are interrupted if they are on school grounds and in school activities.

Teachers are well aware of the intimidating intent of their activities and need to be supported in their attempts to disperse and monitor such groups. The issue of 'rights' can be contradictory and is, of course, always discussed in relation to relevant 'responsibilities'. Does the bully gang have a greater 'right' to assembly in threatening packs than the victims have to a safe environment, free of

The Courier Mail – August 2, 2008, 12:00 noon

TUCK THOMPSON and GREG STOLZ

Violent youth gangs take control of streets

DRIVE-by beatings and random 'swarming' attacks by teens armed with knives and poles are leaving a bloody trail across southeast Queensland.

This week's meat cleaver attack by a gang of youths at a Brisbane boys' college is the latest major episode illustrating youth violence is becoming more blatant and unpredictable. Seven teens, linked to a gang called the Jay Jays, were arrested after a student at St Laurence's College at South Brisbane was hit in the face with the cleaver and another stabbed. On the Gold Coast, a child gang operating "like a pack of animals" attacked a young couple in a Coolangatta park. One gang member used a fence to give himself extra leverage to stomp on one of his hapless victims. The gang, whose members are as young as 11, celebrated with high-fives and disappeared into the night, leaving the couple bruised and bloodied.

harassment? Rights and responsibility need to be weighted in favour of the safety of all students. Intimidation has no part in a 'group' activity.

Certainly, gangs have a long history in Australia. The first criminal gangs in Australia were probably the bushrangers, with the Ned Kelly Gang being the most famous (White, 2003).Recently, there has been a push to outlaw 'bikie' gangs across Australia, in an attempt to deter their criminal and violent activities. The response from these obviously anti-social and dangerous gangs has been surprising. They declare themselves to be simply groups of individuals interested in a shared love of riding motorbikes, and they have formulated legal defence based on their 'right to assembly' for legitimate purposes like country rides and social gatherings.

While this may be a reasonable description of the activities of 'biker' groups, whose intention is not intimidation, we need to be prepared to differentiate these groups and confront their true intent. While the right to assemble for legitimate, peaceful, non-criminal activity cannot be denied to any group, the problem here is in the purpose and intent of the gang. Indeed, the behaviour of outlaw 'bikie' gangs in riding together in mass numbers through communities can be described as 'swarming' and it is not unreasonable for law enforcement agents to confront them for this obviously threatening activity.

The obviously intimidating attire of outlaw 'biker' gangs is similarly dismissed by them as merely a means to identify each others' 'group'. There is a co-ordinated effort now to also outlaw these distinguishing outfits which are intended to intimidate the opposition gang, but in the process also intimidate the general community. There are already regulated and legislated restrictions regarding suitable attire within society, including the outlawing of Nazi paraphernalia and activities, which are obviously designed for intimidation effects. Banning particular garb to ensure that the general population feels secure is not new and should not be viewed as discriminatory. In schools, the issue of intimidation by gangs needs to be confronted and addressed when it arises, irrespective of the attire of the group, bearing in mind the intention of the group is the key. The similarities between outlawed gangs and the developing behaviours and intentions of school gangs need to be identified and addressed.

The so –called 'Cronulla riot' in December 2005 resulted from youth gangs of Lebanese, Middle Eastern and Australian origins in territorial conflict at the beachside suburb of Cronulla (see Healey 2006). Unfortunately it was the innocent citizens of the suburb who were blamed for racism when the conflict turned to physical attacks on local white Anglo-Saxon residents and businesses. In fact both gangs comprised youths from outlying suburbs who met and clashed in Cronulla about cultural and social differences. These were gangs without uniforms but with strong cultural allegiances to their individual flags. Much confused commentary followed and many Cronulla residents were left feeling guilty for racism they did not express or feel. Overall there was a refusal to accept that anti-Australian racism is just as unacceptable as any other form. Gang membership denial was a key issue here.

So, What is a Gang?

There are a number of salient points here to understand and address in relation to bullying. Gangs, groups and teams all fulfil a particular need and purpose within their own communities, some of which are legitimate and endorsed by society and others not. To pretend that violent and disruptive assemblies of like-minded individuals are serving the same function as law-abiding and genuinely pro-social groups is to ignore the obvious consequences of their activities. Gangs differ from other groups on a number of dimensions. Schools, teachers and the community may need to become familiar with these differences in order to validate their rejection of so-called 'groups' engaging in unacceptable behaviours.

There are six key features that comprise a gang, according to recent research. These include: being organized; having identifiable leadership; identifying with a territory; continual association; having a specific purpose; and engaging in illegal activities.

Goldstein and Kodluboy, (1998), describe a gang as:

> *'a visible group of youths who engage at least some of the time in behaviours that are troublesome---and sometimes illegal (page 2)*

Collins et al. (*2000*) address the issue of gangs by exploring specific factors:

> 'we need to separate what constitutes gangs of organised crime from gangs of youth. ..... we really need to interrogate the issue of youth gangs. Are they just friendship groups of kids hanging out mainly in public spaces who occasionally engage in criminal or anti-social behaviour? (Are they) gangs in the sense that they have membership rituals, hierarchal structure of power and patterns of systematic criminal activities?'

These issues impact on our understanding of the role of gang membership in bullying incidents. For the purposes of this discussion, the relevant factors are the differences in the legitimacy and intent of the 'group' as they impact on the running of the school or on the community. Teachers, parents and community members must be prepared to reject and report disruptive groups whose aggressive and threatening behaviour and illegitimate activities clearly identify them as a 'gang'. We cannot be distracted by cries of 'unfair' from groups whose intentions are clearly harmful. In particular, gangs of bullies who roam together with the sole intention of attacking others can quite legitimately be identified as such and called to account. Teachers and others do not have to accept the self-applied description of 'group' when clearly there is a 'gang' in operation. Students also need to be able to differentiate acceptable and friendship groups and activities from those of socially delinquent 'gangs'. The overall relevance of this issue is to empower teachers, schools and parents to report and reject the 'gang's they can readily identify and to have the courage to refuse them legitimacy in childhood activities.

White (2003) believes that intervention needs to be embedded within a therapeutic system to be effective,

> 'While for tactical purposes, coercive force may occasionally be necessary, positive approaches to gang issues also require developmental strategies and active community involvement'.

We need, therefore to offer remedial intervention to guide members who want to move beyond illegal activity and re-enter mainstream society. In particular, school-aged gang members need educational intervention to alert them to the consequences and impact of their activities.

Factors Differentiating Gangs, Teams and Groups

In *Figure 4*, certain factors are compared which show a differentiation in focus between gangs and legitimate teams or harmless friendship groups. These criteria may be applied when dealing with bullying behaviour by gangs. Fundamentally, responsibility for the management of the activities of abusive peers who operate in gangs falls to the school, the community and ultimately the law. It is very important to understand that while gangs may fit the criteria for the other groups or even teams, the greatest difference is that legitimate groups do not fit the criteria that relate to gangs.

For teachers, schools and community observers, the checklist contained in *Figure 4* can guide their determination of whether a 'group' of individuals actually fits the profile of a legitimate group or team (socially acceptable associations of individuals) or can be indentified as a 'gang' which has negative social and possibly legal implications.

The key defining features of group associations are:

- Leadership
- Membership
- Intention or focus
- Attitude
- Appearance

FIGURE 4: FACTORS DIFFERENTIATING GANGS, TEAMS AND GROUPS (Healey, 2010)

FACTOR	GANG	TEAM	GROUP
LEADERSHIP	• 'elected' based on dominance • power-base focus • punitive • intimidating • frightening	• elected based on performance • guidance focus • by management • collaborative • inspiring	• no formal leader • friendship focus • consensual • co-operative • secure
MEMBERSHIP	• hierarchy of subordinates • recruited based on strict rituals and illegitimate skills and requirements	• specific roles based on criteria • recruited based on strict legitimate requirements and skills	• interest /skill or affection • selected friends based on interest recreation skill or gender
INTENT	• disruption • criminal activity • harm to others • indoctrination	• cohesion • legitimate activity • establish spirit/ goals	• enjoyment • fun/pleasure • shared interests
ATTITUDE	• rejecting authority • aggressive • threatening/defiant	• strict adherence to rules/authority • co-operative	• work with authority • supportive
APPEARANCE	• strict uniform code to unite members but intimidate others; • insignia and flags to unite and identify	• strict uniform code to identify and unite members • insignia and flags unite and identify	• no uniform or • benign outfits • few identifying insignia

FIGURE 4. Factors differentiating gangs, teams and groups (Healey, 2010)

> **LEADERSHIP**
>
> ... *refers to a guiding and supportive role which takes followers from a particular stage of development or skill to a more advanced and rewarding stage. 'Leadership' is not something bullies do well, since their focus is mainly to dominate and coerce for compliance and obedience. Using the term in relation to a team or group of individuals, the form that leadership takes is likely to involve cooperative, collaborative and mutually satisfactory decisions, even when those decisions may impact on followers with a requirement for greater effort or sacrifice.*
>
> *' when the best leader's work is done*
> *the people say 'we did it ourselves' Lao Tse*

The masterful leader is persuasive and inspires the follower to engage for their own benefit and the greater good. Encouragement, support and positive interactions will usually prevail in such encounters. Fundamentally this is all undertaken with the purpose of achieving improvements or attainment in socially endorsed and acceptable activities. Typical groups in this category would include sporting teams, dance groups, etc. In this situation, leaders are usually elected due to their superior performance and popularity or respect amongst fellow team and group members.

'Gang' leaders may also meet some of these criteria. They may 'lead' through charisma and 'persuasion' but it is much more likely to be persuasion to engage in socially unacceptable activities and compliance is usually predicated upon threats of harm. Gang leaders are much more likely to be 'elected' due to threats and dominance rather than a democratic and positive process. Gang leaders nevertheless enjoy high levels of loyalty, and secure compliance as a key indicator of their superior position. Bully gangs display all of these characteristics, and cannot be tolerated within the community or school as a concession to their democratic right to 'play together'.

> **MEMBERSHIP**
>
> *... in a team or friendship/interest group membership is usually reliant upon specific socially acceptable criteria and/or performance. The Orchid Society, for example, will be pleased to welcome new members who either wish to show their expertise or learn the skills they offer. Similarly, most sporting organisations will provide team membership at the elite and beginner levels to encourage membership.*

Gang membership can also be offered to novices. However, induction often involves serious rituals and pain or satisfaction of specified socially unacceptable or criminal criteria for membership to be granted. Membership in the '5T' Asian gang based in Sydney and other cities in Australia in the 80's was predicated on the satisfaction of five specific 'achievements' including fathering a child and murder (personal research with gang members during their incarceration in juvenile detention).

Membership in teams and groups is generally voluntary, however gang membership may include the expectation of lifetime commitment and priority over all other aspects of life including family and work. Childhood bully gangs are probably not quite so stringent, however loyalty is expected, defection may be punished and disclosure seriously punished.

> **INTENTION OR FOCUS**
>
> *... is a critical defining feature of the 'gang', and in particular the socially negative aspects of their activities. 'Outlaw bikie gangs' are familiar to us as they are frequently referred to in the media and are known to exist to engage in anti-social and criminal activities just as much as friendly 'outings'. Childhood bully gangs are less familiar and less often reported, but also have as their major focus negative and harmful intent.*

Differentiating such groups from social interest and friendship groups and legitimate teams is a key role now for educators, families and the community.

> **ATTITUDE TOWARDS AUTHORITY**
>
> ... is a key indicator of the social deviance of gangs. An interest or friendship group will have no intention of rejecting social mores and norms as they conduct their activities; similarly, teams are far more likely to endorse the relevant social and industry regulations which underpin their activities. By contrast, 'gangs' are rebellious and see the rejection or defiance of authority as critical to their image, purpose and intent.

> **APPEARANCE**
>
> ... as defined by specific and regulated garb is a further critical indicator of anti-social gang membership in society, as a rule. However, in school and childhood gangs, particularly in Australia where school uniform is the norm, gang 'colours' such as those evident in gangs in the USA are rare. However, school-aged gang members may redesign their uniform to indicate their membership by subtle changes to trouser length, size, exposure of buttocks/underwear and other indicators. The intention is not intimidation in this case but affiliation and loyalty. Nevertheless, if it is an indicator of membership in a gang, the practice needs to be discouraged. Team membership also usually involves some identification by garb but the genuine intention there is to differentiate them from other teams. Social groups may wear benign outfits to identify membership and affiliation. Flags and insignia or emblems are common cohesive devices used by gangs as well as teams, but for very different effects and messages.

Fundamentally, this information is provided to support teachers in their identification of specific criteria by which to classify groups of individuals according to their intention. Groups and teams have positive intent (even if that is to legitimately defeat the opposition) while gangs have negative intentions to cause harm or hurt or disruption to others in their social milieu. Differentiating these is a valuable skill in terms of management of bullying practices.

WHAT WE KNOW ABOUT VICTIMS OF BULLYING

Further discussion of the key elements of the definition of bullying brings us to the next issues which concern victims:

■ *'Against an individual who cannot effectively resist'*

Victims of bullying cannot be identified as a single group, as their ability to resist the bully differs along a continuum from passivity and surrender to resilience and recovery. Further discussion of this element of the paradigm is continued in the chapter related to 'resiliency'. Victims of bullying may be poor at interpersonal peer relationships and sustaining friendships. They are often seen as 'loners' and may appear self-sufficient in that they do not seem to need friends and to be able and happy to learn, play and engage in activities without the need for peer supporters. They may be labelled socially isolated and 'different' and this rejection, whether overt or secretive, places the individual in a vulnerable position to the jibes of others. A large part of the behaviour resides in the lack of tolerance and acceptance of others' individuality during childhood developmental periods. Children and young people have immature and incompletely developed concepts of 'norms' and peer pressure is still a real and tangible influence on their attitudes and behaviour. *Heidke-Miller* (*2009*) describes this as being 'caught in the crowd'.

■ *And 'who does not reciprocate the actions'*

A lack of reciprocity was identified as a key factor whereby bullying is conceptualised to involve the hurtful actions of one person or a group towards another whom, though sometimes resistant, is not aggressive in return. Attention to the factor of lack of reciprocity enables the differentiation of bullying from fighting. Additionally, capacity for resistance or resilience is also a critical factor, since bullied individuals differ in their ability to cope with and effectively resist the victimisation.

Columbine occurred after a reportedly long history of peer abuse however, and illustrates the element of precipitation which is often a consequence of sustained bullying. Victims are encouraged to 'fight back' and to 'stick up' for themselves, and in some cases this has tragic outcomes. They may retaliate against the bully, changing the dynamic of the interaction from abuse to fighting, or they may turn on themselves. What is certain is that at present there is no process in place to establish when, and if, the problem is likely precipitate an escalation of events. This is a critical component for consideration in a comprehensive intervention such as that proposed here. Accessing suicide prevention literature and other legal and medical advice can be a valuable inclusion in intervention.

Victims of Bullying:

- *Have low social/group status*
- *Have low peer support*

Negative and derogatory descriptors are far more likely to be used by peers in relation to victims of bullying, than they are for bullies. Words used by a large sample of students across a range of school settings responding to a peer abuse questionnaire included 'nerds', 'spotty', 'fat', 'ugly', 'no friends', 'unfashionable clothes and hair' and 'no good at sport' (Healey, 2004). Victims of bullying often find their access to peers blocked by bullies or denied because of the fears of peers that their own status may be affected by association with the victim. The isolation resulting from these attitudes leaves the victim exposed and vulnerable without a friendship group to rely on for support or company. The loneliness of the long-suffering victim of bullying is tragic and can eventuate in depression or even suicide.

Examination of responses to students surveyed indicates that victims of bullying are often viewed as being in some way deserving of the bullying because of their 'obvious' social incompetence, unattractiveness and lack of personality. Many viewed students who were "different" in unspecified ways, as targets for bullying and lack of popularity and the consequent lack of friends were also seen as indicative. Ethnicity was also seen as relevant and other contributing factors included poor self-esteem and personal attributes. The overall impression gained from examination of these responses is that, without the support of carefully inducted peers whose attitudes towards those being victimised had been addressed systematically, there is little hope for the safety and well-being of victims of bullying from their less than sympathetic non-abusive peers.

- **May be highly competent and resilient**
- **Exhibit a continuum of responses (passive to assertive)**

On the other hand, victims of bullying can be shown to be socially competent and resilient in the opinion of others. They may be assertive but ignored in their social environment; may be resilient but unsupported. For example, targets of bullying who continue to attend school, engage in the programs offered, sustain their relationships with peers and teachers and continue to develop skills despite the abuse, are undoubtedly resilient. This concept is examined in greater detail further in this discussion but in general, socially competent and resourceful victims are not advantaged by their responses if they find their position is further compromised by a lack of support and intervention. Victims of peer abuse cannot solve their abuse alone however, and given the lack of established and effective consistent intervention and responses within their social environment, their psychological strength is soon depleted. Not all victims of bullying are incapable of responding in a self protective manner, but those who do have the skills to report and seek help nevertheless need support and protective intervention to successfully overcome the abuse.

- **May be inadvertently unsupported by authority**

Instead of carefully monitoring the reported behaviours to identify abusive or physically harmful activities, those in authority often permit the social competency and status of bullies to shield them from detection. As shown earlier, their dominance is often misinterpreted, or viewed as conflict and fighting with the victim, leading to unfair blaming and punishment of victims.

Victims of bullying are not necessarily all passive, ineffectual individuals incapable of resistance. However, the capacity to resist in a non-aggressive, socially acceptable manner often does not afford the victim any protection at all. Their help-seeking and reporting of incidents or their resilient behaviours in continuing to attend school and attempt to get on with their lives must be supported within their social environment to be effective. Unfortunately, this is often not the case, as such individuals are often viewed as coping and therefore not in need of assistance or support.

In summary, the psychology of peer abuse is a complex and serious concern for parents, educators and the community. It can no longer be seen as matter of little consequence since we are now, throughout the world, witnessing the awful and deadly outcomes of sustained bullying in childhood. It can be shown that bullies require urgent specialised and individual behaviour remediation, within a supportive school and community context, if their future as genuine model citizens is to be secured. To date, nobody seems to be addressing the matter this comprehensively. It can also be shown that victims of bullying require supportive and protective intervention, and to be heard when they assertively and resiliently report and resist their abuser.

The following chapters elaborate on the key theoretical perspectives, pragmatically applied, which may assist effective intervention.

NEW PSYCHOLOGICAL PERSPECTIVES

Several new psychological perspectives emerge with reflection upon on recent research of this author and others and are discussed in terms of the development of practical responses to the management of peer abuse.

Specifically:

■ *Bullying as abuse not conflict*

A critical revelation from examining research, media reports and deaths associated with bullying is that viewing peer abuse as conflict is tragically mistaken. Bullying is entirely about abuse and responsibility for the all-too-frequent lethal consequences of the abuse rests with the bully or bullies engaged in the abusive behaviours. Accepting this paradigm shift is essential to an understanding of the underlying philosophy of this text which is that education underpins the solutions to bullying and that supportive and at times punitive intervention must also be put in place to provide the security and safety to which victims of peer abuse are entitled.

■ *Peer abuse as child abuse*

It is proposed for the first time here that peer abuse is a type of child abuse and should be addressed accordingly. The applicability of child protection legislation to the issue is also, therefore, explored. The realignment of bullying from the conflict into the abuse paradigm is a critical and innovative change in the current discourse. The applicability of child protection legislation and processes to bullying intervention is proposed as a pragmatic solution to bullying. Further, the impact of peer abuse as comparable to other forms of child abuse is validated and discussion of a range of legislative responses undertaken.

■ *Resilience as a critical factor in resisting bullying*

As a critical factor in resisting bullying and the practicability of teaching this attribute to victims, this is a major perspective and component of intervention proposed. Resiliency training underpins the interventions recommended for victims of bullying. The key indicative behaviours and personal attributes evident in the characteristics of resilient individuals, it is proposed, may be taught and rehearsed until the actor becomes genuinely resilient. The

BULLYWATCH™ SELF GUARD PROGRAM provides the opportunity to develop these skills.

■ *Peer Advocacy©*

The notion of using positive peer advocacy as a supportive response for victims of bullying is explored in this text. It is apparent from a broad spectrum of research that the support of peers is the key sustaining factor in bullying and this phenomenon is addressed as a critical issue for bullying intervention. The approach taken here is to introduce peer advocacy as a positive factor offering systematic support and guidance for victims of bullying. The introduction of Peer Advocacy© training as an intervention to support victims is described.

And, finally:

■ *Impact of violence viewing*

As an influence on young people, motivating them to engage in violence or bullying is examined in light of research which seems to indicate that only those with a predisposition towards violence and abuse may learn and adopt new skills as an outcome of violent media viewing. The impact of viewing simulated violence by most individuals is highly unlikely to lead to violence and bullying in interpersonal interactions unless a predisposition is already evident or potential. The purpose of this discussion is to focus attention not on general viewing but on the specific choices abusive individuals are likely to make in order to supplement their repertoire of abusive behaviours.

Of these, bullying as a form of abuse removed entirely from the 'conflict' paradigm is the most significant.

All other perspectives are addressed in following chapters.

4   Peer Abuse as Child Abuse

Introduction

Over recent years profiles of the school bully and the victim of school bullying have become daily features of news reports and the increasing number of suicide deaths attributable to bullying has grown alarmingly. No longer can bullying be considered a minor nuisance of childhood. In particular, the teenage years expose young people to sophisticated levels of peer abuse and harassment, often with tragic consequences. Litigation against schools, but also individuals and families, for the damaging effects of systematic abuse is increasing daily, as the parents of children and young people seriously effected psychologically, socially and academically, now routinely use the legal system to address the issue. A range of legal avenues are currently explored to seek protection for abused children including stalking legislation in Victoria, sexual harassment legislation in Queensland and apprehended violence legislation elsewhere.

It is suggested here that the most relevant legislation to use in such cases, applicable across Australia, is child protection legislation, which already mandates teachers and other professionals in most states to report suspected or reported incidents of abuse. Teachers are trained in their professional courses to be aware of abuse indicators, and certainly in all states except Queensland to report suspected or notified abuse of children. It would seem self-evident therefore that peer abuse, which is equivalent to other forms of child abuse in terms of ongoing damage, would be included in those recommendations for reporting.

National – *May 9, 2010 EXCLUSIVE*

BY STEPHANIE PEATLING

New Bullying Laws

- Young victims of cyber bullying and tormenting classmates will be given legal protection under new anti-harassment laws to be introduced by the Federal government.
- The changes will mean victims under the age of 16 will be able to use sexual harassment laws to pursue their tormentors.
- "These are sensible changes but they reflect the fact that young people are, unfortunately, the victims of sexual harassment," Minister for Women Tanya Plibersek said.
- "It's a terrible thing for parents and adults to realise how vulnerable children are and that they can be harassed at home in their bedrooms through Face book or chat rooms."
- Now, a 15-year-old girl whose former boyfriend sends naked cyber images of her to their classmates has no protection under federal sexual harassment legislation. But a 16-year-old girl is protected under the existing act.
- "'Younger children are often the most at risk from online bullying or harassment," Sex Discrimination Commissioner, Elizabeth Broderick said.
- Ms Plibersek said the changes would mean tormentors would no longer be able to get away with harassment.
- "The anonymity of [the internet] gives people a licence to behave very, very badly but the effect of it on the victim is very, very public," she said.

It would seem unnecessary to introduce new legislation, when current laws are already in place to protect children and young people.

Since bullying or peer abuse is now recognised as an endemic feature of school life and efforts are being made to address the issue at the school level through policy and curriculum development as well as individual interventions (Healey, 2009), the incorporation of bullying into child protection training and processes should not pose too great a challenge. Legislation across Australia mandates early notification of all forms of abuse, and increases both the level of responsibility and liability for litigation of teachers and schools for failure to offer an appropriate level of protection to victims. Schools are actively seeking advice and direction on the introduction of research-based customised bullying intervention procedures (Healey, 2003b) which should provide adequate protections for students. Nevertheless, serious and harmful incidents may still occur and in these cases the application of the protective legislation provisions ought to be considered.

Few researchers have addressed the issue of bullying in the context of child protection or abuse. However, evidence is now readily available in the literature that peer abuse correlates closely with child abuse in terms of negative social and psychological impact and outcomes. The application of the legislation specifically to the abuse of children and young people by their peers and the responsibility of schools under this law to provide protection is a new and challenging interpretation of duty of care. It is suggested that the use of child protection processes in dealing with bullying, may help avoid litigation in future but more importantly, could provide early protection for victims of serious peer abuse.

Behaviours can be classified as abusive if there is actual harm or the threat of harm, the intention of the perpetrator is to cause harm and outcomes for the abused individual are negative. It now seems that the critical defining features of child maltreatment by adults are also applicable to peer abuse. *Duncan (1999)* suggests that bullying is often viewed by society to be at the 'milder end of the trauma spectrum' and that it is viewed as 'merely a bothersome part of a normal childhood'. However, this view cannot be sustained given that research clearly indicates that experiences of bullying result in damaging outcomes that are the same as other forms of abuse including long and short term negative psychological impact, physical harm, school failure and social exclusion. Further, recent events clearly show that lethal outcomes are not uncommon.

In defining either peer abuse or the more commonly acknowledged abuse of children by adults, the similarities are far more noteworthy than the differences. Not only are the actual behaviours often the same, there is ample evidence that peer abuse can have equally as serious and permanent repercussions as other forms of abuse (*Ambert, 1995*).

PEER ABUSE AS CHILD ABUSE — HOW ARE THEY THE SAME?

Child abuse is clearly shown in a range of research, to have negative psychological and social impact and implications for development (*Finkelhor and Korbin, 1998*) and it is difficult to differentiate these outcomes from those identified as resulting from peer abuse or bullying. Certain characteristics of abuse are common to both bullying (peer abuse), and child abuse, which is often perpetrated by known and trusted adults. Included in these are the types of behaviours endured, the psychological impact of the abuse, the power relationship between victim and abuser and the lack of availability of support for the victim such as access to professionals who can intervene on their behalf. Further, the non-accidental nature of the injury, although not as obvious or readily identified between 'peers', and the harm or threatened harm which characterises peer victimisation, equates to child abuse on all levels of analysis.

Child abuse literature describes the impact of emotional abuse on the psychological functioning and well being of children and includes: "acts of rejection" (*Rutter, 1993*), spurning, terrorizing, isolating, exploitation and denial of emotional responses and states that it is often the repetitive, sustained nature of the behaviour that is most harmful. Bullying or peer abuse is similarly described as involving "repeated taunting" "put downs, insults, laughing and gesturing in derogatory ways" "social exclusion and demeaning" all of which behaviours would be acknowledged as abusive if conducted by an adult against a child as a form of psychological abuse. *Hodges and Perry* (*1996*) confirm that peer abuse has the effect of causing depression, low self-esteem and avoidance of school, while *Olweus*, (*1995*) and others (*Morita, Harud, Haruo and Taki, 1999*) also found elevated levels of depressive tendencies and poor self-esteem which continued into young adulthood in victims of peer abuse. This is also a defining feature of child abuse (*O'Toole, Webster, O'Toole and Lucal, 1999*).

Rigby (1996) indicates that the general health of self-reported victims of bullying is significantly poorer than that of non-victims, with many psychological effects reported including lost sleep due to worry, constant strain and feeling worthless. Victims of bullying have been reported to exhibit higher rates of depression, withdrawal and suicidal thoughts in response to the abuse and to experience emotional disturbances such as anxiety, panic, loneliness and rejection.

Others report that victims feel humiliated, ashamed and degraded by the rejection they endure and develop introverted and socially avoidant behaviour. Furthermore there is evidence of long-term impact and the potential for difficulties in interpersonal relationships in adult life as a result of bullying in childhood (Doll and Lyon, 1998[7]). On each measure, peer abuse echoes the damaging outcomes of other forms of child abuse.

Duncan (1999) describes a retrospective study in which 46% of college students reported frequent flashbacks to childhood bullying even as young adults, while *Matsui, Kakuyama, Tsuzuki and Onglatco (1996)* found continued depression and low self-esteem in Japanese males victimised as children. Bullying also increases the likelihood of psychiatric referral in later life. Peer abuse, as can now be documented, contributes to suicide attempts and completions. Indeed historically, the issue of peer abuse was first brought to international attention with the suicides of three 10-14 year old boys in late 1982 in Norway, as a consequence of bullying (Olweus, 1993). The development of fear, anxiety or withdrawal in victims are all reported as outcomes of severe peer abuse just as they are reported in the child abuse literature. Psychopathology and future criminal behaviour are also implicated in both peer abuse and child abuse in reference to the prognosis for the victim and the perpetrator (*Spatz-Widom, 1995*).

Ambert (1995) suggests that peer abuse is seen to differ from other forms of abuse on three key factors: the age of the abuser, formal power and neglect, all of which she believes are factors which are generally used to diminish the impact of the behaviour. Since the abuse is undertaken by minors, the effect may therefore be viewed as minor; since there is no recognised power differential, no abusive relationship is identified and since peers are not responsible for their age mates, neglect cannot be attributed to them.

It is apparent, however that these arguments are fast losing their credibility as the impact of peer abuse is documented and the legal responsibilities of teachers and other carers is challenged. It is clear that peer abuse, as with other forms of abuse, is defined by a difference in social status or power of the abuser compared to the victim, even though there may be no obvious power difference between the victim and their age-mate abuser. In peer abuse the power does not reside necessarily in the physical size difference between the bully and victim, although some researchers have identified inferior physical development as a factor in bullying victimisation (Olweus, 1993). Rather, it is perceived social position and status which bullies use to their advantage (Espelage, 2003).

Fundamentally, the six key factors by which child abuse can be identified and analysed comprise: type of abuse, severity, frequency, age of the victim, age of the abuser and the types of intervention available. Peer abuse can also be measured and analysed on each of these dimensions providing a comprehensive picture of its similarity to other forms of child abuse and its correspondence with child abuse across types, severity and impact.

Peer abuse may be perpetrated by age peers, by older social contacts such as the friends of older siblings or students in higher year levels at the same school. Children are generally vulnerable and have few choices about with whom they associate, particularly during the school day and travelling to and from school when peer abuse often occurs. Peer abuse is facilitated by both the restricted range of social contacts for young people, and by social structures which ensure that age peers spend the majority of their time together. As with child abuse, access by the perpetrator is socially defined with few opportunities available for victims to select safe companions or refuse contact with their abuser.

On each of these dimensions peer abuse can be seen to correlate with child abuse. The capacity of peers to abuse their age mates is not questioned; rather it is the failure to interpret this behaviour as abusive and the subsequent responses of teachers in terms of their mandated responsibilities to report the abuse, which is examined here. While it is apparent that peer abuse or bullying unquestionably fits the definitions and parameters of child abuse, there still seems to be some doubt about the application of the mandated legal processes in respect to intervention in peer abuse. Teachers may not, of course include such behaviours in their reporting until the legislation is amended. Alternatively, they could seek protection for themselves by using the legislation to report serious peer abuse as a recognised form of child abuse.

In relation to peer abuse, data are not generally available regarding reporting and legal interventions under child protection provisions, since the phenomenon has never been acknowledged or recorded in the child abuse statistics. Child abuse on the other hand is officially and systematically recorded in Australia by the Australian Institute for Health and Welfare among other agencies. The main criteria for assembly of the data are to protect children and young people who are seen as at risk of harm, and 'whose parents are unable to provide adequate care and protection'. This of course means that the child must not only be abused in a particular way but also neglected. The argument here with regard to peer abuse is that parents are unable to provide the safe environment for their children because the school is not a safe environment, yet they are obliged to send their children there despite the abuse.

Furthermore, the list of professionals and others who are either mandated to report or who take responsibility for reporting child abuse is impressive. Child abuse notifications to Community services are either required or accepted from: parents /guardians; siblings; other relatives; friends and neighbours; doctors; hospital and other health workers; social workers; teachers and school personnel; childcare workers; police; outside agencies and anonymous reporters.

Despite the disproportionate number of peer abuse incidents, however, which far outweigh the number of other reports of abuse, no formal process is in place for receiving or recording complaints.

Comparing the Data

What are the notable similarities and differences in the nature and extent of reported peer abuse and other forms of abuse?

The first distinction to be made is that AIHW data is recognised as legitimate and substantiated for the purposes of legal, therapeutic and government intervention in child abuse. The data are collected with the intention that support and protective intervention will be made available to those individual children and young people in need. Indeed, a substantial body of further data is provided in their reports to describe the types and parameters of intervention implemented in response to the reports of abuse. Nevertheless, there is also an acknowledged underreporting of abuse and many victims are not offered assistance.

The data gathered at schools with regard to peer abuse does not hold the same status however, despite being collected for the same purpose. There is no government response anticipated for reports of peer abuse and certainly no funding or services are offered to sustain individual intervention, other than those initiated at the school level. At the most fundamental level, the existence, impact and validity of the data referring to peer abuse is neither recognised nor recorded other than within the school itself.

Table 3 indicates that in Victoria, Queensland, South Australia and ACT a high proportion of investigated reports of child abuse were substantiated as being emotional abuse, but it is clear from the peer abuse data that the major source of emotional abuse of young people is bullying.

Table 3: *Number and % of children and young people (0-17 years) across Australia who were the subject of substantiated reports by type of abuse (2000-2001)*

Type of abuse or neglect substantiated	NSW	Vic	Qld	WA	SA	Tas	ACT	NT
	Number							
Physical	2,336	1,995	2,019	404	663	46	97	186
Sexual	1,903	608	398	311	223	34	20	42
Emotional	609	3,158	1,743	112	309	5	53	38
Neglect	1,087	1,598	2,759	342	890	12	63	127
Other [a]	542	- -	- -	- -	- -	- -	- -	- -
Total substantiations	6,477	7,359	6,919	1,169	2,085	97	233	393
	Per cent							
Physical	36	27	29	35	32	47	42	47
Sexual	39	8	6	27	11	35	9	11
Emotional	9	43	25	10	15	5	23	10
Neglect	17	22	40	29	43	12	27	32
Other [a]	8	- -	- -	- -	- -	- -	- -	- -
Total substantiations	100	100	100	100	100	100	100-	100

(a) The category 'Other' used for NSW comprises children identified as being at high risk but with no identifiable injury or harm
(b) Later tables of data were presented in bar graph form and are not as informative as this style.

The evidence also indicates that a high percentage of abuse across all states and territories is physical abuse while 33.3% of males and 15% of females in the peer abuse data also endured physical abuse (see Table 4). The problem of peer physical abuse is very comparable to levels of physical abuse reported and substantiated under legislative mandates, and indeed it is clear that young people are being abused to a much greater extent than is currently acknowledged, if both sets of data are considered together.

Analyses were undertaken to examine responses of students to the School Safety Survey (Healey, 2004) which sought to identify the nature of bullying by nine specific types of bullying behaviour. The responses of bullied students only are presented in the following table.

In four of the five cases where gender differences were significant, the differences indicated males reported experiencing more bullying. Typically, the categories of bullying behaviour which closely resemble other forms of abuse yielded the following results from bullied respondents:

Table 4: *Responses of bullied students to the School Safety Survey 2003 which sought to identify the nature of bullying by examining nine specific types of behaviour (Healey, 2004)*

Q4 Part	Type of Bullying Behaviour	% Males	% Females
4.1	Being teased and called names	**64.3**	**52.9**
4.2	Receiving negative comments about family, country, religion	**26.1**	**17.3**
4.3	Being left out or excluded on purpose	**19.6**	**25.5**
4.4	Being verbally threatened	**20.8**	**10.0**
4.5	Being physically hit, punched or kicked	**33.3**	**15.7**
4.6	Being forced to give money or belongings	6.0	7.9
4.7	Receiving negative comments on personal appearance	44.8	51.0
4.8	Being touched in ways they do not want to be touched	9.0	8.2
4.9	Deliberate damage to personal property	15.4	15.4

It is evident that peer abuse not only occurs more frequently and therefore has a greater impact than other forms of abuse, it happens more frequently to males, which is not the case for other forms of abuse. If peer abuse were to be reported under the legislative guidelines for child protection, it may acquire the equivalent status and command similar responsive intervention, and it may afford males greater protection than is currently available to them. Overall there is a close comparability between the nature and parameters of peer abuse as reported in independent research with adolescent populations in schools and the officially recorded data for reported and substantiated abuse perpetrated by adults against young people. Peer abuse can certainly be classified as a form of abuse and should therefore be included in mandated provisions for protective intervention. It is also fair to say that peer abuse resulting in the suicide of the victim is a far more serious concern than other forms of child abuse.

APPLYING CHILD PROTECTION LEGISLATION TO PEER ABUSE

Child abuse issues were afforded a high profile in NSW in the wake of the *Wood Royal Commission (1996)*. *The Wood Report (1997)* implicated a number of educators in child abuse matters and resulted in prosecution and incarceration for some, on the basis of failure to notify suspected cases of abuse of children and young people in their care.

The focus of the Children and Young Persons (Care and Protection) Act 1998, proclaimed in December 2000, is the provision and maintenance of protective services to children in abusive situations with an emphasis on preventative intervention. Further protective measures were instigated as an outcome of the Wood Royal Commission recommendations with the establishment of the Commission for Children and Young People Act 1998 and the Child Protection (Prohibited Employment) Act 1998.

In Australia, most states and territories mandate reporting of child abuse on the basis of 'reasonable grounds to suspect' that abuse is occurring and the legislation therefore could be applied in the case of severe peer abuse. The definitions of abuse incorporated into the child protection legislation are broad enough that any harmful act towards a child or young person could be included and they could therefore be applicable to peer abuse. Peer abuse has been the subject of legal action in Australia and overseas, although not through child protection provisions.

The NSW Act also defines both children and young people by age (child as a person under the age of 16 years and young person as between 16 and 18 years) which permits application at both the high school and primary school levels. Peer abuse is well documented at both systems levels (*Healey 2001(a)); Rigby and Slee 1993*). It is therefore suggested that knowledge of systematic, frequent and harmful abusive behaviour by peers unquestionably implicates teachers in notification under these legislative guidelines.

The *NSW Act* (*1998*) states:

> *"that all institutions responsible for the care and protection of children and young people, provide an environment for them that is free of violence and exploitation and provide services that foster their health, developmental needs and dignity"* Chapter 2, Article 8 a, b

In terms of decision-making with regard to reporting peer abuse, it could be argued that teachers are mandated to consider this aspect of the child's safety under this law. Further, the Act states that a child or young person is at risk of harm,

> *"If current concerns exist for the safety, welfare or well-being of the child or young person"* Chapter 3, 23

because of the presence of such circumstances as:

> *"The child or young person's basic physical or psychological needs are not being met or are at risk of not being met"* and *"the child or young person has been, or is at risk of being physically or sexually abused or ill-treated".*

The specific obligation to notify under the mandatory notification provisions (part 27 of the Act) further states that:

> "(a) a person to whom this section applies has reasonable grounds to suspect that a child is at risk of harm, and (b) those grounds arise during the course of or from the person's work,"

must make a report as soon as practicable.

It is clear that these mandates cannot be ignored in the case of severe peer abuse when the criteria for risk and harm are met and documented. Bearing in mind that definitions of bullying refer to an *ongoing* abusive process, not a *single incident* of assault, peer abuse fits the criteria for sustained and current concerns for welfare & safety.

Since the NSW Act mandates that all persons listed, including teachers, must report the concern as soon as practicable there seems to be no reason to exclude the abusive behaviours of peers from this directive. The onus of proof, as stated in the legislation, is irrelevant to notification. This provision applies in all situations where a crime is suspected-the individual reporting the crime does not have to provide 'proof' since they are simply notifying the authorities of a situation requiring their attention.

Teachers and others are being asked to do no more with regard to this crime than all community members are expected to do in relation to any suspected crime – that is, to report their suspicions to those with the authority and expertise to investigate. Teachers are often protected from prosecution under legislation since they are not required to provide evidence. The use of the mandated provisions in the case of peer abuse may well help prevent legal proceedings being taken against schools and teachers who are seen to have failed to protect their students from peer abuse, or to have misinterpreted the behaviour.

Teachers need to be informed that while they cannot be prosecuted for reporting abuse they suspect or know is occurring, they can be prosecuted for failing to report known instances of abuse. This may well apply to peer abusive situations. In the case of peer abuse, however, teachers often do have extensive documentation, formal and informal observations of abusive interactions whereby individual children have been exposed to harm by their peers. Peer abuse is often known to teachers, though rarely identified as abusive, and this implicates teachers in terms of child protection mandates. *Schene (1998)* suggests that the protection of children has been established historically as a government function and, it is argued here, since more children may be at risk from their peers than abusive adults, protection must now be extended to include peer abuse as a legislated child protection issue.

South Australian legislation uses phraseology which could also readily be applied to cases of peer abuse in that intervention can be undertaken when:

> *"there is some information or evidence leading to a reasonable suspicion that a child is at risk; that the child is in a situation such that ... the child's safety would be in serious danger" and " that the child is not in the company of any of his or her guardians" (Children's Protection Act 1993 Section 20 South Australian Consolidated Acts).*

In the Tasmanian Child Protection Act 1974, it is stated that "any person is entitled to report the fact" (Section 8) of maltreatment on the basis of reasonable grounds to suspect that it is occurring.

In Queensland, reporting has not been mandated for teachers, but has been formalised for other sections of the professional community, including doctors. Peer abuse has not yet been considered to be notifiable under the Queensland Child Protection Act 1999 legislation.

In the UK legislative intervention is commonly used to address matters of serious or lethal bullying.

In Victoria, the Children and Young Person's Act 1989 legal requirements relate only to sexual and physical abuse and states that the professional must report the abuse only when they have 'formed the belief on reasonable grounds' that abuse is happening. This permits an element of judgement or discretion enabling the observer to opt out of reporting if they claim not to believe the indicators presented, including disclosure.

One case heard under these guidelines subsequently found the child to have been abused, however the prosecution for non-reporting was unsuccessful because it could not be shown that a 'belief was formed' (Swain, 1998). In this situation, peer abuse may be far less likely to be viewed as a child protection issue but the legislation does not preclude this application. In Victoria, remarkably, the amended Crimes (Family Violence) Act 1987 Stalking provision (section 21A (2) has been implemented in over 600 cases between children as a means of addressing the problem of victimisation (*Coate, 2001*).

The law is being used to seek protection in a way which was never considered at its inception, clearly indicating a need to formalise legal intervention for peer abuse. *Coate* expresses some concern that this should be the case, and prescribes mediation and other conflict resolution interventions instead.

> **Two teenage girls have been found guilty of causing the death of a vicar's daughter who jumped from a window in south-east London.**
>
> Kemi Ajose, 19, and Hatice Can, 15, were found guilty of the manslaughter of 19-year-old Rosimeiri Boxall.
>
> Miss Boxall died after falling from the third-floor window of Ajose's flat. She was beaten and bullied by the teenagers, the Old Bailey was told. Rosimeiri's parents said they have forgiven the two girls. The judge lifted an order banning identification of the younger defendant Can, of Belvedere, south-east London.
>
> **'Forgive them'**
>
> Following the verdict, Rosimeiri's parents Simon and Rachel Boxall released a statement saying they "forgave" Ajose and Can.
>
> "We continue to pray for those who are responsible for Rosi's death. We want them to know that we forgive them."
>
> Simon Boxall says he forgives the killers but they 'need to face up to the consequences'.
>
> "That does not mean that what they did 'doesn't matter'. Of course it does," the statement continued.
>
> "For justice to be seen to be done it had to happen and those responsible have to face up to the consequences of their choices."
>
> The two teenagers, who were 17 and 13 at the time, blamed each other for telling Miss Boxall to jump when she climbed up to the window after she was attacked.
>
> Roger Smart, prosecuting, said the three had been arguing over a boy.
>
> Part of the attack on Miss Boxall by Ajose, from Coleraine Road, Blackheath, which was filmed by a neighbour on a mobile phone, was played to the jury. The video showed her hair being pulled and hairspray aimed at her face. The sound of her being slapped and punched could also be heard in the film.

However, given the long term impact, children and young people are entitled to the same rights to protection under the law as adults in abusive situations and legal provisions ensuring personal safety must be extended to young people who are at risk.

Generally, private litigation for neglect of duty is sought when parents and individual students believe they have been poorly served in terms of safety and protection at school. Increasingly, reference is made to children's rights to protection from harm (Anderson and Fraser, 2002) freedom of association, adequate educational and safety provisions, when issues of peer abuse arise. The Northern Territory legislation *(Care and Protection of Children Act 2007* (NT) does not specifically mandate teachers and there is no consideration of all forms of abuse for protective intervention. Certainly it would involve a major shift of legislative intent to incorporate peer abuse in this law; Western Australia (Children and Community Services Act, 2000 WA) operates under guiding principles including:

(c) the principle that every child should be cared for and protected from harm;

(d) the principle that every child should live in an environment free from violence; (part 2, 9)

There is no reference to mandated reporting, however, the concept of abuse refers to effects on

k) the child's physical, emotional, intellectual, spiritual, developmental and educational needs;

and this could incorporate peer abuse. There is the provision for protection under the law for disclosure of abuse given in good faith.

In the Australian Capital Territory legislation, (*Children and Young People Act, 2008* (ACT) amended 2010) teachers are mandated reporters of abuse of children and young people and the wording of this act would permit peer abuse to be included. There are penalties for the non-reporting of known abuse which could implicate teachers and others mandatory reporters if peer abuse is known to be causing distress and psychological harm, yet is not addressed.

Logistically, because of the prevalence of the behaviours as demonstrated in this research, it may not be possible to offer the same level of protection to all abused individuals under the terms of the legislation. Realistically also, all abused individuals may not require the level of protective intervention afforded through the processes prescribed, and it can be anticipated that for students with some measure of resiliency (*Carver, 1998; Kinard, 1998*) and strong family and school supports, such intervention may not be necessary. *English* (*1998*) and *Tomison, 2002* also caution about the demands placed on child protection agencies and the need to ration their involvement, a consideration which is likely to be compounded by the inclusion of peer abuse as a category of abuse. Other researchers suggest the responsibility for intervention in child protection, though not specifically peer abuse, may need to be spread into the community (*Munro, 1998; Schene, 1998; Waldfogel, 1998*) rather than simply relying on agency supports. Anti-bullying interventions in many countries, in particular the Scandinavian sector, have produced advertising campaigns, systems-wide programs and specific legislation to prevent peer abuse (Smith, 1994) with documented success, but such approaches are yet to be tried in Australia.

Legal intervention is considered usually only when the school system is deemed to have failed to provide adequate protection. Reluctance to become involved may stem from an inaccurate understanding by teachers of their legal responsibilities for child protection and in particular their resistance to defining peer abuse as either serious or abusive or related to child protection. The introduction of protections under the law for reporting according to mandated provisions will hopefully assist in the acceptance of peer abuse as a phenomenon requiring serious professional attention and early intervention in the context of legislated child abuse provisions.

Other countries such as Finland (*Bjorkvist and Osterman, 1999*) Japan (*Morita et al, 1999*), the United States of America, (*Haratchi, Catalano and Hawkins 1999*), and Sweden (*Olweus, 1999*) have enacted specific legislation against bullying which can lead to prosecution of the perpetrators. Others use existing legislation to deter and punish peer abuse as it is not seen as a distinct offence.

In Canada, for example, legislation governing young offenders is often used to deal with cases of bullying (Anderson and Fraser, 2002). Such legal provisions may act as a deterrent assuming the peer abuser is aware of their existence. However this approach is less likely to offer protection to the victim and does not negate litigation against schools.

The introduction of specific anti-bullying legislation therefore, unless presented as a mandatory notification procedure would not improve the current situation. Teachers would only be in a position to advise parents and victims of their right to litigate under those provisions, given that they identify behaviours as peer abuse. This cannot increase the protection offered the victim or staff within the school setting and is merely punitive in nature, whereas the use of child protection interventions should provide an avenue for remediation of inadequate behaviours in bullies and victims. It can also enable the teacher to continue a supportive educative roll while other authorities provide support and investigate the abuse reports. In other words, legislation can be utilised by teachers for their own protection as well as for the well-being of victims of peer abuse.

It is suggested here that the current legislation provides the best means of protection and intervention for teachers, since it can be invoked at the school level and provide immediate notification. Child protection legislation therefore provides a more direct and effective pathway for protection. However, an examination of the use and effectiveness of the child protection legislation indicates that although peer abuse qualifies on all counts as notifiable under the legislation, invocation of the relevant act has thus far been noticeably absent in such cases.

The capacity of young people to abuse their peers cannot be questioned in view of the substantial evidence available. Rather it is the failure of educators to interpret the behaviour as abusive and their subsequent failure to invoke protective interventions, which gives rise to the proposition that child protection legislation should be utilised. While a case can be made that peer abuse unquestionably fits the definitions for child abuse there is still some reluctance to apply the mandated legal procedures in the matter of peer abuse.

More refined examinations of the legislature may reinforce the proposition however and offer the protections necessary to ensure the safety and well being of young people in all circumstances.

When considering issues of protection, and given that teachers are more likely to witness this type of child abuse than other forms which occur outside school boundaries and hours, their ability to recognise the indicators is a critical factor. If current definitions of bullying are known to the observer: the lack of reciprocity, intention to harm, repeated nature of the actions and obvious distress ensuing (*Besag, 1989; Tattum, 1993*) there would be no dilemma in addressing the behaviour as abusive and it is not unreasonable to expect such an interpretation despite the social or developmental status of the perpetrators. Name-calling, taunting and overt rejection of individual children would readily be interpreted as abusive if inflicted by an adult within the hearing and observation of the teacher, and it is suggested here that no other evidence is needed of abuse when such behaviours are observed in peers towards an individual.

Peer abuse as a child protection issue has been canvassed here and recommended as a response strategy for mobilising resources and supports for victimised individuals. Concerns for the disruption to family and social group cohesion, however, precipitated by notification of abuse have been expressed (*Heatherton and Beardsall, 1998; Sheerin, 1998*). While the welfare of the victim is held to be paramount, nevertheless the individual functions within a complex social environment throughout which the ripple effect of notification of abuse can have very damaging effect. Teachers are concerned to maintain close bonds between peers in the belief that this scaffolds future relationships. Further, despite their mandated responsibilities, teachers are often reluctant to report abuse and even less likely to support peer abuse.

The time has come to place peer abuse firmly within the child protection framework, giving access to all of the legislative provisions which are afforded other types of child abuse. It is not difficult to establish the correlation between bullying and other forms of abuse in terms of the behaviours, their impact and outcomes. By combining the literature relating to bullying behaviour and that describing other behaviours traditionally viewed as abusive, a strong case can be made for peer abuse as child abuse.

In terms of the perceived impact outcomes and support requirements necessary for the protection of children and young persons from long term damage as a result of abuse, the provisions of the legislation and the procedures and requirements delineated by teacher employing bodies are clearly applicable to severe peer abuse and should now be implemented as a protective intervention. In terms of this discussion, it is suggested that the application of the same guidelines proposed for the notification of all forms of suspected or identified child abuse be applied in instances of peer abuse. Currently it is most unlikely that a safe environment will be provided for the abused child other than temporarily, by removal of the peer abuse perpetrator such as in a school suspension.

For this reason it is proposed that the Bullywatch reporting mechanism – the Logbook – be utilised as a record of incidents that can be used to verify the details of the abuse should the legislation change to include peer abuse, or should other legislation be employed to seek compensation or redress.

5 Resiliency – A Critical Factor in Resisting Bullying

Introduction

Victims of bullying cannot be identified as a single group, as their ability to resist the bully differs along a continuum from passivity and surrender to resilience and recovery. A descriptive model for intervention is presented in Figure 1 (page 47) which illustrates this phenomenon. Here, discussion centres on defining resilience and the possibility of teaching resiliency skills to individuals who do not demonstrate a natural psychological capacity to recover from adversity. It is also necessary to explore the notion that resistance to bullying is not simply an interpersonal skill, but that it depends very much on the social environment which may well support the abuser. Consideration is given to the effects of abuse on both resilient and non-resilient individuals to determine whether resilience provides protection from distress as well as the capacity to resist or avoid bullying.

Discussing resilience in relation to abuse generally, can equally be applied to discussions of the development of resilience in response to bullying. The capacity for young people to survive abuse through the acquisition of resilient behaviour is applicable to the experience of abuse at the hands of peers, just as much as to that experienced from adult abusers.

The following key issues need consideration:

- An understanding of what constitutes resilience in relation to bullying

- Identifying protective factors in the social environment which may assist in the development of resilience if provided to victims of bullying

- Exploring the possibility that resiliency can be taught to victims of bullying to assist in the development of responses which facilitate resistance and recovery.

RESILIENCY DEFINED

A standard definition of resilience is that it represents a capacity to 'rebound or readily recover from adversity or pressure' (Macquarie Dictionary). In describing resilience in individuals the definition refers to their psychological responses in these situations.

Resilience in individuals is broadly defined in two opposing ways as:

- a predisposition towards positive expectations and outcomes despite adverse experiences, which refers to individuals who are generally optimistic in their responses to life experiences, despite hardships;

and,

- the development of the capacity to overcome adversity despite a natural predisposition to stress responses, referring to individuals who are more inclined to be pessimistic but who nevertheless try to 'battle on' in the face of difficulty.

The first definition refers to an innate positive capacity to endure adversity and to carry on coping. The second refers to the individual who struggles to cope but nevertheless persists. Both are to be admired as they deal with the abusive experiences to which they are subject. It should also be noted however, that the capacity to demonstrate natural resiliency in relation to bullying should not preclude victims from protective intervention, and does not negate the stressful impact of the bullying behaviour. Just because the individual 'copes' it does not mean they do not suffer or require support. Further, the competency of the victim in seeking assistance should not in any way reduce the level of responsibility attributable to the bully.

It can be seen that these two distinctly opposite personal characteristics are both relevant in the discussion about responses to bullying. In particular, these definitions should guide adult intervention with children and young people experiencing peer abuse, and attempting to deal with its impact. Identifying resiliency in the abused individual may be the critical defining factor in survival of the experience. Irrespective of whether it is innate or acquired, resilience represents a critical factor in resisting bullying.

Further, the terms 'resilience' and 'resiliency' are used to indicate separate concepts within the framework of this discussion. While *'resilience'* or *'resilient'* are terms used to describe an individual's apparent psychological state, *'resiliency'* is used to refer to the actual behaviours evident in those who seem to have resilience. The purpose of making the distinction is to support the argument that resiliency 'behaviours' can be taught and acquired, then used as a means of resisting bullying, irrespective of whether the individual actually is resilient. This discussion takes place in the context of an effort to establish the efficacy of a program of intervention for bullying which includes resiliency training (Healey, 2004).

Resilience is seen as an attribute which is measurable and therefore clearly identifiable as a personality and behavioural trait in particular individuals. *Kinard (1998)* points out that the factors which define resilience are sometimes also reported as capacities which lead to the development of resilience. Having good self-esteem, for example, may indicate resilience is present or it may facilitate the establishment of resilient behaviour where none was previously demonstrated, perhaps due to the absence of adversity. This becomes a critical matter in the discussion of responses to, and the impact of bullying.

While some children may experience chronic life stressors such as poverty, inadequate parenting, maltreatment and school failure, others may be exposed to relatively mild adversity, the key being the presence of adversity to validate the presence of resilience. The literature with regard to resilience more often refers to the former and the reasons why some individuals develop such skills given the negative outcomes of abuse which are usual for the child (Carver 1998).

Resiliency, on the other hand is the term used to describe the process of behaving with resilience in the event of adversity such as bullying. In other words, the child can be taught to demonstrate specific behaviours which indicate resilience even before they actually feel and are resilient. This would include remaining at school, taking part in education programs, maintaining friendships and trying new activities, as well as actively resisting bullying through help-seeking and reporting.

Broadly speaking, then the literature establishes that the term *'resilience'* describes the capacity to 'bounce back' from adverse experiences, retain psychological equilibrium, continue to perform in a competent manner and generally give little overt indication of the impact of an adverse event. This is a result either of a naturally positive predisposition or from a deliberate effort to present this impression despite the stress endured. Various researchers have defined resilience, and *Masten, Best and Garmezy (1990)* describe resilience on three separate dimensions:-

- positive outcomes despite experiencing high risk environments,
- competent functioning in the face of acute and chronic life stressors

and

- recovery from trauma.

Children who are able to function within normal and acceptable expectations with respect to behavioural, social and/or cognitive functioning, despite adverse experiences (Kinard, 1998) are identified as resilient.

Resiliency in this context refers to the behaviours which seem to indicate that the victim of abuse has resilience and is able to continue to function as an adaptive individual.

Various personal attributes have been reported to correlate with, or some argue, be pre-requisite to, the ability to recover from adversity. These factors, evident in the behaviour of the abused individual include: positive self-regard, academic success, positive social and emotional adjustment and adaptive social skills. In the context of bullying intervention and resistance, for those who are not naturally resilient it may be necessary to teach the competencies associated with resilience, thereby equipping victims with psychological strengths with which to respond with resiliency in an assertive and effective manner. However individuals who attempt to continue their activities despite having minimal self-confidence, success or social support are particularly resilient and deserve the greatest level of protective intervention.

The terms resiliency and thriving are often used interchangeably but can be differentiated essentially on the basis that thriving can develop in the absence of adversity, while resiliency is only identified in terms of adverse experiences (*Cohen, Cimbolic, Armeli, and Hettler, 1998*). Unless or until the individual is placed under stress, the competencies of resiliency are not required. However, thriving is often a continuous process illustrating a relatively uninterrupted life course leading to social and emotional competency.

For victims of bullying it may be that developmental thriving will facilitate resiliency development if none has previously been demonstrated. Some of the key characteristics identified by *Carver* (*1998*) as indicative of thriving include tolerance for stressful events, faster recovery from stress, optimism and confidence, as well as social indicators like consistently high social functioning and security in interpersonal relationships.

However, while it is commonly assumed that traumatic events such as psychological or physical abuse inevitably result in psychological harm, some researchers see the need to challenge this in the light of evidence of resilience (*Monaghan-Blout, 1997*). The concept of 'suffering in order to grow' a popularly expressed view in community discussions of bullying, needs some refinement if young people are to be protected from bullying and other forms of abuse. *Cohen, Cimbolic, Armeli, & Hettler,* (*1998*) discuss this controversial aspect of resilience –that of 'stress related growth' or 'post-traumatic growth ' and the concept of 'benefit' as a result of trauma, but care must be taken to determine whether and under what circumstances such positive outcomes can be expected. Generally speaking, such an interpretation reinforces the behaviour of the abuser.

There is an underlying contradiction in the notion that victims who demonstrate resilience by reporting the abuse are in fact demonstrating weakness by complaining about their plight instead of 'getting on with it' or 'getting over it'. Bullies and their supporters are the most likely to use this interpretation. Victims of abuse are not deemed brave, resilient or strong following disclosure of their abuse, but instead are deemed to be 'whingeing ' and 'complaining ' when they should be 'fighting back'. Supporters of the abuser will reinforce this view and so add further to the abusive outcomes. Resiliency, then, is not universally admired or supported within the abusive environment.

Differences in Resiliency Responses

Evidence related to cultural differences in girls' resiliency to bullying (Healey, 2002) was also found in the research underpinning this text, to support the concept that there are differences in the resiliency of individuals in their responses to bullying behaviour. The responses of girls to bullying were examined more closely as they formed the majority of participants in the research undertaken. Results suggested that some female students who were bullied nevertheless did not view the behaviour as a serious problem, whereas others revealed a greater degree of disaffection. The research data recorded responses across the types and intensity of bullying and illustrated the percentage of girls from each cultural group who experienced the type of bullying listed. This provided evidence of the intensity of the bullying endured. It is clear that for some cultural groups, girls reported experiencing all of the listed behaviours, while for others only some of the behaviours were evident. The results yielded some apparently contradictory findings that may be explained by cultural differences in girls' resiliency to bullying.

It would seem reasonable to expect that those students who are seriously bullied in school would view the matter as a serious or major problem and would be willing to report the behaviours and assist others they saw being bullied. It would also seem reasonable that they would believe that experiencing such behaviours in the school would mean that the school does not help students feel good. Nevertheless, while some sections of respondents expressed deep concerns for the impact and seriousness of the bullying they endured at school, others did not view bullying as a serious or major problem and felt that some or most students felt good about themselves at school. They were willing to assist and to report in regards to bullying, but the overall cumulative impression revealed in the data was that their own experiences of bullying had not impacted on their views about school or on their appropriate functioning. This seems to support the notion of resiliency in the face of the adverse experience of bullying. It could also, however, indicate a greater tolerance of bullying as an expected behaviour while at school.

The findings of the research provide support for the view that there are qualitative differences in the responses of bullied individuals in terms of impact. The most salient explanation for this is that some individuals respond with resilience to the abuse, in that they continue their lives with little outward evidence of trauma. Others respond with a degree of hopelessness and see their world as dominated by the bullying episodes. The research base for the suggestion that bullied individuals may be trained in the development or demonstration of resiliency is validated by these analyses.

What Relevant Theory Underpins Resilience?

In considering the application of resilience to intervention in bullying, the relevance and efficacy of a range of theoretical constructs of resilience require examination. This is in order to provide justification and verification for the teaching of resilient behaviours and skills. Theorists variously describe resilience as a psychological protective facility (*Jew 1998; McCubbin 1998*), a social skill and a developmental indicator in an attempt to unravel the key components. In terms of this discussion, resiliency is seen as a set of capacities which can be acquired and applied in a situation in which there is trauma through bullying, and several theorists appear to support this view.

Flow theory has been discussed as a model for enhancing student resilience (*Parr, Montgomery and DeBell, 1998*) through a process of alerting them to their individual interpretations of life experiences. The theory has been applied by the original theorist, *Csikszentmihalyi (1990)* to a wide range of risk-oriented activities such as mountain climbing, ocean racing and other peak experiences as a means of analysing growth through challenge. *Parr, et al.* suggest that the capacity for resilience may develop in the same way that solitary ordeals contribute to personal growth in that the individual takes a pro-active perspective which sees challenge in hardship and meets hardship by formulating goals for recovery. The capacity to formulate goals for action within the challenging environment and the belief that the self has the interpersonal resources to overcome the challenge results in "flow" or an ordering of consciousness towards a positive outcome.

According to *Parr, et al* in a matrix they formulate consisting of the key elements of challenge and skill at high and low levels, they state that psychological flow:

> 'depends on achieving the right balance between how challenging one's goals are and how effective one's skills are in meeting those challenges' (pg 28)

High challenge coupled with high skill will result in 'flow' or a positive outcome while high challenge with low skill will result in anxiety.

The theory is relevant to this discussion of resiliency in relation to bullying as it acknowledges the need for skills development or acquisition in the areas of positive self-talk, self-belief and goal-setting in order to successfully meet challenges, and this capacity can certainly be trained or taught, for example in cognitive restructuring approaches.

Flow theory however, is premised on the engagement of individuals in often deliberately selected challenging experiences, which of course is not the case in victimisation through bullying. Nevertheless, if the victim of bullying can be assisted to view their experience as a challenge to be overcome, and for which they need to set goals for resistance, the outcome may be more positive. "Flow" will develop in victims of bullying who can restructure their thinking about the experience towards an interpretation which is empowering and proactive rather than anxiety-producing. Parr, *et al.* believe that the

> development of a high level of skills, in this case psychological resistance, will facilitate meeting any challenge and it could be argued that this would also apply to bullying. This portrays the individual as resourceful, thoughtful and pro-active even though they may not be fully equipped to meet the challenge and this is probably a more realistic appraisal than that so often expressed that victims of bullying are ineffectual and passive in their responses.

Many factors combine to prevent a victim avoiding bullying, not the least of which is the non-supportive environment in which the events occur, but this does not mean the victimised individual is passive. If the challenge of bullying is compounded by the further challenge of an unsupportive peer group, unsafe or unmonitored environment and uninvolved adults, there is a multiplication of the original challenge by several factors which may overwhelm the individual.

Flow theory explains the capacity of the individual to devise means to meet the challenge of bullying given interpersonal competencies and skills such as goal directed behaviour. Resiliency results from the achievement of these goals despite hostile or neglectful environments.

McCubbin, et al (*1998*) applies *Antonovsky's Salutogenic Theory* (*1987*) to the concept of resiliency. They discuss several factors believed to counteract the tendency towards stress including three psychological aspects which contribute to a resilient response to adversity:

- comprehension of the current adverse situation,

- manageability or the capacity to use current skills to address the current challenge and

- meaningfulness or the ability to derive meaning from the demands confronted.

- Fundamentally, if applied to the event of bullying:

- the bullying experience will be compounded by a lack of knowledge about bullying, particularly if others in the victim's environment interpret the behaviours differently. If the victim can recognise the behaviour as bullying they will be better prepared for an assertive response. If the victim is made to feel that their interaction with the bully is a 'conflict' or 'fight' or insignificant event however, due to misinterpretation of the behaviour by others in their environment, they will not be encouraged to respond appropriately. At the most basic level, the victim and others in their social environment must be able to identify bullying and differentiate it from conflict, fighting, play and other reciprocal interactions;

- a lack of skills for resistance will result in a negative outcome, which is why the proposition is made that such skills and knowledge be acquired through a training program. If the victim of abuse believes they have the skills to cope with the situation, including reporting skills, they will develop resistance and resiliency in the event of the abuse. This is dependent, of course, on the responses they receive when they engage in appropriate reporting and other behaviours.

- if victims can emerge from the experience with an interpretation which provides meaningfulness-for example that locates the deficit within the bully and not within themselves – the outcome is more likely to be positive and resilient.

- As a psychological theory, salutogenics has found support because of the emphasis on the sense of coherence in individuals and the departure from an illness/failure-based model to one which recognises innate capacities for resilience. *McCubbin, et al.* present discussions which relate the sense of coherence to the management of stress and change, which are particularly relevant here.

'The inherent abilities of the human system to counteract the tendency towards stress and disease' (*McCubbin, et al.*) is the foundation belief linking this model to the proposed intervention whereby individuals can be taught to draw on or further develop this capacity to counteract victimisation. This theory supports the notion that victims of bullying may have or develop an innate predisposition to resist stress and anxiety and validates the efficacy of teaching resilient behaviours.

Cowan, Cowan & Schulz (1996) consider multiple risk factors in families and discuss protection and buffering mechanisms as a means to develop resilience. In this context, resilience unfolds over time as the individual practices resistant behaviours which are met with positive responses in their environment, which in turn leads to the development of competence through resiliency.

Luthar (1993) and others however, discuss a multi-dimensional model of resiliency whereby stress levels are not necessarily reduced by the demonstration of skills. Resiliency comprises interpersonal, developmental and psychological capacities as well as socially acquired skills and young people may remain competent in some areas such as academic achievement, maintenance of social status through sports etc., yet nonetheless be experiencing high levels of stress and anxiety in response to adversity. This perspective supports the view expressed elsewhere in this document that overt compensatory behaviours which appear to be effective, may well mask underlying severe stress reactions to bullying or other adverse situations and cannot be viewed as evidence that resilience inoculates individuals from stress. Nevertheless, the acquisition and application of resilient behaviours can result in demonstrable resiliency despite internal stress, and if this deters a bully from further interference, the victim will benefit.

Consideration also needs to be given to the perception of abuse or adversity held by the 'victim', and correspondingly to the evidence of resiliency observed. If the 'victim 'does not perceive the situation or event to be adverse or abusive, can their responses be described as resilient and coping? In the popular literature individuals are frequently described as resilient and as 'overcoming adversity' if, for example, they are successful despite disability.

Caution needs to be exercised in this regard since although there can be no question that to succeed despite a disability is to achieve, unless the disability is perceived as an obstacle by the individual there is nothing to overcome. These individuals focus upon their capacities and the development of their skills to the same extent that non-disabled individuals do, and in the process become successful. We cannot assume that their efforts are based on a determination to overcome 'adversity' if their circumstances are natural for them. Successful disabled athletes need to be as resilient in the face of defeat as successful non-disabled athletes, but their response is related to their perception of their capacity to perform, not their incapacity to do so.

Resiliency as a set of social skills rather than an innate capacity evolving from psychological character traits, is an attractive theory since it proposes a pragmatic solution. If resiliency comprises specific demonstrable skills, behaviours and attitudes, it is likely that it can be taught and acquired. Several researchers take this view and examine social problem-solving skills in relation to levels of adjustment and resiliency.

The purpose of developing resistant behaviours is not to deny the impact of the bullying behaviour but to provide an interim response which may divert the bully and thereby give some relief from stress temporarily. Victims need to behave as though they are resilient in order to secure relief from the victimisation.

In summary, theoretical discussions of what constitutes resiliency are only valuable if they guide intervention. While it can be established that there are particular indicators of psychological *'resilience'* as well as observable and measurable indicators of *'resiliency'* in terms of the behaviours engaged, the challenge is to induct victims of bullying into the resilient community by teaching the appropriate skills for resistance.

Resilience is a skill which can be acquired as well as a personality trait evident in populations of abused and non-abused individuals (*Cicchetti and Rogosch, 1997*). It is suggested that resilience does not emanate from practice with suffering but rather is genetically programmed as a resource on which abused individuals can draw in times of need (*Klarreich 1998; Freitas 1998; Banishek 1997*). There is also, however, the possibility of the propensity to develop the skills of resiliency and to train young people to acquire resilient behaviours as a defence to threats and abuse, even when their natural inclination is to respond differently. Research indicates the possibility of the development of resilience which supports the notion of training for the acquisition of resilient behaviours, and this can be extended to include a peer group which demonstrably resists bullying by behaving in a resilient manner (*Catterall 1998; Shulman 1998*).

Resilience does not mean learning to 'put up with' certain events and to stoically withhold a legitimate response indicating hurt. Rather, resilience means actually developing strategies to protect the self from the hurt intended, and replacing the natural inclination to feel hurt with a more assertive resistant response.

Resilience means developing an inner strength which affords protection in the face of harm and the propensity for recovery from harmful incidents. Peer Advocacy© facilitates the development of this capacity by providing a reinforcing partnership of resistance to the hurt experienced through bullying.

6 Peer Advocacy© as a Key Strategy in Bullying Intervention

Introduction

Peer Advocacy© represents an innovative and research-based approach to the preparation of young people for the shared responsibility of protection and support of their peers. These discussions locate Peer Advocacy© within the framework of a comprehensive approach to intervention in bullying in schools. The intervention is implemented ideally within a supportive environment which acknowledges the damaging effects of peer abuse. It is embedded within the school-wide anti-bullying program and follows on from the BULLYWATCH™ curriculum which assists young people to develop relevant knowledge and attitudes towards bullying. This curriculum provides foundation information in preparation for the development of personal competencies and interpersonal skills in the role of Peer Advocate© (see *Figure 5* in Appendix for diagram overview of the BULLYWATCH Comprehensive intervention).

The components of Peer Advocacy© are discussed in relation to the:

- theoretical constructs
- empirical basis and
- structure and processes.

The theoretical constructs and empirical basis for the approach are discussed here. The theoretical underpinnings of Peer Advocacy© and the empirical basis are linked to original research which identified peer attitudes and competencies as relevant in relation to bullying intervention (Healey, 2004).

The structure and processes components of the Peer Advocacy© intervention are described in detail in 'BULLYWATCH: Programs and Resources for Coping with Bullying'© publication available at www.bullywatch.com.au.

The Peer Advocacy© program at the primary school level is the 'Guardians'™ program, and at the secondary level the 'Defenders'™ program. Peer Advocacy© is a training program comprising a set of guiding principles, operational principles, knowledge and procedures related to the role of advocacy as a bullying intervention. The program equips young people with the skills, motivation and commitment to assist their bullied peers in the quest for protective intervention. The objective is for relevant personal attributes, specific knowledge and informed advocacy skills to be developed and demonstrated as a result of inclusion in the program. It is an innovative and advanced program of intervention reliant upon the courage, skill and tenacity of young people in defence of each other even when those in authority may be unresponsive to the need or requests for protection.

BACKGROUND TO THE PRACTICE OF ADVOCACY

Advocacy has been accepted in the literature as an established and effective means of providing qualified support for needy individuals in the quest for improved services otherwise denied them as a consequence of their personal incapacities or lack of skills (*Ward and Page-Hanify 1986*).

Advocacy is proposed in a range of circumstances including advocacy for children who are abused, neglected or exhibiting mental health difficulties or disabilities (*Paull, 1998; Watkins, 1997*). It is described as a process whereby a skilled individual acts clearly on behalf of a person with disadvantage to ensure their rights and welfare are protected (*Stroeve, 1998*). It can range from this personal and individualised process to one which advocates support for causes through legislative change (Doueck,1997, Shore,1998) and policymaking (Zirpoli,1995,) support for families and parents of individuals with specific needs (*Litzelfelner 1997*) and encouragement of self-advocacy in a wide range of areas of need including learning disability (*Aspis 1997;White,1997*).

There is a strong tradition of advocacy practice in the field of special education and disability services which provides a substantial framework and foundation for the introduction of Peer Advocacy© as a bullying intervention.

Peer Advocacy© AS AN APPROACH TO BULLYING

Peer Advocacy© is a helping strategy which provides victims of bullying with an individual mentor to assist them in their efforts to resist bullying. It is an innovative adaptation of the advocacy process successfully employed to support individuals with disability and other community members who seek justice through the aid of skilled, knowledgeable and capable others. It is a new approach to intervention in bullying as it recognises that without the acceptance and assistance of peers for the problems faced by victims of bullying, very little will change in terms of current social responses to bullying and victimisation.

The processes of Peer Advocacy© are discussed elsewhere in relation to field research, which sought student opinions on the seriousness of bullying in their school, their inclination to report bullying they were aware of, to a teacher, the capacity of the school to make students feel good about themselves and student willingness to assist others they saw being bullied. Significant differences were found in the attitudes and perceptions of bullied students and the general populations of the schools and between particular schools.

Peer Advocacy© requires the adoption of specific operational and philosophical principles related to bullying intervention as a responsibility of the peers of victimised individuals (see *Figure 3*).The intervention specifies processes and procedures which guide the interaction between the advocate and partner, and which require commitment, the acquisition of certain competencies and a mature understanding of the emotional and social support needs of the victim. Relevant theories can be shown to support the notion that young people can secure the assistance and intervention to which they are entitled by working in partnership with their peers, and that such advocacy is paramount in addressing the bullying issue.

Peer Advocacy© is grounded in a range of theoretical constructs including those related to the psychology of victimisation and resilience, the concept of social capital, child protection issues and practices including programs for skills development and advocacy. An examination of the relevance of each theoretical perspective demonstrates the contribution each makes to a strong foundation for the approach and this provides a range of concepts from which to create a new composite theoretical construct which describes the process of Peer Advocacy©. This program represents a new approach to intervention for victims of bullying as it proposes the inclusion of peers in a systematic process which demands a morally and legally conscientious response from those in authority. It necessitates the induction of young people into a training program to develop the attitudes, skills, knowledge, motivation and empathy to speak out and secure assistance for individuals who are being hurt through bullying.

Peer Advocacy© draws on the successful tradition of having others act on behalf of those in need and applies similar principles and practices to the training of young people to take responsibility for assisting peers who are victims of bullying. The specific application of Peer Advocacy© to bullying intervention evolved as a result of research which indicates that victims of bullying would seek the help of peers but hold unfavourable views of the capacity and willingness of teachers to assist them when complaints about bullying are made. It does not preclude the application of Peer Advocacy© for other purposes such as student rights issues (e.g. uniform, homework, fees) and support programs (e.g. remediation and therapy for behaviour problems) in other situations.

While advocacy as a practice has generally involved a partnership between an individual whose needs are not being met because of their inability to advocate for themselves and another individual who has relatively superior power, status, knowledge, ability or skills, Peer Advocacy© represents a relationship between individuals of like status. Both the Peer Advocate© and the victim of bullying are young people whose social status, power, knowledge and capacities are obviously inferior to those from whom they must seek assistance.

In advocacy programs which support individuals with limitations of intellectual, physical, social or psychological capacities it is essential to select an advocate who can act on their behalf in circumstances where they may otherwise be denied their rights and due processes (Smith 1997).Such advocates undertake to obtain justice and services for their partner in situations where particular organisational or procedural intricacies may require the intervention of someone with the necessary skill or knowledge to achieve access to the requisite service Similarly in the case of Peer Advocates® a young person is trained to understand and operate the procedures necessary for the victim of bullying to receive a fair hearing from the adults with the authority to intervene particularly within the school,family and social system. This obviously represents a substantial level of responsibility and commitment.

Within schools the Peer Advocacy© program is immersed within the anti-bullying program and there is necessarily a supportive community to which to appeal for intervention. Peer Advocates® are expected to put the case for and with their partners to adults whose receptivity and responses must reinforce the practice.

PEER PARTNERSHIP PROGRAMS

There is a plethora of programs and training packages available now for schools which have been introduced over recent years in an attempt to equip young people with the skills necessary to facilitate the development of mature interpersonal interactions. Many of these approaches are highly successful if appropriately applied and have been responsible for the development of significant and effective skills in formerly naive young people. Peer Advocacy© has a specific focus and implementation process which makes it preferable or complimentary to other skills bases for the purpose of intervention in bullying.

While each of these approaches is designed to introduce co-operative skills and deter aggressive interactions between peers, (Long, 1998; Beland,1992) it is their dependence upon the reciprocal nature of disputation and conflict in interactions which makes them unsuitable for bullying intervention.

Peer Advocacy© can provide young people with foundation skills including empathy and communication, which will assist in the acquisition of Peer Advocacy© competencies. The positive and supportive attitudes developed through a peer support program will facilitate the processes and procedures which comprise the Peer Advocacy© approach. In particular, Peer Advocacy© is not proposed as a generic set of skills, but as one specifically introduced to provide victims of bullying with an intermediary to formally put their case to those with the authority and inclination to intervene.

The purpose of the inclusion of Peer Advocacy© in an anti-bullying program is the establishment of a partnership which teaches a self-protective response to abusive behaviour, not a dependent relationship whereby passivity is reinforced. The processes of access and engagement of the Peer Advocate© are in themselves assertive and proactive behaviours required on the part of the victim.

Peer Advocacy©, provides a partner with whom to jointly advocate for protection rather than to represent their needs to those in authority. Further, *Blankenship (1998)* believes that social status predetermines the likelihood that individuals will face challenges through which their capacity to thrive will be developed and that race, gender and class are all salient conditions to consider. Other research indicates that irrespective of social position, resiliency and coping mechanisms can be developed

In preparation for the introduction of the Peer Advocacy© training (Healey, 2000) program several intervention and personal competencies are introduced including reporting, help seeking, resilience, assertiveness and introspection, each of which provides a skill base for the acquisition of the responsible position of Peer Advocate® in bullying intervention.

The processes and component of Peer Advocacy© are set out further in the *BULLYWATCH* program manuals.

SOCIAL RESPONSIBILITY

Peer Advocacy© rests upon the principle of community and social responsibility for maintaining a fair and equitable environment, at least in terms of opportunities for success and survival. Without recognition of the cost to the community of failure to support and assist those being bullied, substantial fiscal and social costs will ensue. During childhood and often into adulthood, individuals who have been severely victimised by bullies require additional social, medical and legal resources which could be avoided if early intervention was offered when bullying was first identified.

However, as with untreated health and ecological deficits, the postponement of intervention leads to gradually increasing service requirements for recovery or remediation. Additionally, the continuation of the bullying behaviour in a climate which endorses it inevitably leads to further costs as bullies relocate eventually to adult vocations as managers and executives reinforced for their capacity to disregard the human and focus on the fiscal investment in their organization. Stress, absenteeism, harassment claims and the incapacitation of workers through psychological damage, all deplete social capital as well as adding to the financial costs of the workplace (*De Maria, 1996; Mann 1996; Lennane, 1996*). It is the perceived lack of investment of interpersonal and other necessary resources which eventually incapacitates the victim and reduces trust.

In relation to investment, which involves Peer Advocacy© training for a ready resource of available peers to advocate on their own behalf, the social capital gained is disproportionately positive. The underlying theory of the importance of sustaining social capital in an economically rational society fits well with the production of Peer Advocates® at little cost and enormous gain in the effort to eliminate bullying. Peer Advocacy© contributes to social capital and therefore to the well being of the broader community, by encouraging young people to provide each other with assistance, therefore preventing the additional costs which result from the abandonment of victims of bullying.

Victimisation often results from the social isolation of the target individual in the bullying paradigm and this disconnectedness from a supportive community in turn enables the bully to continue since social isolation facilitates the abuse of young people (*Garbarino 1976, Tomison, 1996*). Establishing and maintaining supportive social networks can, on the other hand, equip young people with the resources to seek and access the help they need to resist bullying. Peer Advocacy© focuses on increasing the investment of young people in each others' welfare when supportive adults are not available or not concerned to intervene in what are often regarded as childish 'disputes'. It is only with great difficulty that young people are able to convince those with the authority to intervene that their help is necessary to protect a young person from harm (Healey, 2000).

As discussed earlier, current social attitudes and responses to bullying correlate closely with those evident in child abuse generally including the tendency to discount the incidence and impact of the activity, to maintain the social status and privileges of the perpetrator and to minimize the responsibility and capacity of others to intervene (Finkelhor,1995). Peer Advocacy© empowers young people to work together to demand protection and the prohibition of abusive activities to which they are vulnerable and exposed. The process enables young people to access the protective provisions already available through legislation for children who are being abused. Peer Advocacy© prepares young people by educating them about their rights to protection under this legislation as well as the provisions of anti-discrimination, harassment and assault legislation. In the absence of proactive and responsible authorities, Peer Advocacy© empowers young people to act on their own or others' behalf to secure their rights and safety are maintained.

7 Challenging the Effects of Media Influences

Introduction

Despite an apparently widely accepted belief that viewing violence influences young people generally, to engage in violent and bullying behaviour, a critical analysis of current research demonstrates that the evidence for such an assertion is weak and unsubstantiated. Fundamental to the mistaken claim is a failure to differentiate real from simulated violence in experimental, observational and analytical studies of the aggressive behaviours of young people. Further, what such analyses fail to do is recognise the implementation of real aggression and abuse by those with a predisposition to violence and bullying, irrespective of their viewing habits. In other words, abusive individuals do not need tutoring via the media in order to engage in their destructive behaviours.

Despite sometimes excessive and always unnecessary viewing of violent media images, the vast majority of viewers of violence will never engage in similar behaviour. A more practical approach is to examine the psychological and developmental buffers which seem to protect most young people from the influence of the media and maintain acceptable and non-violent behaviours for the majority. This information may contribute substantially to an understanding of the development of aggressive behaviour in abusive individuals and suitable intervention strategies.

Further, the issue of desensitisation to violence, often seen as a consequence of violence viewing for young people, is discussed here as a critical consideration when reflecting on the motivating forces which result in bullying and violence amongst young people. Fundamentally, it is argued that desensitisation to real violence almost never occurs, but desensitisation to the pain of others is almost certainly a defining feature in the psychology of bullies.

Researchers in a broad range of studies have ascribed aggressive play in children and young people to destructive media influences; they extrapolate from minor aggressive incidents to the likelihood of major acts of aggression in later life; they attempt to demonstrate that any overt aggression observed in the behaviours of young people is a consequence of abstract media influences. These links however, have not been established and much more careful analysis of current research is warranted. There are specific recurrent themes in the professional literature and social discourse on violence viewing, the most frequent of which are:

- watching media violence causes young people to become violent or aggressive (*Ballard and Weist, 1995, Arnow 1995*) watching media violence de-sensitises young people to violence (*Levine 1994, Moliter 1994, Botha 1993, Young and Young 1997*);

These mistaken beliefs in an unfounded central allegation, require redress in order to provide a new analysis of the more usual response to violence viewing which is not aggressive. This then facilitates reflection on two main considerations:

- what protects young people from the assumed negative impact of violence viewing?
- what does influence young people to engage in real and harmful behaviour?

VIOLENCE VIEWING AS AN INFLUENCE ON BEHAVIOUR

There seems to be a prevailing community view, often reinforced by newspaper analyses of crime, that there is a causal link between violence in society and violence portrayed in the entertainment media (Goldsmith 1997). The simplicity of the analysis does not detract from its impact and a plethora of research studies and reports – up to 3,000 by recent accounts (Oaks 1995) – seem to reinforce the connection. At least in the print media there appears to be no doubt that viewing violence inevitably makes young people violent.

Given that millions of young people, and others, daily view on-screen violence in a variety of forms-cinema, video, computer games etc-without exhibiting violence, however, it would seem much more parsimonious to conclude that such links are at best tenuous. Very few violence viewers engage in real violence in real life. Were it the case that violence viewing did in fact influence viewers to engage in violence, society would have long since been overwhelmed to a much greater degree than is currently evident, and violence would surely have been expunged from the screen.

Judging by the reactions of a majority of the viewing population it seems self-evident that a causal link has not been established, for the most part, between violence viewing and subsequent violent behaviour. While violence viewing obviously contributes nothing of value to the social and moral development of young people, it is argued here that nor does it precipitate violence in most viewers. Evidently, there are strong mitigating factors at work in society and in particular in the world of young people, which ensures that despite regular exposure to on-screen violence, the vast majority of young viewers do not seek to emulate what they view.

It is far more informative therefore, to consider why such viewing does not encourage most viewers to behave violently. Identification of the under-lying social, moral and psychological underpinnings which produce this result may well provide the essential components of a successful education program or other intervention for the vulnerable few for whom violence viewing does have a negative impact by reinforcing their individual violent propensities.

Nevertheless recent media reports indicate that some researchers believe that viewing simulated violence on video can indeed lead to realistic re-enactments, sometimes with lethal consequences.

YOU BE THE JUDGE

Excerpt taken from the Daily Telegraph (previous article)

Hollywood the villain of violence

Article from: **Daily Telegraph**
By Gemma Jones
February 26, 2009 12:00am

TEENAGERS filming and posting violent videos on the internet from after-school fight clubs are copying Hollywood movies, a youth behavioural expert said yesterday.

The claim came after The Daily Telegraph revealed a teenager died of head injuries after participating in an after-school fight club meeting.

Bullying expert Roberto Parada from the University of Western Sydney said boys were using the clubs to show how tough they were.

There are numerous videos on YouTube showing teenagers bare knuckled and some in boxing gloves bashing each other in parks as onlookers cheer.

"They are making it a form of cyber bullying so everyone else can see the person being picked on. YouTube is a way for it to be glorified," Mr Parada said yesterday.

"By videoing it and distributing it, it says 'Look at me, look how tough I am'. The reality is we look at it so often in various movies. I think the consensus of the research would say exposure to aggressive media generates more likelihood of a teenager being aggressive."

Internet videos show shocking violence, with many of the fights put to music and watched by thousands of viewers, who give the violence a star rating.

Fight Club: The movie that inspired the violence.

Experts said yesterday people who went willingly to join a fight club were not being bullied but it would be difficult for spectators to speak up and stop a confrontation.

"A lot of kids will report they don't intervene because they fear being a target themselves," Sydney University Associate Professor Caroline Hunt said.

"One of the things that protect targets of bullying is having friends who are a little bit more outgoing than you are who might be brave enough to stand up."

Continued next page

Dr Jean Healey, Bullying Researcher and Consultant, said there was often reluctance on the part of teachers to intervene in fights and bullying out of school hours. She said the fight clubs had to be tackled by police and the community. "What schools need to do, if they are not already doing it, is define how far they are prepared to be involved in activities outside school grounds and school time," she said.

"They are not really responsible for what is happening in the park even if they are in school uniform. You can understand them being reluctant. It is a community responsibility"

Extreme danger: *A teenage fight club video posted on YouTube. This is not the fatal fight.*

THE REALITY FACTOR

The fundamental issue in discussing the impact of violence viewing is to differentiate real from simulated violence. If young people watch 'pretend' violence, and then re-enact the 'pretend' behaviours observed, usually without incurring or causing injury, this cannot be interpreted as media violence viewing causing violent behaviour. Simulated violence is not violence. Pretending to be violent is not actually being violent. Nevertheless the example here seems to contradict this theory as the fighters in this event have apparently specifically copied a particular film. This actually illustrates quite well the argument that violence viewing may influence those who already have a propensity to violence, as the story shows.

Most students in this example, are not physically involved in the brutal fighting. They are engaged, as usual, observing the fight, and possibly vicariously enjoying it. Nevertheless, it becomes apparent when someone is actually hurt or shockingly in the case of these fights, tragically killed, the attitudes of the observers changes to shock and disbelief. The observation of 'violence' is tolerable when the 'actors' are not actually hurt. Simulated violence is acceptable and exciting, but real violence leading to damage or death is clearly not. De-sensitisation to real violence has not occurred if the observer responds appropriately to these socially unacceptable events. Furthermore, in the case of the fights illustrated, participation is generally seen as voluntary, and therefore the fighters not entitled to sympathy. Even if one of the participants has been bullied into participation, the observers interpret their participation as chosen and therefore that they are not in need of protection or intervention.

The *intentionality* of the act is critical to the definition. There must be real harm, hurt, damage, or other consequences for the act to be a violent act. Violent simulations – unless enacted in order to be threatening – are not real violence. Even quite young people are capable of differentiating real and 'pretend' violence, contrary to popular belief. Further, it cannot be assumed that the simulated violence young people view in various forms of media is generalised to their real world and lives.

"Violent' video games for example are viewed as:

- *"sort of funny – 'cos you know it's not real"*
- *"it looks funny when you just grab the neck and rip off their heads and you see the spine dangling"*
- *"it's not really people – it's guys, but they're monsters"*
- *"it's like blowing a hole in them and they keep walking – real people couldn't do that"*

Young & Young (1997)

While these are not attractive depictions, nor are they evidence that viewers will try to emulate them. Young people are clearly capable of recognising the exaggeration and 'entertainment' intended in such media, and the unlikelihood of the activities occurring in reality – there are no blurred boundaries in their perception. Given the hundreds of thousands of young people engaged in daily 'violent' interactive video games and video film viewing the failure of the medium to incite violent behaviour in contravention of social mores and norms is compelling evidence of its ineffectiveness. Watching 'violence' obviously does not make young people violent, no matter how excessively 'violent' they may seem to adult viewers. Even young people identified as 'at risk' through their educational and minor criminal backgrounds, when interviewed about the impact of violent video games indicated:

- *"fighting games don't lead to street fighting – people worry about that but it's just paranoia"*
- *"I don't need a video game to be violent – it's not games, it's other people that set you off"*
- *"there are no repercussions from the computer, but if you did it in real life it would be real sad"*

(Young & Young, 1997)

Griffiths (1997) suggests that computer game playing is an "absorbing and harmless activity" which may be problematic for a small minority of young people. The views expressed in their study reinforce the classic early research findings by *Lefkowitz, et al, (1973)* that young people prone to violent behaviours will select violence viewing, but that violence viewing does not create the violent tendency. *Cesarone (1994)* suggests that the interactive nature of video games may have a more harmful effect than passively watching 'violent acts' on television, however, the interviews conducted by *Young and Young (1997)* seem to indicate that entertainment and recreation are the major priorities and outcomes for young people engaged in viewing 'violence'. The concern for 'protection' of young people from video 'violence' may have reached extreme proportions when we consider that *Chen (1994)* found that of forty videos rated, only twelve met his vigorous non-violent criteria and several Disney corporation products were rejected as unsuitable even though they were prescribed for pre-schoolers. Such sanitization of content for young minds may well result in a generation of young people without resilience.

Strasburger, et al. (1993) point to video games and rock music videos and songs and other media as potential influences on adolescent aggression, and while there can be no doubt that some rock lyrics illustrate violent attitudes and behaviours:

> *"Beat her til she's red and raw, crack the whip, it hardly stings the bitch". ("She Likes it Rough". Thrasher quoted in Goldsmith, 1997)*

There is no evidence that this incites young people to engage in such behaviour. Sadly, such lyrics may well be a reflection of reality for some young people and do not introduce new concepts or ideas. In this case the reality of the experiences, not the recording of them in a song is likely to have the greater impact. Nevertheless, while there can be no justification for the distribution of such offensive material, it is unlikely to lead to similar behaviour.

Some researchers take a particularly glum view of society suggesting that young people are generally being "conditioned to violence and hatred through war toys, video games and mass media" *(Arnow 1998)*. While pro-peace and anti-violence approaches (Jenkin, 1996) are certainly to be encouraged, the effective psychological conditioning which happens in most families, even where there are such toys and games, are evidently sufficient to maintain the majority non-violent *status quo.*

Ballard and Weist, (*1995*) seemed surprised to find that male college students registered higher cardiovascular reactions after playing a highly stimulating 'violent' video game than after playing billiards and cautions that the level of 'violence' watched causes the biological reaction. Without discussing the implications of these results with the students to discover whether in fact they felt inclined to engage in real violence as a result of the game, it is very difficult to identify a connection. Many activities result in psychological stimulation without inciting violent behaviours and based on cardiovascular responses alone it is difficult to estimate the impact. Any number of engagements may produce a similar reaction, and in the final analysis the purpose of the 'game' is to generate excitement, though certainly not violence.

Throughout the last forty years of research a key factor in differentiating the responses of young people to violence viewing seems to have been overlooked.

MODELLING AGGRESSION — THE ORIGINAL SOURCE OF THE MYTH

The notion of 'modelling' aggressive or violent behaviour can be traced back to the classic experiments of *Bandura* (*1973*) and his observation of young children in a laboratory situation, whereby an adult experimenter was viewed behaving 'aggressively' towards a large plastic Bobo doll. The adult female subject was observed by children from an observation platform, and was seen to hit, push and punch the doll while it bounced and returned to its position.

When allowed into the experimental environment with the doll, their responses after watching, were predicably enthusiastic. They too, when given the opportunity enjoyed 'beating' the model. Indeed, some children improvised by using a toy mallet to ensure the doll received a thorough 'beating'! To deduce from this, however, that these children had observed 'violence' and had subsequently adopted 'violent 'behaviours is highly questionable. They watched and engaged in *simulated violenc*e, usually sanctioned by adults and indeed, in this case observed to be enacted by an adult. To extrapolate further from this, that young people who watch 'violence' will model 'violence' is completely unsubstantiated.

Not only did the doll not show any distress or pain – in fact it grinned vacuously throughout the ordeal – it just kept coming back for more as it was designed to do! These children watched and engaged in *simulated violence* and no evidence is presented that they then or subsequently developed into violent individuals.

Analyses of these observations did not seem to take account of several important factors:

- the children were well aware of the function of a Bobo Doll and therefore would not have been surprised, let alone distressed, to see it "beaten"

- the doll is an inanimate plaything designed for the purpose so of course the children were likely to copy the observed behaviours, which were not only fun but also sanctioned by adults

- the adult engaged in the 'violent' behaviour was not angry or frightening to the children, and was engaged in vigorous play familiar to the children, which was quite appealing to them

- her behaviour was not interpreted by them as' violent 'as it was neither harmful nor socially inappropriate

The critical question, which needed to be answered in this situation, was whether those same children, after viewing an adult in an angry or aggressive mood physically abusing a real person or child would have responded differently? There is little doubt that they would have been distressed, afraid and anxious. Viewing *real* and *simulated* violence is not the same and there must be grave doubt that they would have taken the opportunity to emulate the adult were it offered in a genuinely violent situation. Young people may well simulate 'violence' particularly when so much is sanctioned by society, but they nevertheless retain their links to reality by refraining from engaging in real acts of violence. Even young people who are exposed to real violence or abuse in their family or community rarely respond by developing violent behaviours themselves (Spatz-Widom 1998; Roberts, 1998). Instead, most respond with trauma, withdrawal and depression.

IMPACT OF REAL VIOLENCE

Rather, examined on a continuum from real-life, personally experienced violence to the least effective cartoon-style antics of various characters, it becomes clear that nothing matches the impact of real-life violence. If it was true that the more realistic the violence viewed, the greater the likelihood of the young viewer becoming violent, then those young people who witness and experience real life violence on a daily basis would be most likely to become violent. Very few such individuals do indeed develop violent skills and strategies. The majority of children exposed to real life violence do not become violent – they become withdrawn and depressed (Spatz-Widom, 1998). Children in international areas of civil unrest and wars remain silently traumatised for many years, as did the adult soldiers before them. *Van der Voort* and *Beentjes* (*1997*) express concern for the emotional reactions elicited from young people viewing extremely violent movies, films and games. Theirs and other substantial research now documents the fact that young people are much more likely to respond with fear and anxiety, often persisting long after the program is ended, than they are to respond with pro-violent feelings.

Cantor (*1997*) has thoroughly examined children's reactions across various age groups and has determined that there are close developmental links to the fear response. Young children are likely to be afraid of the appearance of violent characters, while older children become afraid when they apply their cognitive predictions and analysis processes to the drama – particularly if the violence could happen in reality. *Ramsden* (*1997*) found that 48% of children interviewed were uncomfortable when they watched 'people being shot', 'killing' and 'blood' as well as animals hunting each other. None reported an urge to go forth and emulate.

Fear of becoming a victim, rather than identification with the perpetrator, was a much more likely response by children in these studies. *Buckingham* (*1997*) found viewers did not 'become Freddy Kruger' but more usually feared becoming his next target. In this study, various coping strategies such as declaring blood to be tomato sauce, and hiding behind large cushions or companions seemed to ease the anxiety but little – and while there was a vicarious thrill attached to suffering the visual impact of the 'violence', nobody expressed a desire to copy the character. *Valkenburg (1997)* quite sensibly states that it is not a serious problem for children to be a little afraid when viewing television or videos – and that this can contribute to the development of resilience and competence in later life. She does not advocate regular or intense doses of fear-inducing video violence and prescribes adult supervision and discussion with children to alleviate real concerns.

Certainly in recent years there have been a number of mass murders committed by juveniles, particularly in the United States where access to means and access to victims combine with individual psychopathology and result in tragic young deaths. The overriding evidence in each of the murders, however, seems to indicate that the youthful felons were no more generally violent than any of their peers – described as 'weird', perhaps, unpopular usually and often rejected – but none were reportedly violent prior to the murders. These most violent of juvenile crimes do not seem to be in any way related to violence viewing. Nor can we demonstrate in these extreme cases that these juveniles were anymore likely than others to watch violence. The link that can be established, however, is that already violent individuals are likely to select violent videos. Violent individuals are also likely to engage in behaviour leading to criminal convictions.

Chesney-Lind, Sheldon and Joe, (1996) and *Artz (1997)* are concerned with the media images portrayed of violent adolescent girls, but agree that these young women may well have a similarly violent orientation to their male counterparts and are more like violent males than non-violent females, although they resist using biological determinism to account for similarities. However, what can also be established is that some violent young offenders come from family backgrounds where crime and violence were frequent and researchers can demonstrate links between familial violence and subsequent criminal and violent behaviour in some children. *Salby (1997)* advocates early intervention to avoid the long-term impact of violence in the lives of children. In *Spatz–Widom's*, research 26% of juveniles identified as abused and neglected had been arrested and involved in criminal activity at a young age. These are the young people who have been indoctrinated and reinforced into a violent culture and who adopt the requisite skills to survive in their environment. Child soldiers are sadly also indoctrinated, drugged, trained and reinforced to engage in involuntary killing and violence in real camps with real weapons and real victims. This is a clear example of the force of education principles in establishing socially acceptable behaviours, for the particular environment.

Petrie (*1994*) addresses the media-influence theory in his review of the murder of James Bulger in the UK, and examines the concept of the 'evil within'. Given the social and familial backgrounds of the two juvenile murderers, violence viewing probably played a negligible role. Indeed, *Mathews* (*1994*) contends that no connection with the child's murder could be identified in a systematic examination by censors of the video "Chucky 3" which was widely believed to have influenced the boys. The anti-social, pro-violence attitudes portrayed in the video may have reinforced their own perceptions, but they did not create them. James Ferman of the *British Board of Film Classification* says: "What has never been demonstrated is that media violence is either a necessary or sufficient cause of violence in real life" (*Videodrome, 1994*). Nor does the correlation between violence viewed and violent behaviour prove causality.

Despite this concern for identifying and intervening in genuinely aggressive activity among young people, it is also apparent that there is a failure to identify potentially dangerous individuals. Martin Bryant, who was responsible for the massacre at Port Arthur, was reportedly a quiet though 'strange' and withdrawn student at school; the Columbine high school mass murderers in USA have been variously described as 'walking time bombs' and ordinary kids; the murderers of James Bulger in the UK were troubled children who nevertheless slipped through the net. Irrespective of the video viewing habits of such individuals it is unlikely their murderous behaviour was triggered in this way, and while violent behaviour during childhood may signal future problems, so can withdrawn, depressed and isolated demeanours. The personality and interaction styles of such individuals are far more indicative than their viewing habits.

One rather controversial proposition is that maleness is a *cause* of violence rather than simply a correlation factor (*Eggar, 1995*). Of concern to feminist analysts, certainly are the portrayal of women in submissive and victimised roles in the media and the consequent reinforcement of sexist attitudes. It cannot be demonstrated, however, that such portrayals initiate pro-violent attitudes where none existed previous to viewing. Overall, the individual psychology rationale has greater credibility than any explanation focussing on external influences.

Katz (*1988*) while considering social and environmental factors in youth alienation focuses most strongly on a lack of moral and ethical standards as the driving forces in young people's involvement in violence. *Spatz-Widom* (*1998*) also examines individual characteristics and capacities as possible 'buffers ' against the long-term negative consequences of real life violent experiences – in fact most victims of familial violence do not engage in violence in later life. It is very apparent that a wide range of contingent factors must be present in violent individuals before violence is perpetrated and that violence viewing is, at most, incidental. Nevertheless, there can be no edifying reason for the creation, presentation and sale of violent media products to young people.

SO, HOW IS VIOLENT BEHAVIOUR DEVELOPED?

Violent and abusive behaviours are learned behaviours. Understanding the process of learning to behave in a violent manner is fundamental to understanding why media violence is generally unlikely to teach young people to behave in such a way. Developmentally, children are programmed from birth for learning and indeed, having discovered the principles of learning which guarantee our messages will be absorbed by children, teachers and parents devote countless hours reinforcing usually pro-social information and behaviour. Most children follow a predictable pathway of intellectual, moral and social development.

The essential components for teaching any skill or behaviour include:

- motivation,
- instruction,
- demonstration,
- practice,
- opportunity,
- reinforcement and
- approval

(*Berk 1998*)

Children are exposed to each of these processes through their continuous interactions with their parents, peers and others and these usually positive influences assist in the development of appropriate behaviours and attitudes.

There are some young people, however, whose major influences are neither appropriate nor positive. For such individuals, the key influential persons in their lives may consistently engage in violent or abusive behaviours. For this small minority abusive and aggressive behaviours may well be demonstrated, practised and vicariously instructed, as well as resulting in reinforcement and approval when the child engages in the behaviour. The scene is set for the creation of a violent individual. The individual will more than likely also have positive role models for life – at school, in the community and even on television, however the major influence is his home environment and the significant adults therein. Having established for the child the acceptable range of behaviours for the particular environment (the violent home) the child will inevitably seek out opportunities for reinforcement inside or outside the home. There is evidence therefore that for a sample of young people, the overwhelming influence in their lives of an abusive significant other, may lead to the learning of those behaviours through the process described. Violence viewing alone cannot provide all of the elements of learning outlined.

Let's examine these factors in relation to violent or abusive behaviour enacted by the young person:

There first needs to be *motivation* to be violent or abusive towards another. The internal psychological pre-disposition towards aggressive behaviour is a pre-requisite for the enactment of the behaviour. Next, the presence of *instruction*, through personal observation of the *demonstration* of real or simulated violent or abusive acts; then *opportunities* for *practice* to abuse others needs to be provided. This must be followed by *reinforcement and approval* of the abusive behaviour in order for the abusive behaviour to firmly established within the range of behaviour of the learner.

It is highly unlikely that viewing simulated violence in and of itself, will satisfy all of these conditions. However, *real* abuse or violence may.

Motivation is sustained by either 'intrinsic' or 'extrinsic' reinforcement (Healey, 2008). Either the act is 'intrinsically' rewarding and therefore sustains involvement, or some external or 'extrinsic' reinforcing element sustains the behaviour. In the case in point, this would mean that violent or abusive behaviours would be felt to be intrinsically rewarding and therefore would become a regular part of the behaviour of the individual. In terms of social and psychological profiles, only the most damaged individual will be motivated towards violent and abusive behaviour because it in intrinsically reinforcing. This does not include most people who view violence but does include those few deviant individuals for whom hurting others is pleasurable. Hurting others will often result in them achieving power and goods they would otherwise not have. Fundamentally, then, violent and abusive behaviour will be enacted by individuals who are exposed to all of the key elements of learning such behaviour and who are motivated to engage in learning the behaviours.

There are some individuals who prefer to engage in behaviour that is threatening and violent sometimes because they have no other repertoire upon which to draw. They will be delighted to observe similar behaviour and situations on television or other screens and may well append their own violent range of behaviour with effective demonstrations they have viewed.

Violent behaviour, having been established through a thorough process of training during their early development, simply requires reinforcement in order to be maintained. Violent behaviour is often selected, according to violent individuals, for the gratification of their needs for power, domination and sadism – they learn to enjoy hurting others. While the majority of young people in our society are effectively immunised against the impact of violent viewing therefore, through pro-social experiences and expectations, young people who are subject to inadequate parenting, or who have developed a psychological or personal orientation towards violence, are likely to select violent viewing to reinforce their world view, as well as for entertainment.

Lefkowitz, et al. (1977) was one of the first to demonstrate that violent media viewing is unlikely to have the effect of causing violent behaviour, but may well supplement the already violent behaviour of susceptible individuals. This may account for the low correlation between watching video violence and performing real violence among most individuals who engage in the activity of viewing.

Individuals are likely to select video viewing for a number of reasons including interest, curiosity, entertainment and instruction. Keen gardeners will no doubt happily select videos on rose pruning or Great Gardeners of the World, which in turn may improve their skills; the average driver may be keen to watch Grand Prix films in the hope of increasing their own driving skills or self image; fitness videos are selected by those motivated to become fit, or at least watch someone else do so! The key here is the motivation to specifically add to your own range of behaviours by viewing others with more advanced or different skills.

It should come as no surprise, then to find, that violence viewing is selected by those who have a propensity or preference for violent behaviour nor that such individuals may well select such viewing in order to increase their own range of behaviour – the key factor again being motivation. In each instance the already motivated viewer selects the product which 'fits' their own situation, sometimes to improve their skills, sometimes for entertainment. There are many others who select the same video for entertainment alone – without any motivation to develop or acquire the skills demonstrated.

Ageback (*1997*) suggests a mutual cause and effect relationship in which more aggressive children tend to gravitate towards media violence. She is convinced that 90% – 95% of the aggression, however, stems from psychological, familial and environmental factors.

Schramm (*1996*) assures us that movies can rarely be blamed as the sole cause of anti-social conduct but cites instances of the effect on susceptible youngsters, supporting the view that the pathology is more likely to be present prior to viewing. Parental supervision, monitoring and censorship are also critical factors in violence viewing. Parents who reinforce and engage in violence themselves are less likely to find violent videos objectionable, or to feel the need to 'protect' young people from them. Access is a critical factor. *Krcmar and Cantor* (*1997*) examined parent/child viewing choice conversations and found that effective parents used more negative affect when discussing violent videos, while children were likely to request or favour programs with more restrictive ratings.

Many of the young people interviewed in the *Young and Young* (*1997*) study were unaware that there were restrictions on video games and claimed they could play with any of the games. *Biggins* (*1997*) states, that when young people choose a diet of heavy violence it is an indication of poor conditions at home – "when no-one monitors what children watch, they are in danger for other reasons – a lack of caretaking".

Such neglect coupled with spasmodic though violent parental attention could provide the ideal condition for the development of a violent individual. Support for the view that parental and environmental factors can mitigate the influence of violence viewing can be found in an early report by *Huesmann and Bachrach (1986)*. They found that there was a significant difference between the responses of city children and children living in Kibbutz, with city children more likely to be aggressive. Kibbutz children were not influenced to engage in aggressive behaviour following violence viewing – a factor attributed to the close familial environment of the Kibbutz.

On this point, researchers have been diligent in recent years documenting the non-violent responses of young people to the simulated violence they view. The 'reality factor' is a critical issue though not in confirming that the more realistically violent the fiction the more violent the young person is likely to become.

DESENSITISATION

The issue of desensitisation is a recurrent and again poorly supported contention regarding the influence of violent media. It is impossible to imagine most young people, or even older viewers, becoming desensitised to real violence as a result of watching simulated violence. *Moliter (1994)* expresses the concern that exposure to media violence *desensitised* children to real-life aggression since children tended to 'tolerate' more aggressive behaviour in others if they have first viewed violence on film. This could however indicate a passive response rather than aggression. *Levine (1995)* quotes numerous studies, which have shown that viewing media violence "encourages aggression and desensitisation" but she also concluded that a greater tolerance for or acceptance of simulated violence is more likely.

Violence viewing more likely results in desensitisation to *simulated* violence – hence the desire to view more graphic depictions of simulated 'violence' at each sitting – but there is no evidence that watching simulated violence desensitises young people to real violence. It is apparent that much of the research undertaken has not differentiated real from simulated violence. Ideally, viewers would all become desensitised to simulated violence to the extent that it becomes rejected as boring and repetitious. Even in this circumstance it is most unlikely that any individual seeing violence against another person or animal in real life would be unmoved.

Ageback (1997) agrees

> 'evidence proving familiarisation with media violence leads to indifference towards violence in real life, is yet to be unveiled'.

BUT ADVERTISING WORKS, DOESN'T IT?

Another common argument put forward regarding the impact of media viewing is that product advertisers can clearly demonstrate that their efforts lead to increases in the purchase and profile of their product and that therefore viewing can be highly influential and can dictate behaviour. Advertising costs are expended with the express purpose of encouraging changes to the purchasing habits of the population to which the advertising is targeted, or, in the case of children, their parents.

However, it cannot be assumed that it is just as easy to influence individuals to engage in neutral behaviour (e.g. buying goods) as it is to influence them to engage in anti-social, violent or criminal behaviour. Unless pre-conditions are present, such as propensity for or training in violence, most people will not be influenced by media images which contravene all of their moral and social beliefs, to engage in the demonstrated violent behaviours. The mediating factors for most young people are their powerful moral and social, psychological and intellectual development and learning, most of which occurs long before violence viewing is experienced.

Being influenced to buy pizza, a new car, alcohol and furniture is undoubtedly increased by clever and consistent advertising. Nevertheless, this behaviour, which is socially sanctioned and desirable, cannot be equated with media images which illustrate clearly antisocial and often criminal behaviours which harm others. The viewer is not a 'tabula rasa' having no pre-conceived notions of what is right and wrong. Indeed, by the time they begin viewing, children are not blank slates upon which to write any message irrespective of its social consequences. Children have already developed a set of acceptable social behaviours, mores and values by the time they begin to watch violence. It is apparently this buffer which ensures that violence viewing remains fantasy for the majority of young viewers and which prevents the adoption of clearly unacceptable behaviours for which they know they will 'get into trouble'. In any case, they will never become desensitised to the reality of abuse and violence in their real lives.

Youth violence, popularly believed to be influenced if not caused by violence viewing is often reported in the print media is such a way as to suggest increases of crime–wave proportions. As *Polk (1997)* points out, youth involvement in violent crimes has been stable over the past ten years. However, in homicide the age group 0 – 19 years accounts for 18% of offences. It is disastrous that such young people should be involved in murder and community concerns reflect this. The most likely negative influences impacting on their involvement however, are alcohol consumption (Egger 1995), the ready availability of weapons such as knives and the presence of young people in unsupervised often public spaces in search of recreation (Polk 1997).

The data relating to violent incidents involving young people are much more likely to show that they had recently exited a hotel than a cinema showing a violent movie. Youth conflicts leading to violence are likely to be provoked by verbal interchanges which threaten their fragile self-concepts and newly emerging 'masculinity' given that such young offenders are most often male (Polk,1997) and that their concept of masculinity is often poorly constructed.

Young males are most at risk from each other in our society and this is related to social perceptions of what constitutes "a real man". We need to establish a view that strength and masculinity are not compatible with violence towards others, particularly women and children. The notion that violence can be resolved through education (*Jenkin, 1996*) is well supported by the evidence that the majority of young people do not engage in violence irrespective of their experiences via the family or media (*Spatz-Widom, 1998*). In 1990-1991 16% of all homicide victims nationally were under the age of 19 (*Strang 1992*), with children under age one year disproportionately represented. Young victims and perpetrators of violence are usually involved as a result of a spontaneous and rapidly escalating dispute with no evidence of pre-meditation or systematic planning such as may be anticipated were they to use viewed violence as their reference and mentor. "Copy cat" crimes of violence are a print media invention with no evidence of such deliberations available in the crime statistics data.

SUMMARY

From the extensive literature available it is clear, then, that the following statements can be substantiated:

- young people who do not have a violent orientation or behaviours are highly unlikely to copy violence viewed.

- the 'reality factor' in fact, increases sensitivity to violence – the more realistic the violence, the more fearful and distressed most young viewers become.

- most young people are effectively socialised, moral and discerning individuals who capably distinguish real from simulated violence and show no inclination toward violent behaviour.

- Violence viewing cannot be shown to increase violent behaviour in the vast majority of viewers, young and older.

However,

- young people who already have a propensity for violence will choose violence viewing. The boys in the *Lefkowitz* (*1977*) study clearly preferred violence viewing and this correlated with assessments of their own already established levels of violence.

- these young people may supplement their repertoire of violent behaviour through violence viewing

- violent young people are more likely to become involved in criminal activity and are more likely to be arrested.

Violence in all forms of media does not contribute to the appropriate socialisation of young people, does not represent reality nor, in fact offer any redeeming reasons for its own existence. Violent media images are unnecessary and intrusive, taking the place of works which could be more entertaining, more constructive and more valuable for the young people who view them. Media creators need to stop catering to the lowest common denominator of expectations, moral values, intellect and sophistication, and begin to produce media images that will live long in the memory for positive reasons. But they will not. They know very well that violence on screen is profitable – and they care not that a vulnerable few may find the ideas presented instructive. Instead, of concentrating time, energy and resources in researching and agitating for more responsible media products – society needs to focus on the major genesis of the violent individual – the home, the family and the influence they reflect.

8 Cyber bullying – Impact and Management

Introduction

The proliferation of technology as the major communication tool for young people in society and education today has introduced a further dimension for abuse. There is no limit to the access and opportunity provided by web-based social networks, chat rooms, email and personal profiles for abusive peers and predatory individuals to engage in bullying. Research and initiatives by communication and media authorities as well as education and other government organisations provide a sound platform for the management of bullying on the internet. However, responsibility for exposure, the sharing of private information and pictures rests with the user of the internet and a major focus of intervention in this arena needs to be on the education of young people in safe and responsible usage. Sharing private pictures and information with others whose access to the internet enables them to share even more broadly given particular circumstances, means that young people can be exposed by their ' friends' without further reference. Young people are fully competent in the use of cyber-networking, but may not be 'cyber-smart' unless they have the advantage of education to protect them online.

Young people have adopted social networking by 'proxy' as a replacement or supplement to social networking in person. To adults, teachers, parents and the community this is something of a concern. It was recently suggested that soon we will no longer need the local 'park' for young people to hang out together-they can now do it without leaving their home or bedroom and the company of their computer. Alarm bells must be sounded if this is the extent of social interaction for a young person, but as a means of meeting and communicating with others of similar age and interests, it may complement the real world of relationships. *Gennaro and Dutton (2007)* express concern for the social development of young people engaged in isolating internet usage, and suggest the activity may exacerbate anti-social behaviours.

Lenhart et al. (2010), state that in the USA, 73% of young people 12–17 used internet social networking sites in 2009 and this represents an increase from 58% in 2007. They also state that 82% of young people 14–17 and 55% of younger adolescents have a social networking profile page. Australia is a global leader in the use of SMS text messaging and mobile phones are the most common medium used here for cyber-bullying. (*Dooley, et al. 2009*)

In recent years some government and education authority efforts have been undertaken to educate young networkers about their privacy and security online. *Hinduja and Patchin (2010)* discovered that *MySpace* users are increasingly likely to choose to restrict access to their profiles by making them 'private'. In 2006, 39% did so while their research showed that in 2009, 85% used this facility. However their research also discovered that a significant number of users include their full name and sometimes their home city and /or school in their profiles making them very easy to locate for predatory users. This indicates a need to consider safety online and the means by which these participants can be assisted to ensure their safety is not compromised while they communicate.

The Australian Communications and Media Authority provide guides for students on 'Socialising on the Internet' and 'Internet Safety'. These free brochures make it clear that parental responsibility is paramount and their vigilance in observing their children's internet usage is a key factor in protection from online abuse and predators. It is concerning, however that meeting new acquaintances online and then arranging real-life social meetings is not discouraged rather, it is suggested such meeting be planned and organised with a 'parent'. It would seem that such an experience would be best deferred until the young person is mature enough to make judgments about the individual requesting the meeting.

These brochures offer advice for parents of children and young people regarding their usage and include these general hints and tips:

- spend time online
- help your kids use the internet as an effective research tool
- teach your children 'netiquette'
- set rules (for usage)

They also suggest parents teach children:

- that not all internet information is reliable
- there are ways to deal with upsetting or disturbing content and
- to be aware of strangers and their real identity.

(ACMA, Cybersmart Guide)

Numerous websites are now available to offer support and guidance for parents and users in relation to safety online. The most comprehensive and valuable list of such sites is contained in the appendices of the report by Dooley et al (2009). These sites advise what protective programs are available and how to install and use them. In the end it is a shared responsibility and the avoidance of abuse relies on the resilient and proactive measures taken by users, by parents and school personnel to ensure that online experiences are valuable and productive rather than destructive.

DEFINITIONS

Cyber-bullying is defined by *Hinduja and Patchin (2010)* as:

> wilful and repeated harm inflicted through the use of computers, cell phones (mobiles) and other electronic devices'

They add further that cyber-bullying refers to:

> 'incidents where adolescents use technology,.....to harass, threaten, humiliate or otherwise hassle peers'.

Dooley, et al. (2009) simply refer to cyber-bullying with reference to traditional definitions and add that it constitutes,

> 'bullying in an electronic medium or via technology'

The similarity to other forms of peer abuse is obvious, however the major defining feature is the involvement of technology to frighten and abuse others. Other key components of the accepted definitions of bullying or peer abuse, are probably also relevant to cyber-bullying. These include intentional harm, repetition and power differences. Some analysts however, question this. *Belsy* (*2004*) omits reference to power differences in the definition he provided:

> 'the use of information and communication technologies to support deliberate, repeated and hostile behaviour by an individual or group, intended to harm another'

This may indicate that the power differential is seen as negligible when the abuse is distant and impersonal. Also the social power status of the abuser may be less than that of the victim, but the anonymity and reach of the technology as a weapon for abuse invests the socially less-powerful individual with a greater degree of control and power than they usually receive.

Further the criteria for 'repeated' abuse changes with the internet environment. If the image or message is posted only once, but the recipients and viewers are numerous, is this the same as repeated bullying? (*Cross, et al., 2009*). *Kowalski, Limber & Agaston*. (*2008*) notes that the methodologies are varied and therefore impact may differ. Young people can use their personal profiles to vilify others, list people they don't like and denigrate others; they can assume virtual personalities or use online game and chat rooms to spread rumours, exclude individuals and disseminate abuse and private information. To some extent the limits of the usual definitions of peer abuse become apparent with further analysis. Interestingly, however there is no mention of conflict in any definition currently offered of cyber-bullying.

There are a number of salient factors which differentiate cyber-bullying from others forms of abuse, including the fact that the abuse can be undertaken anonymously. The bully can screen their identity by using anonymous email identities, pseudonyms and other internet veils. At least when bullying occurs in a social environment, the victim and others are witness to the abuse and may well initiate intervention. In some ways the internet facilitates the abuse but also changes the dynamics. The bully cannot see the immediate response of the victim, but may hear from others how upset they are. This style of secretive, sneaky abuse, which relieves the abuser of the immediate responsibility for upsetting the victim, suits the covert bully.

It is a major focus for educators and parents to provide the information necessary for young people to be protected, to be encouraged to be vigilant and to take responsibility for their postings. However, it is true to say that many teachers and parents do not feel they are as computer – and online – savvy as the young people they are trying to protect. For this reason, general messages about self-protective behaviours need to be reinforced beyond the computer, and the acceptance of responsibility in all phases of life and behaviour needs to be encouraged. This includes developing an awareness of the types of predatory behaviour that can eventuate from casual meetings online, and of course is relevant to the discussion about bullying in cyberspace.

IMPACT AND OUTCOMES

A recent Australian review of cyber-safety research (*Dooley, Cross, Hearn and Treyvaud, 2009*) indicates that rates of cyber-bullying are comparatively low in Australia at <10%, whereas international rates are up to 52% and that 82% of victims know the identity of the perpetrator (page 59). *Hinduja and Patchin* (*2010*) found that 20% of 11-18 year old students in their research indicated they had been a victim of cyber-bullying and about the same number admitted bullying others on the internet.

The impact of cyber-bullying compares to other forms of abuse and bullying as described further in this text. Those individuals exposed to this form of abuse develop depression, withdrawal and suicidal ideation to the same extent as other victims whose abuse is more personal and face-to face. Low self-esteem, feelings of worthlessness and humiliation all result from the often public denigration of the victim. Fear and distress at returning to school where their reputations and private information were, they believed widely known and scorned, leads to school refusal and social withdrawal.

Distress is compounded since the opportunity to spread the abusive message in limitless to the determined bully and the victim has no way of controlling where the abusive messages are distributed. The impact of the abuse can also be greatly boosted by the language used and the participation of many others who may contribute their opinions. Finally, because of the humiliation they feel, the victim may keep the abuse secret from their family and those who can assist and protect them. All of these elements indicate a serious and severe response is highly likely for the abused individual and there have been a number of reported deaths as a result.

In 2009 MTV conducted a 'Digital Abuse Study', and found that 10% of 14–24-year-old users had sent naked photos of themselves via the internet. *Lenhart (2009)* also found that 15% of 12–17-year-olds with mobile phones had sent nude or near nude photos to their friends. This form of interaction called 'sexting' is a burgeoning issue for those who are charged with protecting young people from themselves and others who would harm them. Unfortunately, the photos often become public when friendships sour and the individual concerned cannot retrieve the images. Prosecutions and severe outcomes such as the suicide of Jesse Logan shown here, are the punitive and tragic outcome of this new method for abusing others. Educating young people to protect themselves from such embarrassment is a critical measure in protecting them from cyber-bullying.

INTERVENTIONS

In terms of intervention it would seem that a simple solution lies in the ability of the receiver to identify the sender prior to opening the offensive material, whether email, text or SNS posting. In a similar manner to avoiding the bully when they are seen approaching, the recipient of these messages can be trained to take responsibility for their own protection by not opening the offensive material and/or forwarding it to a third party who can provide protective intervention, such as a parent or school personnel. This is not possible, of course, when postings and texts are sent anonymously. Nevertheless, the possibility of taking control and forwarding such material to a protective third party is an attractive solution for those being effected.

http://news.bbc.co.uk/2/hi/uk_news/england/sussex/7251384.stm

BEBO BULLY VICTIM IN SUICIDE BID: *Monday, 18 February 2008, 17:06 GMT*

A teenage cyber-bully drove his ex-best friend to attempt suicide by tricking him into falling in love with a fake internet boyfriend, a court has heard.

The 17-year-old posted a fake profile on the social networking site Bebo, then told friends and teachers intimate details of their online conversations.

The 16-year-old victim, from Brighton, East Sussex, swallowed 60 painkillers.

The cyber-bully, who cannot be named, was given a 12-month referral order and told to pay his victim £250. Brighton Youth Court was told the victim's life was saved by his mother, who took him to hospital.

"I feel 100% sorry for the amount of pain I have caused you and your family"
Defendant to victim

Psychologists later said he had made a serious and genuine attempt to end his life.

The court heard the pair fell out after the victim revealed secrets and told lies about the defendant. The youth then set up the Bebo profile of the fake character and lured his former friend into a cyber relationship where explicit messages were exchanged. He was found out when he accidentally sent the victim an e-mail purporting to be from the fake character from his own address.

"The victim was then told by the defendant that not only had he made up the identity but he had been talking to their friends and others around him, including his teachers," said Suzanne Sorros, prosecuting.

"Effectively he was told that all those people were colluding against him andlaughing at him. "What caused specific distress was that this included his teachers."

Laptop confiscated

A statement read on behalf of the victim's mother said it had turned her son from a fun-loving teenager into someone who was untrusting and withdrawn.

The defendant, who pleaded guilty last month to harassment, apologised in court on Monday to the victim.

"I feel 100% sorry for the amount of pain I have caused you and your family," he said.

Describing it as a prank, his mother also apologised to the victim and his family, saying: "Believe me, it will never happen again."

The court confiscated the defendant's laptop.

Chair of the bench, Tim Chittleburgh, said he hoped the case would send a message to other youngsters.

"This was a piece of planned and sustained harassment in public," he said.

"You involved or at least intimated that teachers were aware, which was vicious."

However, this is generally not what happens and as the example cited earlier indicates, the consistent access of the bully via these electronic means can prove to be the highly destructive. Supportive strategies within the home and school such as limiting access to mobile phones and supervised computer time, can offer protection. Allowing unlimited access to mobile phones and computers without monitoring the content is the equivalent of locking a child in their room with their abuser and this is an inadequate response. Parents may want to consider overnight restrictions on mobile and internet usage to limit access if the child is being bullied by theses means.

MySpace has introduced protective measures such as promoting safe social networking on their sites since 2006. They have employed trained specialist personnel to deal with inappropriate content and have closed down 29000 profiles set up by registered offenders (*Patchin and Hinduja*,2010). They restrict access to sites set up by young people under age 15 and do not permit children under 13 to register. These measures provide some protection from predatory users, and may be a useful barrier to peer abuse.

A major challenge to intervention is the acceptance of responsibility for protective intervention, therapy, education and suitable consequences for misuse of the internet for abusive or harmful purposes. Recent media coverage has made it clear that SNS such as *Facebook* do not accept responsibility for sites which denigrate others be they paedophiles or individuals expressing socially abhorrent opinions about recent legal matters, murders etc. With the level of exposure possible from such a site it is impossible to monitor or police all content and it would seem that only the most virulent postings, rejected by a broad range of users will be expunged. Individuals who have genuine complaints about online bullying to themselves have very little chance of having any such abusive postings removed. It is therefore imperative that young people be taught to ignore online abuse, report or forward it to those with the authority to intervene within their own environment, and basically take full responsibility for their own safety. It is clear that online abusers have far more support and freedom to abuse than other users have to a safe online environment.

The broader social networking community does not appear to feel an overall sense of responsibility for the protection of children and young people from internet abuse, denigration, cruel remarks or misinformation, or indeed for inappropriate and harmful content from a range of sources. The parallel universe that cyberspace has become works from a different social agenda where everyone, irrespective of their level of maturity or intellectual or social development, is held responsible for their own behaviour, social contacts and research outcomes. If the child can search for and find inappropriate content they will not be prevented from doing so by the system. In light of this, parents, teachers and others who have traditionally taken responsibility for children and young people need to arm themselves with information and skills to ensure that they can continue to offer protection and support even in this often alien environment. Children need protection as they explore this complex new world.

THE 'FREEDOM OF SPEECH' ARGUMENT

The advent of open communication via the internet has begun to raise complex legal issues, particularly for schools. A complicating factor in the issue of online abuse, denigration and harmful content against an individual is the much lauded constitutional 'right' to freedom of speech'. Unfortunately, online abusers in the USA and elsewhere seem to be of the opinion that their activities are protected by their constitutional right to freedom of speech irrespective of the right of their victims to protect their own reputation.

The problem with such offensive behaviour is that the strength of the 'free speech' laws in the USA and other places around the world is much greater than that of school regulations about what is acceptable behaviour and language. In almost all the cases cited, Jacobs (2010) reports that the perpetrator, who was often suspended by the school for their behaviour, successfully sued the school for damages and asserted their right to 'free speech'. The infamous 'Tinker' decision in the USA is usually cited which sets the standard as being that the statement must 'materially or substantially disrupt the educational environment or invade the rights of others to be secure'(Tinker et al v Des Moines Independent Community School District, 1969). The amazing fact here is that the decision was made decades before the internet was even created, yet is consistently applied in cases involving internet abuse. The criterion of 'substantial disruption' is most often used to show that although the messages were offensive, they did not disrupt school operations. In other places the right to freedom of speech is tempered by the equally important right to defend one's reputation.

Recent judgements in the USA reinforce the notion that virtually anything goes in terms of abusive personal online messages and opinions. The right to Freedom of Speech is enshrined in the American constitution and various courts have set judgements which support students in this capacity. Obviously, today we would not try to deter any student from expressing political views such as the Tinkers held regardless of their origins, except if those views are held to incite racial abuse, terrorism or criminal activity. Nowhere are these political views sanctioned in an education or social setting. However, when students denigrate their teachers online, set up social networking sites or web pages to abuse, criticise and slander them, the courts are using the 'Freedom of Speech' card to support their activities.

Jacobs (2010) describes a litany of cases wherein school personnel and students have been seriously denigrated, abused and offended by postings by students at the school. Such postings include questioning the sexual orientation and preferences of teachers, describing them as 'hopeless' and making lewd suggestions about their activities. One site included a photo of a teacher whose face morphed into a picture of Adolf Hitler on the site (Jacobs, 2010, page 2). He cites other cases where teachers have been subjected to such abusive activity and have not been supported in their efforts to prevent such negative and harmful information being posted. This includes a student who initiated a website to denigrate his teacher, describing him as 'fat, middle-aged, and favouring those who kiss his ass' (Jacobs, page 42), among other insults and criticisms. After initially being suspended for this activity, the student eventually sued the school and received $30,000 compensation for being suspended over the incident. The school was also ordered to apologise in writing to the student. No such apology was forthcoming for the teacher, whose reputation, self-confidence and professional standing had been damaged. This and other cases points to some corruption of the notion of free speech.

Freedom of speech must be aligned with the responsibility to ensure that exposure of corrupt or unprofessional activity is documented. Public denigration that is unfounded is generally viewed as slander or defamation in Australian law and can be addressed through legal action. In most countries, freedom of speech is aligned with social responsibility for ensuring all criticisms are founded in fact. However, if interpretations of free speech are to be broadened to allow any and all expressions of negative and abusive opinions based on nothing more than personal bias, the internet will indeed become a parallel universe where legal protections and social mores are able to be dismissed or ignored. This issue will continue to be the major focus of cyber-bullying research and intervention in coming years.

9 Theories of Intervention

Introduction

Bullying behaviour develops in abusive individuals in close relation to a range of psychological and social contributory factors including the attitudes, skills and behaviours of peers and those in authority, the individual responses of victims, characteristics of the bullies themselves, observers and broad social influences. All of these need to be considered when attempts are made to instigate or create appropriate and effective interventions. However, intervention in bullying cannot be undertaken before some record and measures of the behaviour are available for analysis. Research-based intervention is targeted to specific factors and can be more efficiently undertaken given relevant data about what is actually happening for the individual victim and the population overall. Intervention ranges from macro-system to individual treatments and processes.

An investigation of current literature and resources indicates that interventions are currently attempted at each of these levels:

- government initiatives including legislative intervention
- government agency interventions including education and health
- school initiatives
- home and family interventions
- individual interventions for victims and perpetrators.

Of all of these interventions, the least well-documented and implemented are the individual initiatives. This may well be because the educational approach which focuses on individual interventions and programs of instruction are still not broadly applicable other than in special education settings and situations. The argument proposed here is that any individual who engages in abusive, aggressive, bullying or violent behaviour unquestionably has a behaviour or social disorder and therefore the principles of individual assessment and instruction are eminently relevant. Bullies need individual instruction in how to change their inappropriate and harmful interaction behaviours; victims need some instruction on how to acquire effective response strategies such as help seeking and reporting.

Approaches to intervention discussed in this text incorporate all of the above and show that what we need are methods that are comprehensive, customised and individually adjusted for protection and support. The social educative process experienced during the childhood of the abusive individual may underpin the development of peer abusive behaviour and needs to be examined and evaluated. This process incorporates teaching principles which are the foundation of all learning, such as demonstration, practice, reinforcement and skills acquisition. What factors in the life of the bully reinforce or precipitate the behaviour? What family and individual characteristics influence the development of bullying? Further, what individual characteristics of the victim of peer abuse are relevant to intervention? The programs of intervention offered to address these matters here are family and individual focussed for bullies and victims and their families, in close collaboration with schools.

The attitude of students towards those perpetrating or experiencing bullying is another critical dimension for consideration. Abusive behaviours originate in individuals who believe their behaviour is endorsed by peers and those in authority or who enjoy a level of social status which facilitates their engagement in harming others with impunity. Additionally, the presence or absence of resiliency skills and behaviours in victims is proposed as a critical factor in intervention in bullying. The acquisition of resilience through education is suggested as a legitimate focus for intervention. All of these issues are addressed in the BULLYWATCH intervention.

Bullying intervention has been systematically addressed in a plethora of research which indicates clearly the parameters and impact of the behaviour. Many interventions, however, lack the comprehensive approach necessary to thoroughly address all component issues in the management of bullying. An attempt has been made to clearly articulate and address these components in the programs outlined here. Given a strong system-wide approach to intervention, the problems associated with peer abuse may be diminished over time.

Bullying has become a major focus of concern for a wide range of social organisations partly as a result of the costs incurred for failure to provide supportive, safe environments for members of the relevant community. Some social institutions, organisations and professions currently demonstrate a commitment to dealing with the bullying affecting their sector through the development of a range of approaches. The range of policy, training, curricular and individual intervention mechanisms and initiatives developed in Australia and overseas require an enormous commitment of resources but often their effectiveness has not been evaluated. Given that bullying behaviours may have their origins in individual psychology as well as social pathology, it is appropriate for the wider community to take responsibility for intervention in the bullying behaviours of young people beyond the school gate, as indeed some social institutions have accepted.

IMPLICATIONS OF INDIVIDUAL CONFLICT-BASED INTERVENTION

Individual interventions are a component of the comprehensive intervention outlined further in this text (see *Figure 5*). However it is only one component in a set of six essential elements to address bullying especially in schools.

As *Gondolf* (*2002*) states:

> 'The key message from the international research on program effectiveness is that, 'the system matters'. Programs for perpetrators are but one component of the co-ordinated response which is required to hold (perpetrators) accountable and to enhance the safety of (victims)'

Gondolf (*2002*) further suggests that the major focus of efforts to intervene with (abusers) must be on building strong systems within which these programs are located. This would suggest that a whole school focus is important to sustain an individual intervention for either the victim or the bully. Nevertheless, the abuse literature does acknowledge the capacity for individual interventions to have an impact on abusers within a holistic approach.

It is a worrying development in contemporary intervention methodologies being discussed, developed and applied in school systems currently with regard to peer abuse, that conflict and dispute resolution programs are seen as a legitimate means of resolving abusive peer relationships. Some analysis of the inappropriateness of such interventions and suggestions for more relevant, efficacious and protective approaches is indicated. It needs to be reiterated that none of the current accepted definitions of bullying use the term 'conflict' to describe the interaction, and for this reason an abuse paradigm is seen as most relevant and informative.

Conflict resolution is a constructive approach to interpersonal and intergroup conflicts that helps people with opposing positions work together to arrive at mutually acceptable solutions. This can involve the assistance of a mediator who interprets the issues of each party and encourages resolution on the basis of compromise. Active listening and acceptance of each others' differences form an essential part of the intervention, as do dealing with anger and accepting that both parties need to 'win' to some extent. As can be seen from this brief analysis, none of these components are relevant in the abuse paradigm. The role of the mediator is to remain uninvolved emotionally, but to guide the antagonists towards a compromise solution. This is not a role which gives any concession to the damage caused by one participant to the other. *Fast (2002)* explores conflict resolution interventions and suggests mediators should use more impartiality and neutrality in conflict resolution practices. This, however, would be unhelpful for those in abusive relationships who require interventions which provide support and protection. Abandoning the abused individual to discussions with the often more articulate and certainly more socially adept bully, does not offer protective intervention, nor does it take into consideration the fear, trauma, or distress of the abuse victim.

O'Toole, Burton and Plunkett (2005) have developed a conflict resolution program as a 'new approach to managing bullying and conflict in schools'. A central principle to the program is that 'students can and should learn about conflict, its causes and effects in a morally neutral way, which takes out the blame and focuses on the behaviour ' (*page 3*). While this may be true of conflict situations, arguably a central principle in bullying or peer abusive intervention must be abuser accountability.

There are several considerations with this approach if we accept the original premise that bullying is about abuse and not conflict:

FIRSTLY	■ *learning about conflict is not relevant in this context, but learning about abuse probably is*
SECONDLY	■ *bullying is not about conflict nor is it caused by conflict*
THIRDLY	■ *bullies do indeed need to learn about 'moral values' in an attempt to expose them to the harm they are causing and indeed their capacity to acquire social mores and values must be questioned in light of their behaviour*
FINALLY	■ *removing 'blame' also removes responsibility and bullies must accept responsibility for their abusive behaviour*

This particular program merits some credit for the introduction of a further conflict resolution approach. However its application in abusive incidents must be questioned. *Sullivan (1998)* remarks negatively on the Cool Schools (Cool Schools, 1994) project in New Zealand which also utilises a conflict-resolution strategy for students in relation to bullying intervention.

Abusers act from personal attitudes and beliefs about ways to interact with others which maintain a self-perception of power and dominance, and this belief is often tolerated and supported in various social environments. Skills acquisition and knowledge provided about interpersonal interactions will provide a better prognosis for recovery. This, combined with the use of effective sanctions and consequences may be a more effective means of discouraging abusive behaviour and this needs to be considered in relation to intervention in peer abuse.

Two particular interventions introduced in recent times attempt to deal with early onset bullying, and are also suitable for dealing with bullying by behaviour disordered and intellectually disabled individuals who need specific instruction in empathetic and socially acceptable peer interactions. These younger or special needs individuals require an individual instructive approach to assist in the acquisition of appropriate interpersonal interactions.

The original 'No Blame' approach was introduced by *Robinson and Maines (1992)* and was initiated for use with behaviour-disordered individuals as a means of training them in empathetic and appropriate interpersonal interactions. With this clientele it was appropriate and necessary. However most students follow a predictable developmental trajectory and can be expected to assume a level of social and moral responsibility for their behaviour as they mature. This approach has been widely endorsed and adopted, however it is not seen here as a suitable general intervention for older children and young people as it does not require the perpetrator to accept responsibility for their actions. Secondary school personnel in particular have expressed concerns that the method will not ensure the bullying is remediated, nor that the focus is suitable for the preparation of young people for non-abusive futures given the limits of application and failure to expect remorse and responsibility.

The term 'blame' is unfortunate and may be better replaced with the term 'responsibility'. In regard to abusive situations, it is obviously nonsense to suggest that no-one is to' blame' for bullying and victimisation, and it is certainly reasonable to expect abusive individuals to develop responsibility for their interactions. Such behaviour represents a choice and a preference which must be addressed for the functionality and ultimate socialisation of the individual in mainstream society. Early indicators, therefore, of genuinely abusive behaviours need early intervention at the most immediate level, to halt further reinforcement and refinement.

There are elements of this approach which are valuable for the bully and the victim. The key focus is on letting the perpetrator of the abuse feel they are still accepted and their needs will be met as they are assisted to develop empathy and concern for the feelings of their victims. However, abusers are ultimately egocentric and are more than happy to be absolved of 'blame' and for the details of their misdemeanours to be overlooked while the victim is supported.

NO BLAME APPROACH (ROBINSON and MAINES 1992)

KEY ELEMENTS
▪ 'Blame' does not have to be apportioned
▪ models a 'pro-social' response to bullying
▪ Bullies are viewed as 'misdirected ' rather than 'pathological'
▪ focus on victim feelings
▪ Intention to develop 'empathy' among social group
▪ Focus on the actions and behaviours of the peer group towards support for the victim
▪ Works with behaviour disordered children / intellectually impaired individuals who need intensive behaviour instruction
▪ Avoids identifying details of the events
▪ No need for extensive and difficult investigations

Opposing Views

- Expecting bullies to take responsibility for their behaviour isn't the same as 'blame'
- Program ignores the bullying and focuses on supporting the victim
- Bullies still need to be re-directed in their interactions and to learn suitable behaviours
- Bullies have great difficulty with 'empathy' and need direction
- Intervention side-steps the behaviour of concern and seeks peer support as a means of overcoming the behaviour
- Does not provide for remediation of bully and victim behaviours

Other researchers have proposed non-punitive approaches to bullying intervention including *Pikas' (1989) Method of Common Concern* which attempts to offer mediation between the victim and abusers.

SHARED CONCERN METHOD – (PIKAS, 2002)

KEY ELEMENTS
■ Do not demonize bully suspects
■ Consider the bullying as conflict between the parties and mediate
■ Summit meeting between those involved
■ Seal the agreement with a communication contract
■ Mediation-centered treatment
■ Method for group bullying 'mobbing'
■ Group members should feel pressure, fear retribution from group, guilt
■ Individual therapeutic 'talks' with group members can loosen the bonds with group

Opposing Views – Watson (1998)

- Abused individuals 'should *not* be referred to or engaged in services in which they must co-operatively participate, such as counselling services, or alternative conflict and dispute resolution and mediation services'.
- She believes that such practices 'pre-suppose an equal relationship in which both parties are free to openly participate'
- There is an obvious imbalance of power in abusive relationships and the abuser's capacity to control and intimidate victims must be a paramount consideration
- It is simply not possible or appropriate to enter into an abuse situation whereby the respective 'needs 'of the participants are 'negotiated'.
- Abusive individuals do not have the right to be heard in respect of their motives for abusive behaviour.

In senior schools and with more mature individuals it is essential that the responsibility for behavioural choices be clearly articulated and intervention include prescriptive programs for developing appropriate non-abusive interaction repertoires. Neither program recommends punitive sanctions, even for the most extreme incidents of bullying leading to severe psychological distress, as a means of deterring the abusive behaviour and both involve the victim in negotiations with their abuser. As previously discussed, this is not an ideal approach to intervention as it disadvantages the victim by placing them in further contact with the bully.

'No Blame 'or generic instructional programs and methods are suitable in early intervention and for individuals with limited social skills and perhaps intellectual disability since they facilitate the introduction and teaching of appropriate interaction behaviours and empathy training. However, with more mature individuals it is essential that the responsibility for behavioural choices be clearly articulated and intervention include prescriptive programs for developing appropriate non-abusive interaction behaviours. Accepting responsibility for the abuse is paramount to resolution but this cannot be achieved through conflict resolution methods.

Similarly, the abusive nature of the relationship between the bully and victim if addressed using mediation or conjoint therapies sustains the view that the interaction is somehow mutual. This form of intervention in abusive relationships is regarded as inappropriate and dangerous (*Austin & Dankwort, 1999b*). Over the last decade, a number of approaches which attempt to address the concerns and risks of conjoint therapy have been described in the literature (*Goldner, 1999; Goldner, Penn, Scheinberg, & Walker, 1990; Lipchik, et al., 1997*)

Morrison (2002) discusses the application of Restorative Justice (*Braithwaite, 1989*) principles and practices to bullying intervention. The primary principles of this approach involve 're-integrative shaming'-a capacity to experience shame and the negative response of the community to the abusive individual in order to sustain their membership in the social context, while addressing their harmful behaviour

As a remedial approach to intervention in general, Restorative Justice may have merit as it has the expectation that the abusive individual will acknowledge and take responsibility for the harm done. However the focus on conflict resolution cited by Morrison in applying the program to peer abuse situations may need further consideration. There is little evidence for example, that bullies feel 'shame', are capable of feeling 'shame' or are expected to feel shame as an outcome of their behaviour. There is also the issue of the incapacity of some abusive individuals to actually see the harm in their behaviour as this pre-supposes an integrated social perspective which may well be lacking. Indeed, learning in detail about the negative impact of their behaviour on their selected target may well be reinforcing for the bully.

Furthermore, this approach relies on community disapproval to establish shame and what is seriously lacking in current social responses towards bullying is disapproval. *Stubbs (1996)*, states:

> *'Nor can it be assumed that the 'community' will totally condemn the violence, rather than minimise it and join in with the victim-blaming by the offender '*

This is a very common response to bullying as the victim is advised often to 'get over' the issue and 'get on with life' and stop complaining! Stubbs is echoed by *Martin (1996)* who believes that having such serious matters dealt with by the 'community' may minimise the issue and could result in the matter being seen as a minor 'dispute ' between minors, even if the abuse leads the young person to suicide. Surely it is time to see the criminal element in this behaviour and have the serious matter of severe peer abuse dealt with through a range of serious interventions including litigation and judicial intervention.

Bullies do not believe they are disapproved of. Indeed, their exploits are reinforced by peers, parental support or disbelief and school responses which tend to neutralise their behaviours away from abuse towards 'fighting'. Until abusive individuals have their abusive behaviours notified and addressed openly, including social disapproval by significant others, their behaviours will not change.

Laing, 2002 states that, despite the apparent 'fit' between restorative justice approaches and notions of community healing, serious questions about the applicability of restorative justice in situations of domestic and family violence have been raised (Greer, 2001; Stubbs, 1997). It is apparent that the abuse research fraternity does not consider this an appropriate response to abusive behaviour and therefore it seems to lack credibility for peer abuse as well.

Martin (1996) cautions about the consequences of restorative justice approaches in the following terms:

Chapter 9 — Theories of Intervention

> *'Restorative justice approaches draw on a range of processes such as mediation (regarded as inappropriate in situations of domestic and family violence where there are power disparities between participants) and the dispute resolution processes used by the Maori in New Zealand'.*

Presser & Gaarder, 2000 express concern that the process relies on what are termed,

> *'healing encounters between victims and offenders'.*

Abused individuals are well acquainted with these situations, which are inevitably followed by further abuse.

Even *Braithwaite* (*1989*) acknowledges concern for the implementation of 're-integrative shaming' in abusive family situations because of the power imbalance which is also of major concern in peer abuse situations. He also recognises 'mediation' as an issue of concern in abuse intervention, for the same reason. If we accept the original premise that bullying is about abuse, then the application of these methods, unacceptable in family abuse theory must be considered unacceptable to address peer abuse. "Self-sanctioning' which is an underlying principle of the approach, is not a skill that bullies will independently develop and this must be an inclusion in individual interventions for abusive individuals. The courage and tenacity of victims to alert those in authority to their plight should not be the sole defining event which leads to justice or protective intervention. At some point the cowardice and dishonesty of the abusive individual must be confronted and accountability required, if a solution is to be found. Restorative programs are essentially dispute and conflict resolution focussed and as such may need careful adaptation in order to address the abuse component.

Mediation programs have similar shortcomings as effective intervention in abusive relationships as they also assume an equivalence in terms of the desire of participants to have their own needs met at the expense of, or some loss to, the other. Abused individuals are not empowered to engage in discussions with their abusers in order to establish their right to safety and protection. Nor should they be required to state their case in formal proceedings where the mediator must remain neutral. There is no advantage to the abused individual in acknowledging or stating an understanding of the abuser's need to abuse, or attempting to see things from their perspective. Further, it may well be reinforcing for the abuser to hear about the harm and hurt they have caused as this is the main purpose of their behaviour. This is another intervention model which needs very careful consideration before inclusion in bullying intervention.

Overall, it seems imperative to focus attention on the destructive, harmful and now often lethal effects of bullying as a type of abusive behaviour which impacts a broad section of childhood and to examine a broad range of processes for intervention.

PREVIOUS INTERVENTIONS

There has been a wealth of interventions developed internationally to address bullying in schools. For example, an approach described as P.E.A.C.E. (Policy, Education, Action, Coping, Evaluation – *Slee, 1996 a and b*), has been attempted, which incorporates several of the key components of the approach described in this paper, to address bullying in Australian schools. The P.E.A.C.E pack provides schools with information on how to raise awareness, develop policy and work with children. Results have been supportive with reports of reductions of at least 25% in bullying in schools utilising the intervention, as well as increased awareness and knowledge about bullying.

Similarly, the Sheffield project addressed "whole school policy, curriculum work, work in playgrounds and work with individual pupils and small groups involved in bullying situations" (*Smith, 1997 p. 68*). This intervention focussed strongly on policy development and implementation, with the other components offered as optional extras. This has been identified as one of the more effective interventions with evaluation indicating 29% of participant schools had developed a separate whole school policy and 58% addressed bullying specifically in welfare and discipline policies. (*Smith and Madsen, 1997*). Sullivan reports on the New Zealand anti-bullying initiative 'Kia Kaha' produced by the NZ police force. Based on the Maori tradition meaning to 'be strong', the resource kit was provided to late primary and early secondary students, which is a prime target group for such interventions. In his analysis of the program, *Sullivan*

(*1998*) points out a long held myth regarding bullies – that they will surrender in the face of opposition, which appears to be proposed in the program. On the contrary, bullies are keen to engage in aggressive interactions and would often welcome a further opportunity to dominate and harm the resistant victim. Although resiliency is a critical skill to learn in response to bullying (Healey, 2001) it does not involve stoically putting up with the victimisation nor being lured into a reciprocal fight. Sullivan supports this view and calls for revision of the program with an emphasis on shared responsibility.

Rigby (*2003*), in his definitive meta-evaluation of early bullying interventions found that, "the commitment of a school to a program and strong involvement by staff in its implementation appears to be an important and possibly crucial factor in reducing bullying" (page 3).He reports on a range of international interventions each of which comprises a number of components, with mixed effectiveness. Indeed, in some instances, increases in bullying behaviour were reported as an outcome.

The Toronto Study implemented by *Pepler* (*1993*) was devised to operate at four levels: the community, whole school, each classroom and individual students. A peer conflict-mediation program was introduced as well as increased supervision by teachers and some curricular intervention. Nevertheless, the results were seen as disappointing with more children reporting bullying after the intervention. This could indicate a greater awareness and capacity to identify bullying which is an important step to reduction.

Peace and peacemaking initiatives also have limited applications as protective interventions in peer abuse. While the intentions are laudable and the need for a peaceful environment and society cannot be denied, the fact that peace evades those being bullied must be recognised and addressed. Spreading a vague and at times spiritual message of the need for peaceful interaction may reach those who desire peace in their lives but this certainly is not the case with bullies, who choose damaging behaviours as a preferred interaction.

Finally, there is the issue of unsubstantiated, un-researched and popular programs being offered by unqualified though well-intentioned individuals with very limited understandings of the key contemporary issues and research. Very few such programs have been evaluated to establish their efficacy and fewer still have stated objectives by which they can be assessed for effectiveness.

Although such 'shock tactics' are rarely evaluated for long term outcomes, and indeed the educational value of such speakers is not established, there can be no doubt that the immediate impact can be forceful. The article cited here is an example of just such a program which may or may not have long term impact for positive outcomes. It is imperative that intervention be predicated on specific criteria which aim to provide secure environments for victims, remediation for abusive individuals or an overall, measurable improvement in the social ethos of the school. Nevertheless, there does not appear to be a structured, systematic, widely applicable approach which offers the requisite foundation philosophies and strategies to ensure efficacy. The *Bullywatch* program may provide the solution.

Inside Out *reporter Des Coleman discovers how shock tactics are being used in a bid to beat bullying in Nottinghamshire schools.*

Government statistics reveal that over half of all primary and secondary pupils believe bullying within school is a big problem.

In some cases the bullying can become so bad that pupils take their own lives.

It's estimated that 16 children a year commit so-called "bullycide", driven to despair by name-calling and abuse.

Scary Guy

Now some schools – including those in Nottingham are turning for help from a most unusual man called – Scary Guy.

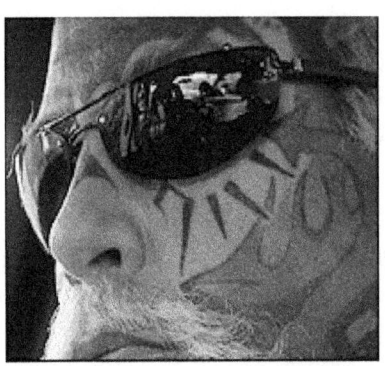

Scary Guy shocks his audience by talking about suicide.

Scary Guy, from Tucson, Arizona, is covered from head to toe in tattoos.

He was born Earl Kaufman, but changed his name 11 years ago when he set out on a mission to eliminate prejudice and bigotry. Inside Out follows this motivational speaker as he tackles a class of tough kids at William Sharp Comprehensive in Bilborough.

Shock tactics

The school is located in one of the most deprived areas of the city and, like all schools, has to deal with the problem of bullying.

All schools have to deal with bullying

Deputy Head Kerry Mills says: "Our main problem with bullying is name calling and verbal sniping."

But Scary Guy who has taken his message of love peace and tolerance to schools all over Britain relishes a challenge. "My experience is that the tougher they are, the harder they fall."

PREVENTATIVE RESPONSES TO INTERVENTION

The preferred approach in bullying intervention programs has customarily been 'bullying prevention'. It is not surprising, therefore, that evaluations of the efficacy of such interventions demonstrate little or no impact in that such interventions clearly do not prevent bullying. The problem lies in the selection of the program emphasis and objectives. Bullying cannot be prevented in the short-term, and certainly not in the short-term offered by a classroom curriculum. Indeed, two studies in Canada demonstrated an increase in reported bullying following implementation of commercially available bullying prevention programs — in one case a rise of 47% was recorded (Artz, 1996). This indicates, in all probability that increased reporting results from the raising of awareness of bullying through the program, rather than an increase in the actual bullying.

However, results reveal that the majority of participants remain non-abusive as they were before the program, and those who are abusive continue to engage in abusive acts. This critical factor validates the educative rather than preventative emphasis in intervention design. Most program participants are not abusive and would not become so even without the program. A clear distinction must be drawn between bullying prevention and anti-bullying initiatives in terms of their objectives, content and impact.

Only long-term socialisation and education processes will help 'prevent' bullying, as is already the case for most members of society. Social competency, empathy, anger management and appropriate communication are all skills usually developed over the years to maturation (King, 1995). For those who do not develop these skills, discrete and specific programs need to be offered to precipitate or induce their acquisition. Goldstein and his colleagues in particular have been influential in securing credibility for the impact and effectiveness of specific interventions for aggression reduction. The Aggression Replacement Training intervention devised by *Goldstein et al. (1998)* has served many abusive youth as has their work with school-based gangs in the USA.

There is an element of precipitation in the intent of these types of programs to develop social skills in young people. They seem to hold the expectation that young people will be able to demonstrate interaction skills at a much more sophisticated level than would have been expected even a decade ago. Bullying is already broadly discouraged by social processes which reject overt bullying within the social environment. The purpose of such programs therefore is to reinforce and extend socially transmitted attitudes and behaviours. However, so-called 'bullying-prevention' programs, which are, in effect, anti-bullying programs, can prepare students to recognise and resist abusive attitudes and behaviours in their peers, if offered within the framework of a comprehensive approach and are competency-based.

Prevention is, however, often the preferred and initial focus for any discussion or examination of bullying intervention. 'Prevention' strategies may relate to some of the following:

- school policy to deter bullying
- a collaborative effort by all stakeholders to ensure the abuse does not continue
- reporting processes established in the school and home
- punitive sanctions to deter further abusive behaviour

Less frequently considered are more personalised or individual measures such as:

- protective measures established within their environment
- specific education programs to establish suitable alternative behaviours and responses.
- Consideration of the psychological orientation and behaviours of the bully
- Consideration of the social skills and responses of the victim

A comprehensive approach to intervention is described further whereby six key components of intervention are implemented in conjunction to address bullying across a whole school. This approach is not identified as 'preventative' in the first instance but as responsive and educative for all school community members. If successfully implemented over time, the cumulative effect may well be 'preventative'. Prevention may follow intervention if the strategies and processes form a barrier to the behaviour.

Prevention is often focussed on the psychological status of the bully and the need to interfere with or halt their inappropriate interpersonal interactions with their peers. Attempts to explain and define the origins of abusiveness in any individual may be made on the basis of psychological or socio-cultural factors. However, each fails to offer a complete definition because, in all likelihood, these elements are both contributory.

Discourse over recent years in this regard has more often centred on the psychological impact of the behaviour for the victim than on its origins and functions for the abusive individual. However, given the psychological, environmental and social influences to which the potentially abusive individual is exposed, it may not be possible to prevent bullying behaviour from developing. *Bowie (1991)* discusses a wide range of explanatory factors relating to psychopathology, genetic and biological determinants, social learning, and environmental sources of abusive orientations and behaviours. Factors suggested also include gender as the key contributor, and some argue, a causal factor (*Egger, 1995; Scutt, 1995; Wallace, 1995*), All of these need to be considered in any intervention that attempts to teach the rejection of abusive behaviour through an educative process, as their impact can determine outcomes.

For those engaged in bullying 'prevention' it is self evident that the abuse is never "provoked", but deliberately embraced by abusive individuals. *Goldstein, et al. (1998)* refer to

> *Aggression addiction – a long-term, repetitively used, stable behaviour" (p. 8)*

These researchers believe aggressive or violent behaviour is typically learned behaviour:

> *"For many youths, its teaching is repetitive, its success is frequent, its rewards are generous and its punishments are few" (p. 1).*

Further, when negative and anti-social experiences are more readily available than pro-social models at critical moments of receptivity during growth and development, learning of such behaviours will inevitably take place. Some individuals will choose abusive behaviour on a regular or episodic basis for self-gratification. Such individuals enjoy the power and prefer to use their abusive capacities to their own advantage. The most salient preventative intervention in this case therefore is to ensure that the experiences and models to which the developing child is exposed are those which will establish pro-social attitudes and behaviours. This role is a shared responsibility of family, educators and the community generally.

Nevertheless, prevention is probably not possible if the individual in question gives no overt or early indication of the abusive propensities they nurture. We rely on the overt indicators, as we must, to inform intervention. Psychological health and well-being are largely assumed on the basis of obvious functional behaviours, and as long as perpetrators are capable of appearing to be socialised we have no evidence on which to assume they are not, until it is too late. Here is the key factor delaying intervention with abusive individuals-their socialisation seems complete and indeed successful, and their abusive behaviour is often overlooked or reinterpreted before it is recognised as harmful.

Ultimately, the question of why certain individuals choose such deviant paths is answered simply by the statement 'because they can'. No other motivation is needed. They engage in these acts because they want to and nobody and nothing including social mores, moral values, empathetic feelings or connectedness to significant others in their lives is a stronger motivating factor at the time. This indicates a genuine dilemma for interventionists because the behaviours they are attempting to inhibit have been firmly established over time prior to the intervention.

Research findings in the preparatory phase of this work also indicated that students' levels of resiliency to bullying differed which suggested that intervention strategies may be strengthened by attempting to account for these differences. A model for teaching the acquisition of attributes such as resiliency, previously considered developmental, also developed in light of the data in relation to variations in student responses to bullying. Further, it became evident that socio-cultural factors including the social status and popularity of bullies, as indicated by peers, were also significant. Analysis of the data revealed that bullies seemed to hold an elevated social status, that peers were, in general, unsympathetic towards victims and that often bullying was facilitated by unsupportive or uninformed authorities.

Indeed, the role of young people as advocates for their bullied peers seemed to be a critical factor in addressing the bullying paradigm, and as a result the concept and curriculum for Peer Advocacy© developed and the social imperative of using this specific strategy to address peer abuse, unfolded. The critical factor in peer abuse or bullying is obviously peer attitudes and behaviours and the most potent intervention is therefore, of necessity, peer-focused. Peer Advocacy© was devised and developed as an adaptive functional response to bullying and as a curricular intervention.

Overall, these perspectives may have the potential to inform new solutions to underpin intervention and also contribute to the formulation of the comprehensive model for intervention. The background to each new perspective identified has been discussed earlier in relation to current research and practice.

EDUCATION AS A RESPONSE TO INTERVENTION

Attempting to rehabilitate individuals who have so obviously been excluded from the usual socialisation processes may well prove financially and psychologically impossible and beyond the scope of such programs as are suggested here. The notion that bullying can be resolved through education is an attractive philosophical proposition. It empowers us to shape environments to prevent destructive acts and to reconstruct individual behavioural orientations to ensure the safety of peers. The proposal here is that the application of a broad educative anti-bullying program coupled with a thorough individual intervention to teach new and appropriate behaviours and orientations is the most promising approach to intervention in bullying in schools and society. A critical issue will be the measurement of the efficacy of such programs in actually reducing peer abuse in schools and in the behaviours of young people.

Evaluation of Programs

Effectiveness of intervention needs to be assessed in the long-term as well as in the short-term, such as the duration of a program. Bullying is endemic in society. It is thoroughly embedded within our culture from kindergarten to the boardroom (McCarthy, 1996). To imagine that an intervention directed at a particular cohort of students in a specific school could have long-lasting effects is unrealistic. What we are really attempting to do is change an entire cultural orientation which supports and encourages individuals who seek and gain social advantage by engaging in abusive and anti-social behaviour. Social change of the magnitude addressed in anti-bullying intervention must be expected to take many years to reach fruition. The level of commitment required to negotiate changes to the bullying culture, which is so much a part of our society, is enormous.

Evaluations of micro-system approaches will inevitably be disappointing when viewed in isolation. However, given the world-wide, persistent, research-based movement against sponsorship of bullying at all levels of society, we can expect change to eventuate in time. Evaluation, therefore, should not necessarily look to reducing bullying behaviours in the short-term only. Other important issues include raising awareness of the problem, identifying and differentiating bullying from other harmful behaviours, creating environments where reports of bullying are taken seriously, and discouraging the dominating behaviour of individuals. This will contribute over time to a society in which the abuse of peers is not accepted, tolerated or endorsed. Until bullies are seen in society as a whole as undesirable and bullying seen as abusive behaviour, small-scale interventions will continue to have limited effectiveness and we can expect decades of work ahead.

SUMMARY

Intervention in bullying is an ongoing process reliant upon the creative and professional efforts of a broad range of individuals across many sectors of society. Criticisms of programs contained in this discussion are meant to indicate that no program, including the BULLYWATCH intervention can supply all of the answers and solutions necessary to ensure the safe passage of all children and young people through childhood to a productive life. Bullying is a high impact abusive behaviour which must now be prioritised for protective intervention.

Based on research findings, it is suggested that methodologies for replacing peer abusive behaviours that comprise knowledge and skills for the acquisition and reinforcement of socially acceptable behaviours and attitudes need to be developed for the Australian context and applied widely. Anti-bullying programs such as those offered here do not claim to be preventative. The focus is to provide education about the origins and impact of bullying and strategies for resistance and avoidance. It aims to change pro-abuse attitudes and deliver relevant information and skills.

Overall, there is ample evidence that intervention in peer abuse currently is broad ranging and complex, although rarely evaluated. There are many interventions applied and attempted in order to address the extensive damage done by the bullying process. This is commendable and contributes to a raising of awareness and a commitment to educating the community about the issue. The underlying theory and practice offer a range of options for both protective intervention and remedial teaching of appropriate peer interactions, which is the underlying problem with bullying. Nevertheless, structuring a comprehensive approach has been the focus of the BULLYWATCH project and the components of the overall intervention shown in *Figure 5* indicate that all levels of involvement and all key stakeholders are included in this approach.

10 Getting Serious about Bullying

Introduction

Bullies should take heed. We are on to you. We know your secrets even better than you know them yourself. Your deadly serious game is under threat and you are on notice to begin your own transformation.

Society needs also to take heed. There is blood on the hands of those who, for whatever reason refuse, delay, neglect or avoid intervention to halt the abuse of young people by their peers and thereby contribute to their deaths by suicide. We can no longer tolerate such neglect and denial. It is time to take responsibility and put the lives of young people before the fear of litigation, guilt and blame.

The focus of this book is on the underlying theory and psychology of peer abusive behaviour, commonly referred to as 'bullying'. Much of the theory and psychology presented here has developed over a substantial period of research, consultancy, reflection and practice. There are controversial and challenging concepts and convictions recorded in this text to hopefully stimulate consideration of new interpretations of the serious – and sometimes deadly serious – matter of peer abuse.

A number of concepts are encapsulated and these are all addressed in a practical way in the supplementary publications of the BULLYWATCH Program. Fundamentally, intervention in bullying at the school, family or community level requires a comprehensive approach presented with commitment in a systematic process which deals with family, school and individual needs for protection, education and recovery. The application of the BULLYWATCH program, which has been developed over a period of fifteen years, must be preceded by an understanding of the key underlying theory and psychology of the problem of peer abuse.

In summary, the key convictions presented in this book are:

- First and foremost, bullying has been incorrectly linked to conflict and conflict solutions for most of the time it has been studied and analysed. This position is rejected here and the focus of the entire program of intervention is embedded in this conviction. Victims of bullying must be granted the respect they deserve and must not be equivalently held responsible for the disruptive, damaging and unwarranted abuse to which they are subjected during bullying episodes.

- Bullying occurs along a continuum of severity (see *Figure 1*) which dictates the responses of the victim and needs to guide the interventions selected. Severe bullying and its most extreme manifestations are not imagined occurrences, but actual and factual tragic incidents including murder, suicide and serious psychological disturbance. We can no longer pretend bullying is just a feature of childhood that enables us to 'develop' into strong adults. On the contrary, the harm done during childhood bullying can stay with the victim for a lifetime and inhibit normal development and growth. It's time to get serious about bullying

- Bullying is a chosen and preferred behaviour for those who indulge their need to control and harm others. From the very earliest signs of this behaviour we must be vigilant and guide the perpetrator away from these behaviours towards empathy, responsibility and tolerance. As the behaviour persists, stronger measures including enforced separation from their victims and punitive sanctions must be incorporated into their intervention to provide protection for their victim.

- The psychology of bullying is related to the personality characteristics and behaviour choices of the abusive individual. Bullies select their victims on the basis of particular criteria which are meant to ensure that they can abuse them with impunity and still retain their status. Bullies do not bully everyone in their lives and indeed they bully very few. This ensures that there will always be a wide range of other associates to declare their loyalty to the bully and their conviction that such behaviour would be 'out of character'.

Additionally, several perspectives underline the approaches developed including:

- Peer abuse as a legislated child protection issue of concern to teachers and others whose role it is to ensure the protection of children and young people in their work in schools and the community. This approach offers protections also for teachers, since they can transfer responsibility to those with the authority and expertise to intervene. This proposition is yet to be widely accepted, but logic and data indicate it is a worthwhile consideration.

- Resiliency is a critical component of protection in the event of bullying and resiliency behaviours may be taught to and acquired by those needing to develop self-protective skills. Further, however, resiliency does not inoculate victims from the fear and distress of bullying, but can provide a platform of responses from which to aid their coping and recovery. Resiliency skills must be supported and reinforced in environments which do not condone, ignore, or worst of all encourage bullying behaviour as a sign of 'strength' or leadership. Resilient individuals deserve to be supported and protected, not spurned and disrespected.

- The role of peers in the whole bullying paradigm cannot be ignored and systematic training of the peers of bullies and their victims is one part of the solution to intervention. The Peer Advocacy© program described here is one attempt to acknowledge the importance of critical peer support to facilitate the recovery of the victim.

- Finally, holding the producers of media violence responsible for the viewing and behaviour of bullies cannot be sustained by the research evidence, and in some ways allows bullies to renege on their responsibilities for the harm they cause. Abusive behaviours are learned and sustained in environments which fail to deter bullies and protect victims.

The purpose of this book is to present the research and theory which underpins the comprehensive and complex intervention developed into the BULLYWATCH Program. The intervention involves the bully and their victim as well as family of both and education personnel who are vital to its successful implementation. The cooperative nature of the program, incorporating as it does a range of new and challenging perspectives may offer a solution to the deadly serious matter of bullying in childhood.

BULLYWATCH™ PROGRAM OF RESEARCH-BASED INTERVENTIONS FOR HOME AND SCHOOL

As evidence mounts of the destructive, pervasive and at times lethal impact of bullying within the education environment and society as a whole, it has become apparent that pragmatic, comprehensive interventions, informed by new and innovative theoretical and psychological perspectives, are urgently required. The interventions presented here have been specifically designed to address these issues.

The BULLYWATCH™ program of intervention comprises a wide range of materials and processes to assist children, young people and the broader community to understand the parameters of peer abuse and develop appropriate attitudes and supportive responses. In addition, specific, individualised materials have been designed to assist victims of bullying to develop adequate skills for resistance and for bullies to develop more appropriate interpersonal behaviours. This fulfils the promise of a comprehensive and customised approach which deals with whole school and family commitment as well as the needs of individuals.

Addressing bullying as a general issue of concern to all teachers, parents and the community is a standard and anticipated approach, informing and advising them of the behaviour and its impact. This information is valuable and educates the general community about this serious matter. However, while it is commendable to offer such educative messages, this does not offer solutions or protection for those being victimised. As with all inappropriate social and criminal behaviours, the majority of the population will never engage in such behaviour and therefore will never require intervention. Internationally, bullying in childhood effects about

20% of school populations personally, leaving 80% who are not involved as bullies or victims. For this large majority, the generic messages rejecting bullying are adequate to sustain appropriate interactions for the most part.

While there is a prevailing social commitment to general 'safety and wellbeing,' stating this obvious fact is neither helpful nor adequate in regard to managing the destructive outcomes of individual peer abuse in childhood. Nevertheless the preferred and often total extent of intervention approaches in schools and organisations seems to be stating that bullying is 'not tolerated' and that everyone is entitled to a 'safe' environment. In terms of effective and meaningful intervention this is quite simply not enough. Genuine commitment which ensures the survival of vulnerable individuals is now an urgent requirement. Furthermore, reluctance to identify individually and remediate thoroughly must be overcome.

No longer can we continue to pretend that children and young people are incapable of managing their own destructive behaviours. We must ensure they have the capacity, motivation and skills to do so. The approach outlined here offers a range of protective interventions to ensure that indeed safety is not just an expectation but an entitlement, guaranteed by moral and social commitment. Further, the program is grounded in remedial intervention which has as its focus the opportunity for all participants to gain new and valuable social skills and interaction behaviours. The main elements of the BULLYWATCH™ intervention are supportive, protective, remedial and socially viable programs for ensuring transformation towards appropriate social competencies of bullies and victims.

BULLYWATCH™ PROCESSES FOR INTERVENTION

BULLYWATCH™ Process for Generic Intervention

The overview in Figure 5 identifies as component 5 'Whole School BULLYWATCH™ Curriculum and Training'.. The term 'generic' is used here to differentiate these programs from the more intensive group and individual interventions discussed later. As part of a whole school and comprehensive intervention, BULLYWATCH™ curricula provide all members of the student body with foundation information, resources and skills to deal with bullying they witness or experience. For most students this level of intervention will provide sufficient knowledge to ensure their safe passage through childhood and avoidance of bullying. Additionally, it is recommended that such curricula be paired with the other four components of the BULLYWATCH™ comprehensive approach, including policy development and organisational changes to supervision etc, to provide a solid foundation for protective intervention.

A further component of the generic approach to intervention in schools is to offer more advanced training in anti-bullying behaviour. The Peer Advocacy©[2] system of training inducts either selected or volunteer participants to accept a more responsible role in bullying intervention by becoming 'GUARDIANS' at the primary school level and 'DEFENDERS' at the secondary level. These two programs have been developed based on substantial research and practice and offer a sophisticated level of proactive intervention processes to empower students to assist and support peers in need as a result of peer abuse. The research and empirical basis for these interventions as well as the structure and processes for delivery are discussed in the supplementary publication. Fundamentally, the interventions provide skills and processes which can ensure that irrespective of the responses of those in authority, victims of peer abuse can be guided towards effective interventions and protection.

BULLYWATCH™ Process for Individual intervention

A cornerstone of education over the past 30 years has been the incorporation of individualised instruction for students with disabilities, or who deviate from expected norms of behaviour. Legislation was introduced across Australia in 2005 in the form of the Disability Standards for Education Act, which enshrined the previously philosophical but not legal requirements for inclusion. Students who require additional support for their special educational, medical, social and psychological needs are no longer deemed too difficult for the mainstream of

---

[2] Several papers are available which describe the theoretical and empirical basis for the intervention as well as the structure and processes. (Healey, 2003)

education. Indeed teachers for the past 20 years have been required to provide suitable education and other intervention programs to ensure the development and inclusion of such students.

The usual response in legal, medical, educational and other key aspects of life in which intervention is required for deviance, is to deal with the individual within the framework of general social norms, values and expectations. It is not sufficient to treat individual aberrations by referring only to normal expectations and requirements. Bank robbers are dealt with by courts on the basis of their individual criminality, not the overall expectation of society that we have 'zero tolerance for bank robbery'. Nevertheless, there is still a school of thought within the bullying intervention movement which is shy of individual intervention and which believes that the generic messages should suffice. That is not the view or approach held or promoted in this text. Deviance in the form of bullying, needs to be addressed by intervention with the bully and their victims after the general messages have been delivered. When the general message fails to educate the individual, then individual instruction is warranted. The foundations of individualised instruction are well documented in the literature and support the inclusion of an individual intervention in this situation.

Further with regard to individual intervention, which underpins the more serious levels of response to peer abuse in this approach, it is helpful to reflect upon contemporary expectations in response to all deviant behaviours in education, medical and legal matters. Within education environments, there are general rules to be followed and a hierarchy of responses for breaches to these rules is applied to the offending individual. Similarly with behaviour deviations, individual programs of remediation are offered to assist the development of appropriate and acceptable behaviours. In terms of medical and psychological problems, each individual exhibiting deviance or concerning behaviours is dealt with and assisted towards an expected norm. Society also expects that those who breach social mores and regulations by engaging in socially unacceptable or criminal behaviour will be dealt with individually in direct relationship to the seriousness of their breach. It is not enough to remind these perpetrators that their behaviour is socially unacceptable. Some measure of therapeutic, remedial and even punitive intervention is usually required to satisfy the community view that such breaches are not tolerated.

The application, therefore, of individual supportive, protective or even consequential responses should be an expected component in peer abuse intervention, to ensure the respective needs of perpetrators and their victims are met. To date, few such programs of intervention have been offered. Both bullies and their victims require individual intervention in the later and more serious stages of abusive interactions. Victims, in particular, need to have their welfare needs identified and addressed and the abusive peer also needs to have their psychological and behaviour needs addressed.

In terms of intervention, the application of different initiatives for a range of progressively more abusive behaviours is well supported in the abuse literature and educational behaviour management theory and practice. When behaviours escalate beyond what can reasonably be tolerated by the mainstream of society and education, specific and targeted intervention needs to be considered and applied.

The application of individual interventions to identified candidates for whom evidence exists of deviance from the norms of accepted behaviours, is a standard response in legal, educational and medical practice in our society. Abusive behaviours indicate a deficit in social and psychological development which must be addressed to secure the safety of others and the social inclusion of those who fail to develop these skills independently. The interventions offered for consideration here take account of the needs of the perpetrator of the abuse as well as the wellbeing of the victim.

The intervention approaches described here are based on personal research, innovative practice and specialised individual assistance. This provides a sound foundation as well as a distinctive approach to the main issues. Approaches that are not based in research and practice probably offer less-well supported programs and questionable outcomes.

BULLYWATCH™ INTERVENTIONS

An overview of the BULLYWATCH™ program of Comprehensive intervention including the whole school, classroom and individual programs for recovery from the abusive situation for all parties, is presented in Figure 5 in the appendix. The BULLYWATCH™ Comprehensive and Customised Program of Intervention is an approach to the management of bullying which incorporates the involvement of the family, the school and broader community. This figure demonstrates the place of each component intervention in the overall structure. This approach illustrates how the whole system, whole school, classroom, peer group and individual interventions can all be incorporated in a comprehensive approach. Furthermore, the BULLYWATCH™ program offers a customised and therefore specifically targeted means of dealing with the issue at the most fundamental level for each location.

The BULLYWATCH™ program of Interventions comprises:

- *The **Whole School Comprehensive and Customised Intervention**, which incorporates all other elements of the program and which is presented to school personnel and the wider community. The overall program comprises six components, which are described in more detail further. Initially, components one to four are presented and include the whole school community and personnel in the collection of relevant school data and making research-based decisions regarding policy, restructuring and curricula.*

- **Classroom Curricula** *which inform and educate all students in important aspects of bullying and the responsibilities of each for the safety and protection of themselves and their peers.*

- **Peer Advocacy© Training** *which offers selected or volunteer students the opportunity to develop further advocacy and protection skills to support bullied peers:*

    * *the BULYWATCH GUARDIANS ™ program at the Primary level and*

    * *the BULLYWATCH DEFENDERS ™ program at the secondary level*

- **Individual Intervention** *for bullies and victims of peer abuse which involves:*

    * *the BULLYWATCH™ SELFGUARD program for victims of peer abuse, teaching resiliency and other critical skills at the secondary or primary level and*

    * *the BULLYWATCH™ SELFWATCH program for bullies teaching responsibility, tolerance and other critical skills at the secondary or primary level*

Each of these components is identified in Figure 5 and each contributes specific skills, training, information and intervention to support the overall intention of the BULLYWATCH™ approach which is to comprehensively deal with the most serious educational issue of our time-childhood bullying. Following are descriptions and details of these key components of the approach. Each component has an available manual and/or other materials and resources for application with groups or individuals at home or school to assist with dealing with peer abuse. ()

The school may implement a program such as the BULLYWATCH™ Comprehensive and Customised Intervention which will inform the whole school community and personnel about bullying in general, about the results of data collection regarding reported bullying and the range of interventions possible. While it is hoped that such a committed program of information would deter bullying, it is the thoroughness of the application, sustained commitment and reinforcement of appropriate peer interactions which do most to encourage safety and protection. A continuum of intervention is embedded within the comprehensive program initiated within the school and community to address the serious –and sometimes deadly serious –matter of bullying. The expectation is that there will be a genuine commitment to an anti-bullying ethos which goes beyond a simple policy or values statement to incorporate effective programs and support. Full details of the program interventions and applications are outlined in 'BULLYWATCH: A Program and Resources for Coping with Bullying'

(ALL MATERIALS WILL BE AVAILABLE AT: www.bullywatch.com.au)

ALL MATERIALS AND LOGOS ARE COPYRIGHT AND TRADEMARKED

EPILOGUE

If there still remains any doubt about the deadly seriousness of childhood bullying and the far-reaching devastating effects, the recently reported double suicide attempt in Denver Colorado by Australian twins Kristin and Candice Hermeler should remove it for all time. In a strange and tragic turn of events, many years after the Columbine massacre, the long term destructive force that is peer abuse again claimed the life of a victim and caused the serious injury, by her own hand, to her twin sister. The sisters had felt an affinity with the Columbine murderers because of their similar experiences "as someone who has been rejected, victimised and ostracised in their life". Their attempted double suicide was not fully successful and one sister remains to live on with the memories and hurt resulting from their abusive experiences at the hands of their peers while at high school. Severe childhood bullying is a life or death sentence for many victims. It's time to see it as a major criminal offence and respond accordingly.

---

www.denverpost.com

DENVER, Colorado: Kristin Hermeler, who took her own life in an attempted suicide pact with her twin sister last week, wrote letters to and phoned one of the survivors of the Columbine High School massacre in 1999. Kristin, then 18, wrote to Brooks Brown, a former friend of the killers, in the months after Dylan Klebold and Eric Harris murdered 12 students and a teacher in April 1999 at the high school in Denver's southern suburbs not far from the gun range where the two women shot themselves last week. In the first of two letters, dated June 12, 1999, Kristin said she was writing "as someone who has been rejected, victimised and ostracised in their life" to thank Brown for giving Harris a second chance at friendship, adding in the second letter, a month later, "not a day goes by that I do not think about what happened. I can't imagine how hard it must be for you, dealing with everything."

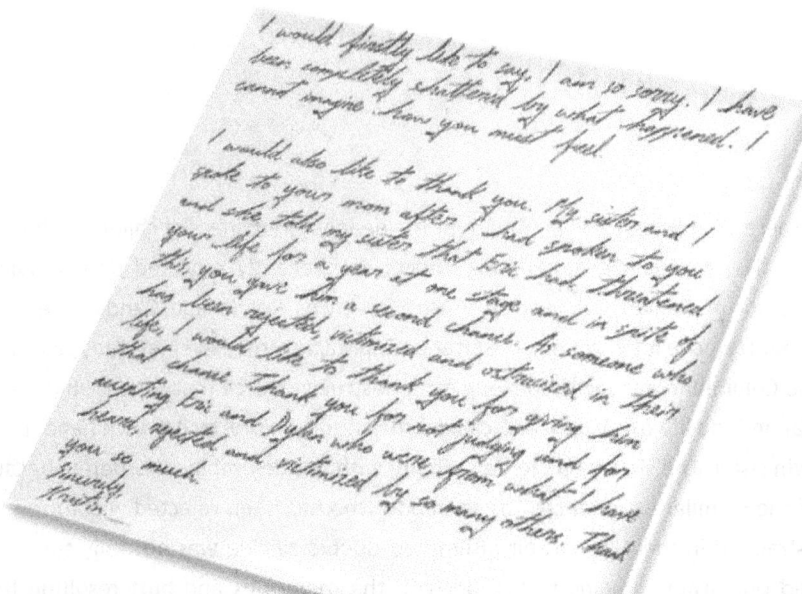

"A sweet letter" ... a part of a letter she wrote to Brooks Brown, a childhood friend of the Columbine killers. Photo: AP

Mr Brown said he had received letters, phone calls and emails from Kristin, who told him she and her sister Candice had been bullied "physically and mentally".

"It was a sweet letter," Mr Brown said. "It was her wanting to know what had happened, trying to understand."

The letters, published by The Denver Post, indicate the twins had a far stronger connection with the city than previously known. The Hermeler twins, the only children of South African-born Ernest and Kelsay, attended secondary school in Bendigo and private schools in Melbourne. They shot themselves at a gun range near Denver last Monday afternoon. Kristin, 29, died at the scene. Candice survived her shooting and remains in a serious condition in a Denver hospital.

Candice was asked about the Columbine connection during her emotional two-hour interview with Araphaoe County Sheriff's office investigators last Thursday. This was after a copy of a

Time magazine cover showing both the killers and victims of the Columbine massacre was found in their luggage. In an early police account, she was said to have responded that she did not care about it and that it happened a long time ago.

The Post report says her actual response was more blunt: "I don't give a f---."

Judy Brown, the mother of Mr Brown, said she recalled long phone conversations with the "sensitive and sympathetic" girls in 1999. Mr Brown, who had been friends from the age of eight with both Klebold and Harris, fell out with the killers in their mid-teens. Harris posted death threats online against Mr Brown.

The threats were known to authorities, but had not been followed up. Mr Brown and Harris had reached a rapprochement of sorts and, after meeting Mr Brown in the school grounds in the minutes before the massacre, Harris warned him that he should go home. Bullying at Columbine, although later discredited, was widely reported as the spark that caused Klebold and Harris to explode. It resonated for Kristin Hermeler, who appeared to recognise a kindred spirit in Mr Brown, and a sounding board in his mother, Judy. "It never goes away," Mrs Brown told the Post. "Bullying changes who you are and who you become."

The release of the letters and the identity of the author are a haunting echo for Denver. Columbine was the worst high school massacre in US history, perpetrated by two suicidal, teenage suburban killers. It was an assault that came out of nowhere and a worldwide media event that touched impressionable and hurting teenagers in unanticipated ways.

"It completely baffles me as to why anyone would hate anyone when they don't know them," Kristin wrote in her second letter to Mr Brown. "It sickens me … The only reason I can think of is, as Charles Spencer said at Princess Diana's funeral, that goodness is threatening to those on the opposite end of the normal spectrum."

The author wishes to extend her sincere sympathy and genuine shock at this tragic episode in the lives of these young women and their family.

The article is included to demonstrate the long-term and devastating impact of the crime of peer abuse, and to ask for Childhood Bullying to now be seen as A Deadly Serious Matter.

Dr. Jean B. Healey, 10/02/11

References

Achenbach, T. M. (1991). *Manual for the child behaviour checklist 4–18 and 1991 profile.* Burlington. VT: University of Vermont, Department of Psychiatry.

Adelaide Advertiser, Adelaide, 03/09/07, page 7, 'Teaching more Difficult'

Ageback, A.K. (1997). *Information and education as weapons.* Paper presented at: Violence, Crime and the Entertainment Media, Australian Institute of Criminology, Canberra, Australia.

Alsaker, F. & Brunner, A. (1999). The nature of bullying in Switzerland. In P. Smith, Y. Morita, J. Junger-Tas, D. Olweus, R. Catalano, & P. Slee, (Eds.), *The nature of school bullying: A cross-national perspective* (pp. 250-263). London: Routledge

Ambert, A.(1995). Towards a Theory of Peer Abuse, *Sociological Studies of Children.* 7, 177-205, JAI Press Inc. London, UK

Anderson, S., &Fraser, S. (2002). Protecting our students (and their teachers too): A Canadian perspective, *Australia and New Zealand Journal of Law and Education,* 7 (2), 55-85

Aspis, S. (1997). Self-advocacy for people with learning difficulties: Does it have a future? *Disability & Society.* 12 (4), Sep 97, 647-657

Arnow, J. (1995). *Teaching peace: How to raise children to live in harmony, without fear, without prejudice, without violence.* Berkeley Publishing Group. N.T.

Artz, S. (1997). *Sex, Power and the Violent School Girl.* TRI Folium Books, Toronto, Canada

Auckland Star Nov 2003 article, by Bramwell, S. & Mussen, D. 'Boy Text Bullied to death'

Australian Commonwealth Government (1994). *Sticks and Stones.* Canberra

Author Unknown, (1994). Videodrome. The Economist, 332 (26), 73

Ballard, M.; & Weist, R. (1995). *Mortal Kombat: The effects of violent video technology on male's hostility and cardiovascular responding.* Paper presented at Society for Research in Child Development, Indianapolis, USA.

Bandura, A. (1973). *Aggression: A Social learning analysis.* Prentice-Hall. Englewood Cliff. NJ.

Banishek, L. A., & Lopez, F. G. (1997). Critical evaluation of hardiness theory: Gender differences, perception of life events, and neuroticism. Work & Stress. vol. 11(1), Jan-Mar 97, (pp. 33-45).

Barnett, D., Manly, J., & Cicchetti, D. (1993). Defining child maltreatment. The Interface between policy & research, In Cicchetti, D., & S. Toth (Eds). *Child abuse, child development and social policy.* 7-73. Norwood, NJ.

Barnett, A., Marsh, H., & Craven, R. (2004). A multi-level analysis of the effects of principal leadership style behaviours on relationship dimensions of school learning environments. Paper presented at SELF Research Centre International Conference and published in conference proceedings Berlin, Germany, July 2004.

Beland, K (1997). Second Step Violence Prevention Program,

Bell, C. C., & Suggs, H. (1998). Using sports to strengthen resiliency in children: Training heart. *Child & Adolescent Psychiatric Clinics of North America, 7* (4), 859–865.

Berk, J. H. (1998). Trauma and resilience during war: A look at the children and humanitarian aid workers of Bosnia. *Psychoanalytic Review, vol 85,* (4) (pp. 639–658).

Besag, V. (1989). *Bullies & victims in schools.* Open University Press, Bucks: UK.

Biggins, B. (1997). *Mitigating risk in film and television: Using parenting to mitigate risks.* Paper presented at: Violence, Crime and the Entertainment Media, Australian Institute of Criminology, Canberra, Australia.

Bjorkvist, K., & Osterman, K. (1999). Finland- the nature of bullying. In Smith, P., Morita, Y., Jungar-Tas, J., Olweus, D., Catalano, R., & Slee, P. (Eds)..*The Nature of School Bullying. A Cross National Perspective,* 56-67, Routledge: London

Bjorkvist,K.,Ekman,K.,& Lagerspetz,K.,(1982) Bullies and victims: Their ego picture, ideal ego picture and normative ego picture. *Scandinavian Journal of Psychology,* 23, 307-313

Blankenship, K. M. (1998). A race, class and gender analysis of thriving. *Journal of Social Issues,* 54, 393-404.

Botha, M., Van Vuuren, D. (1993). *Reactions of black and white children to TV violence in South Africa.* (1987-1991). South African Journal of Psychology 23 (2), 71-80.

Bowen, L., Smith, P. & Binney, V. (1992). Cohesion & power in the families of children involved in bully/victim problems at school. *Journal of Family Therapy, vol 14,* (pp 371–387).

Bowie, V. (1991). *Coping with violence: A guide for the human services.* Sydney : Karabuni Press.

Bradley, R. H., & Whiteside-Mansell, L. (1997). Children in Poverty. In Ammerman, R. T. (Ed), et al. (1997). Hand book of prevention and treatment with children and adolescents: Intervention in the real world context. 13-58. New York, NY, USA: John Wiley & Sons, Inc.

Brinkley, C., Saarnio, D., & Christy, W. (2003). *Involving students in school violence prevention: Are they willing to help?* Paper presented at the meeting of the American Association for Research in Education, Chicago

Buckingham, D. (1997). *Moving Images.* In News on Children and Violence on the Screen Vol.3

Burnage Report (1989). *Murder in the playground.* London: Longsight Press.

Byrne, B. (1993). *Coping with bullying in schools.* Columbia Press, Dublin Eire.

Braithwaite, J & Daly, K, (1995). Masculinities, violence and communitarian control. In D. Chappell & S. Egger, (Eds.), *Australian violence, contemporary perspectives II* 221-252, Canberra: Australian Institute of Criminology

Bryant, Martin. (1996). Port Arthur, Tasmania, massacre April 28th 1996

Reviewed Sydney Morning Herald, April 28th 2009, Paolo Totaro

Cantor, J. (1997). *Children's Fright Responses to Television and Films.* In News on Children and Violence on the Screen Vol. 3.

Catterall, J.S. Risk and resilience in student transitions to high school. *American Journal of Education.* 106(2), Feb 98, 302-333.

Capaldi, D. Patterson, G. (1993). *The Violent Adolescent Male, specialist or generalist.?* Oregon Social Learning Centre, Eugene, paper presented at Society for Research in Child Development. Biennial Meeting, March, 1993.

Carver, C. S., (1998). Resilience and thriving: Issues, models, and linkages. *Journal of Social Issues, 54 (2,)* 245–266

Casdagli, P., Gobey,F., and Griffin, C., (1990) book 'Only Playing Miss', Trentham Books London UK

Cesarone, B. (1994). *Video games and children.* ERIC. Clearinghouse on Elementary and Early Childhood Education. Urbana, Illinios.

Chen, M. (1994). *Practicum report.* N.E. University, Ed.D. Thesis document (unpublished).

Chesney-Lind, M. (2003) Are girls getting meaner? Re-discovering the bad girl. Paper presented at the meeting of the American Association for Research in Education, Chicago, 2003

Chesney-Lind, M. Sheldon, R. Joe, K. (1996). *Girls' delinquency and gang membership*. In Gangs in America, C.R. Huff, Ed. 185-204, Sage Public. CA

Cicchetti, D., & Rogosch, F. A. (1997). The role of self-organization in the promotion of resilience in maltreated children. Development & Psychopathology. 9(4), Fall 97, 797-815.

Care and Protection of Children Act, 2007 (NT)

Children and Young People Act 2008, (ACT)

Children (Care & Protection) Act 1987, NSW. Government Legislative Assembly

Child Protection (Prohibited Employment) Act NSW 1998.

Children and Young Persons (Care and Protection) Act 1998 NSW (2000)

Child Protection Act 1974, Tasmanian Consolidated Acts

Child Protection Act 1999, Queensland Consolidated Acts

Children & Young Persons Act (1989) Victorian Consolidated Acts

Children and Community Services Act 2004, Western Australia

Children's Protection Act 1993, South Australian Consolidated Acts

Coate, J. (2001) *Contemporary Developments in the Law Relating to Children and the Children's Court,* Keynote Address ANZELA Conference, Melbourne Vic.

Cohen, L. H., Cimbolic, K., Armeli, S. R. & Hettler, T. (1998). Quantitative Assessment of Thriving. *Journal of Social Issues,* 54 (2), 323–335.

Columbine Review Commission Report, 2000, Jefferson County, USA

Collins, J., Noble, G., Poynting, S., & Tabar, P., (2001) *Kebabs, Kids, Cops and Crime,* Pluto Press, Annandale, NSW

Commission for Children and Young People While the right to assemble for legitimate, peaceful, non-criminal activity cannot be denied, the problem here is in the purpose and intent of the gang Act NSW, 1998

Cool Schools (1994) *Towards non-violent conflict resolution. Broadsheet Radford Group, In* P. Smith, Y. Morita, J. Junger-Tas, D. Olweus, R. Catalano & P. Slee (Eds.), *The nature of school bullying: A cross-national perspective,* 350. London: Routledge.

Cowan, P. A., Cowan, P. & Schulz, M. S. (1996). Thinking about risk and resilience in families. *Stress, coping and resiliency in children and families. Family research consortium: Advances in family research,* 21–38 Mahwah, NJ, USA: Lawrence Erlbaum Associates, Inc.

Cowen, E., Wyman, P., Work, W., Kim, J., Fagen, D. & Magnus, K. (1997). Follow-up of young stress-affected and stress-resilient urban children. *Development & Psychopathology,* 9 (3) 565–577.

Crimes (Family Violence) Act 1987 Stalking provision, Victorian Consolidated Acts

Csikszentmihalyi, M. (1990). *Flow: The psychology of optimal experience.* New York: Harper & Row.

Cullen, D., (2009), *Columbine.* Twelve Hachette Book Group, New York ,USA

Daily Telegraph, Sydney 03/09/07, page 7 'Girls punched and spat at their teacher'

Daily Telegraph, Sydney 12/04/08, article by Kara Lawrence

Daily Telegraph, Sydney 26/02/09, article by Gemma Jones

Dawkins, J. (1995). Bullying: Another form of abuse. In T. J. David (Ed), *Recent advances in paediatrics,* 103–122. Edinburgh: UK. Livingstone. De Maria, W. (1996) Open spaces, Secret places-Workplace Violence against whistleblowers in McCarthy, et al (Eds) *Bullying from Backyard to Boardroom,* 33-46

De Almeida, M. (1999) The nature of bullying in Portugal. In P. Smith, Y. Morita, J. Junger-Tas, D. Olweus, R. Catalano & P. Slee (Eds.), *The nature of school bullying: A cross-national perspective,* 174- 186. London: Routledge

Dobash, R. E., & Dobash, R. P. (2000). Evaluating Criminal Justice Interventions for Domestic Violence. *Crime & Delinquency,* 46(2), 252-271

Doll, B., & Lyon, M. A. (1998). Risk and resilience: Implications for the delivery of educational and mental health services in school. *School Psychology Review, I 27,* (3), 348–363.

Donald, D., Wallis, J. & Cockburn, A. (1997). An exploration of meanings: Tendencies towards developmental risk and resilience in a group of South African ex-street children. *School Psychology International, 1* (2), 137–154

Dooley, J.J., Cross, D., Hearn, L., Treyvaud, R. (2009) Review of existing Australian and international cyber-safety research. Child Health Promotion Research Centre, Edith Cowan University, Perth

Doueck, H. J., Weston, E. A., Filbert, L., Beekhuis, R., & Redlich, H. F. (1997). A child witness advocacy program: Caretakers' and professionals' views. *Journal of Child Sexual Abuse 6,* 113-132.

Dubow, E. F., Roecker, C. E., & D'Imperio, R. (1997). *Handbook of prevention and treatment with children and adolescents: Intervention in the real world context.* (pp. 259–286). New York, NY, USA: John Wiley & Sons, Inc. xv, (pp. 656).

Dueholm, N., (1999). *The nature of school bullying in Denmark, in* Smith, P., Morita, Y., Junger-Tas, J, Olweus, D., Catalano, R., & Slee, P (Eds.). (1999). *The nature of school bullying: A cross-national perspective.* London: Routledge.

Duncan, R. (1999). Maltreatment by parents & peers: The relationship between child abuse, bully victimisation & psychological distress. *Child Maltreatment,* 4(1), 45–55.

Egger, S. (1995). *Violence and Masculinity a Commentary – in Australian Violence Contemporary Perspective 11.* Chappell, D. Egger, S. Eds.) Australian Institute of Criminology, Canberra ACT.

Elton, D. (1993). Conflict Resolution. Paper Presented to NSW Association of Guidance Counselling of Australia National Conference, Sydney 1993

English, D.J. (1998).The Extent and Consequences of Child Maltreatment, *Future of Children 8(1),* 39-45 Spring

Espelage, D. (2003). Bullying and girl aggression from a social-ecological perspective: Challenging the current methods of inquiry and intervention. Paper presented at the meeting of the American Association for Research in Education, Chicago.

Espelage, D., & Mebane, S. (2003). *Aggression during early adolescence: Does popularity play a role?* Paper presented at the meeting of the American Association for Research in Education, Chicago.

Family Violence Protection Act, Victoria 2008

Fantuzzo, J., Coolahan, K. C. & Weiss, A. D. (1997). Resiliency partnership directed intervention: Enhancing the social competencies of preschool victims of physical abuse by developing peer resources and community strengths. *Developmental perspectives on trauma: Theory, research and intervention. Rochester symposium on development psychology,* 8. 463–489

Fantuzzo, J., Sutton-Smith, B., Atkins, M. & Meyers, R. (1996). Community based resilient peer treatment of withdrawn maltreated preschool children. *Journal of Consulting & Clinical Psychology,* 64 (6).

Finkelhor, D., & Dziuba-Leatherman, J. (1994). Children as victims of violence. *A National Survey, Paediatrics, 94,* 413–420

Finkelhor, D., & Hotaling, G. (1984). Sexual Abuse in the National Incidence Study of Child Abuse & Neglect. *Child Abuse & Neglect.* 8, 23-33.

Finkelhor, D., & Korbin, J. (1998). Child abuse as an international issue: *Child Abuse & Neglect,* 12, 3-23).

Freitas, A.L., & Downey, G. (1998). Resilience: A dynamic perspective. *International Journal of Behavioural Development, 22*(2), 263-285.

Garbarino, J. & Kostelny, K. (1992) Child maltreatment as a community problem. *Child Abuse and Neglect 16,* 455-464

Gardano, A. C. (1998). Risk and resiliency factors among culturally diverse families: Implications for family psychopathology. In L'Abate (Ed.), *Family psychopathology: The relational roots of dysfunctional behaviour 94*–124 New York: Guilford.

Gilligan, R. (2000). Adversity, resilience & young people: The protective value of positive school & spare time experience. *Children & Society, 14,* 37–47

Goldsmith, M. (1997). *Community, consistency or carte blanche, the treatment of media violence.* Paper presented at: Violence, Crime and the Entertainment Media, Australian Institute of Criminology, Canberra, Australia.

Goldstein, A., & Kodluboy,D (1998). *Gangs in schools, Signs, Symbols and Solutions* Research press, Illinois, USA

Gondolf, E. W., & White, R. J. (2000). 'Consumer 'recommendations for batterer programs. *Violence against Women, 6*(2), 198-217.

Griffiths, M. (1997). Computer game playing in early adolescence. *Youth and Society*. 29 (2), 223-237.

Griffiths, M. (1997). Video games and aggression. *Psychologist*, 10 (9), 397-401 September.

Haratchi, T., Catalano, R., & Hawkins, J. (1999). USA- the nature of bullying. In Smith, P., Morita, Y., Jungar-Tas, J., Olweus, D., Catalano, R., & Slee, P. (Eds). *The Nature of School Bullying: A Cross-National Perspective, 279-306,* Routledge: London.

Hart, D., Hofmann, V., Edelstein, W., & Keller, M. (1997). The relation of childhood personality types to adolescent behaviour and development: A longitudinal study of Icelandic children. *Developmental Psychology, 33(2)*, 195–205.

Hart, S., & Brassard, M. (1991). Psychological maltreatment: Progress achieved. *Development & Psychopathology, (3),* 61–70.

Healey, J. (2008) Extrinsic reinforcement as a critical component for motivating students with special needs, in *Motivation and Practice for the Classroom* P. Towndrow, C. Koh, and D. Chan, Sense Publishers, Singapore

Healey, J (2007) Bullying intervention that works in schools, *Principal Matters, Spring,* 2007, 34-38

Healey, J, & Marder, K., (2006a). Reflections on racially-based youth riots in Cronulla, Southern Sydney-is there evidence of racial bullying in Southern Sydney high schools?- refereed publication in Self-Concept Enhancement and Learning Facilitation (SELF) Research Centre Fourth International Conference Proceedings, Ann Arbor, University of Michigan, July 2006

Healey, J., & Marder, K., (2006b). Opening Doors: pre-service teacher professional self-concept in relation to the inclusion of disabled students in mainstream classrooms, refereed publication in Self-Concept Enhancement and Learning Facilitation (SELF) Research Centre Fourth International Conference, Proceedings, Ann Arbor, University of Michigan, July 2006

Healey, J. (2006c). Peer abuse as child abuse and indications for intervention. Refereed paper, AARE Conference Parramatta, 2005 published in conference proceedings, 2006

Healey, J., & Dowson, M (2006d). Adolescents' experiences, perceptions and attitudes towards bullying. Refereed paper, AARE Conference Parramatta, 2005 published in conference proceedings, 2006

Healey, J. (2006e). Peer abuse as a legislated child protection issue for schools. *Australia & New Zealand Journal of Law & Education,* 10 (1), 59-71

Healey, J. (2004a). Peer Advocacy©: A functional response to peer abuse: Structure and Processes. In Marsh, H & Craven, R, (Eds), Collected Papers of the Third Self-Concept Enhancement and Learning Facilitation (SELF) Research Centre International Conference, Berlin, Germany, July 4-7, 2004.

Healey, J. (2004b). A theoretical construct for Peer Advocacy© as a functional response to bullying: Empirical basis. In Marsh, H & Craven, R, (Eds) Collected Papers of the Third Self-Concept Enhancement and Learning Facilitation (SELF) Research Centre International Conference, Berlin, Germany, July 4-7, 2004

Healey, J. (2004c). A theoretical construct for Peer Advocacy© as a functional response to bullying: Contributory theories. In Marsh, H & Craven, R, (Eds) Collected Papers of the Third Self-Concept Enhancement and Learning Facilitation (SELF) Research Centre International Conference, Berlin, Germany, July 4-7, 2004.

Healey, J. B. (2003a). The Macarthur Model for Comprehensive Intervention in Bullying in Schools: A methodology for a customised response. Paper presented at the Joint New Zealand Association for Research in Education and Australian Association for Research in Education conference, Auckland, December,

Healey, J. (2003b). *Bullying in your school: A manual for comprehensive and customised intervention.* In-service manual of Macarthur Model for addressing bullying in schools. In Doctoral Thesis, University of Western Sydney 2003 and published in conference proceedings

Healey, J. (2002a). Resiliency as a critical factor in resisting bullying. Refereed paper presented at 2nd SELF Research Centre Biennial International Conference, Sydney 2002 and published in conference proceedings

Healey, J. (2002b). *Bullying and resiliency: A model for individual intervention.* Paper presented at Protective Behaviours Conference, Australian Catholic University, Sydney, 2002

Healey, J. (2002c). *Cultural differences in girls' resilience to bullying in NSW schools.* Paper presented at British Education Research Association Conference, Exeter

Healey, J. (2000). *Bullying and resiliency: A model for individual intervention.* Paper presented at Protective Behaviours Conference, Australian Catholic University

Healey, J. (1999). *Understanding and managing challenging behaviours for youth in detention.* Training modules: Remedial behaviour management staff training program. Developed and implemented for Reiby Detention Centre Robinson Education Unit for Violent Offenders for the NSW Department of Juvenile Justice

Healey, J. (1996). *Resolving Violence – an Anti-Violence Curriculum for Secondary Schools.* Published ACER, Melbourne, Vic

Heatherton, J. & Beardsall, L. (1998). Decisions and attitudes concerning child sexual abuse-does the gender of the perpetrator make a difference to child protection professionals? *Child Abuse and Neglect, 22(12),* 1265-1283

Hodges, E., & Perry, D. (1996). Victims of Peer Abuse: An Overview *Reclaiming Children & Youth,* Spring**, 23-28**

Huesmann, R. Bachrach, R. (1986). *Differential effects of television on Kibbutz and city children.* Paper presented at the International Television Studies Conference, UK, July, 1986.

Jefferson County Sheriff's Report, 2000

Jenkin, J. (1996). Resolving Violence and Anti-violence Curriculum for Secondary Students. Australian Council for Educational Research, Melbourne. Victoria

Jenkin, J. (now Healey) (1994). A Comprehensive Approach to Intervention in Bullying, paper presented at 1st Bullying Perspectives Conference, Queensland University.

Jenkin, J. (1999). *Bullying of Asian students*. Paper presented at Australia and New Zealand Institute of Criminology Conference, Brisbane, Queensland, July, 1999.

Jew, C. (1998). Effects of Risk Factors on adolecents' resiliency and coping. *School Psychology International, 9,* 189–195.

Kampulainen, K., Rasanen, E., Hentonen, I., Almqvist, F., Kresanov, K., Linna, S., Moilanen, I., Piha, J., Puura, K., & Tamminen, T. (1998). Bullying & psychiatric symptoms among elementary school age children. *Child Abuse & Neglect, 22,* (7), 705–717.

Kass, J.,(2009),*Columbine: A True Crime Story,* Ghost Road Press, Denver, Colorado, USA

Katz, J. (1985). *Seductions of Crime: moral and sensual attractions of doing evil.* Basic Books, New York.

Kent, A., & Waller, G. (1998). Methodological issues in assessing resilience in maltreated children. *Child Abuse & Neglect, 22* (7), 669–680.

Kent, A., & Waller, G. (1998). The impact of childhood emotional abuse: An extension of the child abuse & trauma scale. *Child Abuse & Neglect, 22,* 393-399.

Kinard, E. M., (1998). Depressive symptoms in maltreated children from mother, teacher and child perspectives, Violence & *Victims. 13(2),* 131-147.

Klarreich, S. (Ed), (1998). Handbook of organizational health psychology: Programs to make the workplace healthier. (pp. 219-238). Madison, CT, USA: Psychosocial Press/International Universities Press, Inc. xvii, 296 pp.

Krcmar, M. & Cantor, M. (1997). The role of television advisories and ratings in parent child discussions of TV viewing choices, *Journal of Broadcasting and Electronic Media,* 41 (3), 393-411.

Laing, L. (2002). Responding to men who perpetrate domestic violence: Controversies, interventions and challenges, Australian *Domestic & Family Violence Clearinghouse* Issues Paper 7 2002, 1-31

Lefkowitz, M. Eron, L. Walder, L, & Huesmann, L. (1977). *Growing up to be violent – a longitudinal study of the development of aggression.* Permagon Press. New York.

Lennane, J. (1996). Bullying in Medico- legal Examinations in McCarthy et al (Eds) *Bullying from backyard to Boardroom* Millenium books, Sydney pp 97-118

Levine, M. (1995). *Viewing Violence: How media violence affects your child's and adolescent's development.* Doubleday and Co. New York

Lipchik, E., Sirles, E. A., & Kubicki, A. D. (1997). Multifaceted approach in spouse abuse treatment. In R. Geffner & S. B. Sorenson & P. K. Lunberg-Love (Eds.), *Violence and Sexual Abuse at home: Current issues in Spousal Battering and Child Maltreatment* (pp. 131-148). USA: The Haworth Press Inc.

Litzelfelner, P., & Petr, C. G. (1997). Case advocacy in child welfare, *Social Work.* 42(4), July 97, 392-402.

Long, J., Fabricius, W., Musheno, M., & Palumbo, D. (1998). Exploring the cognitive and affective capacities of child mediators in a "successful" inner-city peer mediation program, Mediation *Quarterly, 15*(4), 289-302.

Lord of the Flies', (1963, 1990) Metro-Goldwyn-Meyer, film of the William Golding novel of the same name

Luthar, S. S. (1997). Socio-demographic disadvantage and psychosocial adjustment: Perspectives from developmental psychopathology. *Developmental Psychopathology: Perspectives on adjustment, risk and disorder.* 459–485. New York, N.Y. USA: Cambridge University Press xxi, 618.

McCarthy, P., Sheehan, M., & Wilkie, W (Eds.) (1996). *Bullying from backyard to boardroom*. Millennium Books, Sydney

McCubbin, H. I., Thompson, E. A., Thompson, A. I., & Fromer, J. E. (1998). Stress, coping and health in families: Sense of coherence and resiliency. *Resiliency in Families Series,* Thousand Oaks, CA, USA: Sage Publications, Inc. xviii, 1, 313

McLean, D. (1971) in Lyrics to 'Vincent", producer Ed Freeman.

Mann, R. (1996). Psychological Abuse in the workplace, in McCarthy et al (Eds) *Bullying from backyard to boardroom,* Millennium books, Sydney, 83-92

Marsh, H., Parada, R., Yeung, A & Healey, J. (2001). Aggressive school troublemakers and victims: A longitudinal model examining the pivotal role of self-concept. *Journal of Educational Psychology, 93*(2), 411-419.

Martin, P. (1996). Restorative justice: a family violence perspective. *Social Policy Journal of New Zealand, 6,* 56-68. *Psychology, 93*(2), 411-419.

Masten, A., Best, K., & Garmezy, N. (1990). Resilience & development: Contributions from the study of children who overcame adversity. *Development & Psychopathology, 2,* 425–444.

Matsui, T., Kakuyama, T., Tsuzuki, Y., & Onglatco, M. (1996). Long term outcomes of early victimisations by peers among Japanese male university students: Model of a vicious cycle. *Psychological Reports, 79,* 711–720.

Matsui, T., Kakuyama, T., Tsuzuki, Y., & Onglatco, M. (1996). Long-term outcomes of early victimisations by peers among Japanese male university students: Model of a vicious cycle. *Psychological Reports, 79,* 711–720.

Matthews, T. (1994). Why censorship isn't child's play. *New Statesman and Society.* 7 (297) 33 April.

Molitor, F. Hirsch, K. (1994). Children's toleration of real life aggression after exposure to media violence: A replication of the Bradman and Thomas Studies. *Child Study Journal,* 24 (3), 191-207.

Monaghan-Blout, S. (1996). Re-examining assumptions about trauma and resilience: Implications for intervention. *Psychotherapy in Private Practice, 15, (4),* 45–68.

Morita, Y., Harud, S., Haruo, K., & Taki, M. (1999). Japan- the nature of bullying. In Smith, P., Morita, Y., Jungar-Tas, J., Olweus, D., Catalano, R., & Slee, P. (Eds). *The Nature of School Bullying. A Cross- National Perspective, 309-323,* Routledge: London.

Morrison, G. M., Robertson, L., & Harding, M. (1998). Resilience factors that support the classroom functioning of acting out and aggressive students. *Psychology in the Schools, 3* (3), 217–227.

Munro, E. (1998). Changing the Response of Professionals to Child Abuse. *British Journal of General Practice 48 (434),* 1609-161

Munthe, E (1989). Bullying in Scandinavia in *Bullying. An International Perspective.* Roland, E., & Munthe, E. (Eds). Fulton Publishers: UK.

Myers, -Briggs; McCaulley H.; Quenk, L.; & Hammer, L. (1998). *MBTI Manual (A guide to the development and use of the Myers Briggs type indicator).* Consulting Psychologists Press; 3rd edition. ISBN 0-89106-130-4.

Neary, A., & Joseph, S. (1994). Peer victimisation and its relationship to self-concept and depression among schoolgirls. *Personality & Individual Differences 16,* 183-186.

New South Wales Government Inquiry into Youth Violence. (1995). A report into youth violence in New South Wales. Sydney: Government Printing Office, NSW

O'Moore, M(2000) Critical Issues for Teacher Training to Counter bullying & Victimisation in Ireland, *Aggressive Behaviour 26,(1),*99-111

O'Toole, J., Burton, B., & Plunkett, A (2005) *Cooling Conflict. A new approach to managing bullying and conflict in schools,* Pearson-Longman, NSW Australia.

O'Toole, R., Webster, S., O'Toole, A., & Lucal, B. (1999). Teachers' recognition & reporting of child abuse: A factorial survey. *Child Abuse and Neglect,* 23, (11), 1083-1101

Oakes, H. (1995). Media violence and young people, *State of the Art.* 7(3), 15-19. Spring.

Olweus, D, (1993). *Bullying at school.* Blackwell Publishers Ltd, Oxford, UK.

Olweus, D. (1999). Sweden–the nature of bullying. In Smith, P., Morita, Y., Jungar-Tas, J., Olweus, D., Catalano, R., & Slee, P. (Eds)... *The Nature of School Bullying: A Cross National Perspective, 7-27,* Routledge: London.

Park, C. (1998).Stress related growth and thriving through coping: the roles of personality and cognitive processes. *Journal of Social Issues,* 54 (2) 267-277

Parr, G. D., Montgomery, M., & DeBell, C. (1998). Flow theory as a model for enhancing student resilience. *Professional School Counselling, 1*(5), 26–31

Paull, J. E. (1998). Case advocacy in child welfare. *Social Work, 43*(2), 190-191.

Pepler, D., Craig, W., Zeigler, S & Carach, A (1993). An evaluation of an anti-Bullying intervention in Toronto schools, *Canadian Journal of Community Mental Health, 13,* 95-110

Petrie, I. (1994). Looking at evil: the Liverpool child murder. *Journal of Emotional and Behavioural Problems.* 3 (1), 20-24. Spring.

Pianta, R. C. & Walsh, D. J. (1998). Applying the construct of resilience in schools: Cautions from a developmental systems perspective. *School Psychology Review,* 27, (3), 407–417.

Pikas, A. (1989). Common concern method for the treatment of mobbing. In Munthe & Roland (Eds.), *Bullying: An International Perspective.* London, David Fulton (pp. 91–104).

Polk, K. (1995). *Youth violence: Myth and reality* in Australian Violence, Contemporary Issues, 11. (Chappell. D. Egger, S. Eds.) Australian Institute of Criminology, Canberra. ACT.

Portwood, S. (1999). Coming to Terms with a consensual definition of child maltreatment, *Child Maltreatment,* Feb.1999, Thousand Oaks, USA

Prewitt. (1988). Dealing with Ijime (Bullying) of Japanese students. *Psychological Reports,* 82(2) April 1998 675-678

Prothrow-Stith, D. (1987). *Violence Prevention Curriculum for Adolescents, Teenage Health, Teaching Modules.* Educational Development Centre, Mass. USA.

Quine, L. (1999). Workplace bullying in NHS Community Trust: Staff questionnaire survey. *British Medical Journal, 23,* 228.

Ramsden, N. (1997). What makes you unhappy when you watch television? A survey carried out in South Africa. In *News on Children and Violence on the Screen,* Vol. 3.

Rigby,K (1996). *Bullying in Schools and what to do about it,* Australian Council for Educational Research, Melbourne,

Rigby, K. (1994). School bullies. *Independent Teacher, 10, (2)* 8–9

Rigby, K. (2003). A meta-evaluation of methods and approaches to reducing bullying in pre-schools and early primary school in Australia. Canberra: Crime Prevention Branch, Commonwealth Attorney General's Department.

Rigby, K., & Slee, P.(1993 a). Dimensions of interpersonal relating among Australian school children & their implications for psychological well-being. *Journal of Social Psychology, 133,* (1), 33–42.

Rigby, K., & Slee, P. (1993 b). Children's attitudes towards victims. In Tattum D. P. (Ed). *Understanding and Managing Bullying.* London: Heineman Books

Rigby, K., & Slee, P. (1993 c). Dimensions of interpersonal relating among Australian school children and their implications for psychological well being. *Journal of Social Psychology 133(*1) 93,33-42

Roberts, G. (1998) *Domestic Violence Victims in Emergency Departments* in Australian Violence, Contemporary Perspectives 11. (Chappell. D. Egger, S. Eds.) Australian Institute of Criminology, Canberra. ACT.

Robinson, G. & Maines, B. (1997) *Crying for help: The no blame approach to bullying.* Bristol: Lucky Duck Publishing.

Roscoe, B, (1990). Defining Child Maltreatment: Rating Parental Behaviours *Adolescence,*99, 517

Rouse, K. A. G., Ingersoll, G. M., & Orr, D. P. (1998). Longitudinal health endangering behaviour risk among resilient and non-resilient early adolescents. *Journal of Adolescent Health, 23, (5)* 297–302.

Royal Commission into NSW Police Service, the Paedophile Inquiry, Final Report (1997) iv,v,vi

Rutter, M. (1993). Resilience: Some conceptual considerations. *Journal of Adolescent Health 14,* 626-631).

Sydney Morning Herald High-school bullying drove teen to suicide, by SAFFRON HOWDEN

Sydney Morning Herald, article by Alex Mc Donald

Schene, P (1998). Past, Present and Future Roles of Child Protection Services, *Future of Children* 8,(1), 23-38 1998 Spring

Schramm, W. (1995). *Motion pictures and real-life violence – what the research says.* Motion Picture Association of America. New York.

Sheerin, D.(1998). Legal options in Ireland for getting adolescent sex offenders into treatment programs and keeping them there, *Irish Journal of Psychology* 19(1),181-189,

Shore, M. F.(1998). Beyond self-interest: Professional advocacy and the integration of theory, research, and practice. *American Psychologist* 53(4), Apr 98, 474-479.

Shulman, E. (1998). Franz Kafka's resistance to acting on suicidal ideation *Omega - Journal of Death & Dying.* 37(1), 98, 15-39

Slee, P. (1995). Peer Victimisation and its relationship to Depression among Australian primary school students. *Personality & Individual Differences, 18,* 57-62.

Slee, P.T. (1993). *Child, Adolescent and Family Development.* Sydney, Harcourt, Brace Janovich

Slee, P.T. (1996). The P.E.A.C.E. Pack: A program for reducing bullying in schools, *Australian Journal for Guidance and Counselling, 6,*63-69

Smith, P.(1999). The nature of Bullying in England and Wales, in Smith, P., Morita, Y., Junger-Tas, J, Olweus, D., Catalano, R., & Slee, P (Eds) (1999) *The Nature of School Bullying: a cross-national perspective.*, Rouledge, London UK,

Smith, P. K. (1994). What we can do to prevent bullying in school. *The Therapist,* Summer 12-15

Smith,P., Morita, Y., Junger-Tas, J, Olweus, D., Catalano, R., & Slee, P (Eds.). (1999). *The nature of school bullying: A cross-national perspective.* London: Routledge.

Smith, P. & Barajas, L (1988). How competent child care workers respond to assaultive incidents, *Journal of Child Care, 3,(4) 29-35*

Smith, P. & Madsen,M. (1997) A Follow-up survey of the DFE Anti-Bullying pack in schools: Its use and the development of anti-bullying work in schools. London, DFE

Sonesson, I. (1998). Television and Children's Fear – A Swedish Perspective. *News on Children and Violence on the Screen.* Vol.2 (1).

Spaccarelli, S., & Kim, S. (1995). Resilience criteria & factors associated with resilience in sexually abused girls. *Child Abuse & Neglect, 19,* 1171–1182.

Spatz-Widom, C. (1995). The cycle of violence. In Chappell & Egger (Eds), *Australian Violence Contemporary Perspectives 2,* Australian Institute of Criminology. Canberra: Australia, 253-270.

Stalking Intervention Orders Act, Victoria 2008.

Stein, N. (2003). Bullying research, zero tolerance and the missing discourse of rights. Paper presented at the meeting of the American Association for Research in Education, Chicago.

Strang, M. (1995). Child abuse homicides in Australia: Incidence, circumstance, prevention & control. In Chappell & Egger (Eds), *Australian Violence Contemporary Perspectives 2,* Australian Institute of Criminology. Canberra: Australia.71-86

Strang,M. (1992). *Homicides in Australia (1990-91--* Australian Institute of Criminology), Canberra. ACT.

Strasburger, V. & Comstock, G. (Eds). (1993). Adolescence and the media. *Adolescent Medicine, State of the Art Reviews.* 4, October

Stroeve, W. (1998). One of the kids – A guide for parents. Sydney: Disability Council of NSW.

Stubbs, J. (1997). Shame, Defiance and Violence Against Women: A critical analysis of 'Communitarian Conferencing'. In C. S. Cook & J. Bessant (Eds.), *Women's Encounters with Violence: Australian Experiences,* 109-126, London: Sage Publications.

Sullivan, K. (1998). 'The David and Goliath routine can backfire-tread carefully': A focus group evaluation of the Kia Kaha anti-bullying kit, *New Zealand Annual Review of Education, 7*

Sullivan, K, (1999). The nature of bullying in Aotearoa/ New Zealand. in Smith, P., Morita, Y., Junger-Tas, J, Olweus, D., Catalano, R., & Slee, P (Eds) (1999) *The Nature of School Bullying: a cross-national perspective.* Rouledge, London UK,

Sulzer-Azaroff, B., & Mayer, G. R. (1977). *Applying Behaviour Analysis Procedures with Children and Youth.* Winston, NY: Holt Rinehart.

Swain, P. (1998). What is "Belief on reasonable grounds?' mandatory reporting of child abuse, *Victoria Alternative Law Journal.* 23, (5)

Swihart, E. W. Jr., & Cotter, P. D. (1997). The manipulative child: How to regain control and raise resilient, resourceful, and independent kids. New York, NY, USA: Macmillan Publishing Co, Inc. xiii, 209

Sydney Morning Herald Article 'Bullied almost to death' by Alex McDonald

Sydney Morning Herald, Article 'High-school bullying drove teen to suicide', by Saffron Howden

Tattum, D. (Ed). (1993). *Understanding & managing bullying.* Heineman, London. *Journal of Public Health,* 84 (4), 628-633.

The Courier-Mail, 02/08/08 article, Violent youth gangs take control of streets, by Tuck Thompson and Greg Stolz

The Sunday Age, April 18, 2004, 'The truth behind youth battles' article by John Elder and Anna Krien

The Sunday Telegraph, Crossbow tragedy haunts students. April 6, 2003,

Tiet, Q. Q., Bird, H. R., Davies, M., Hoven, C., Cohen, P., Jensen, P. S., & Goodman, S. (1998). Adverse life events and resilience. *Journal of the American Academy of Child & Adolescent Psychiatry, 37* (11) 1191–1200

Tomison, A., & Wise, S. (1999). Community based approaches in issues in child abuse prevention. *National Child Protection Clearing House. 11* (99)

Valkenburg, P. (1998). *News on Children and Violence on the Screen.* 2 (1).

Van Der Voort, R. Beentjes, J. (1997). *Effects of extremely violent audiovisual production on young people's aggressive behaviour and emotional reactions.* in New Horizons in Media Psychology. PW Spurk; TVD Voort (Eds.).

Waldfogel, J. (1998) Rethinking the Paradigm for Child Protection, *Future of Children 8(1),* 104-119

Ward. J., & Page-Hanify, Y. (1986). Citizen advocacy in Australia. *Australian Disability Review, 1,* 19-28.

Watkins, T. R., & Callicutt, J. W. (1997). Self-help and advocacy groups in mental health. Watkins, T. R. (Ed), Callicutt, J. W. (Ed), et al. (1997). *Mental health policy and practice today.* (146-162). Thousand Oaks, CA, USA: Sage Publications, Inc. xvii, 397 pp.

Watts, V; & Laskey, L (1994). Preparing teachers for effective child protection: a pre-service curriculum approach, South *Pacific Journal of Teacher Education, 22* (2), 117-127

Werribee Banner, 'Death highlights trauma of cyber bullying', BY MARGARET BURINO 4 Mar, 2009

White, G. W., Thomson, R. J., & Nary, D. E. (1997). An empirical analysis of the effects of a self-administered advocacy letter training program. Rehabilitation Counselling Bulletin. 41(2), Dec 97, 74-87

White, R. (2002). Understanding Youth Gangs, *Trends and Issues in Crime and Criminal Justice*, no. 237, Australian Institute of Criminology, Canberra.

White, R. (2004). Police and community responses to youth gangs, *Trends & Issues in Crime and Criminal Justice* no. 274, 261-280 Canberra: Australian Institute of Criminology,

Wills, T. A., Blechman, and E. A, & McNamara, G. (1996). Family support, coping, and competence. Stress, coping and resiliency in children and families. *Family research consortium: Advances in family research.* 189–228 Mahwah, NJ, USA: Lawrence Erlbaum Associates,

Wilson, B.J., & Gottman, J. M. (1996). Attention: The shuttle between emotion and cognition: Risk, resiliency and physiological bases. *Stress, coping and resiliency in children and families. Family research consortium: Advances in family research.* 189–228). Mahwah, NJ, USA: Lawrence Erlbaum Associates, Inc

Wood, J (1997). Report on Royal Commission into NSW Police Service, the Paedophile Inquiry, Final Report Vols. iv, v and vi. Sydney, Australia: NSW Government publications

World Health Organisation. (2002). *World report on violence and health: summary,* Geneva:

Young, S. and Young, K. (1997). Young player's perceptions and experiences of computer game playing. Paper presented at: Violence, Crime and the Entertainment Media, Australian Institute of Criminology, Canberra, Australia.

Zirpoli, T., & Melloy, K. (2001). *Behaviour management applications for teachers.* New York: Prentice-Hall

Appendix 1

TABLE 1: LOW OR VERY LOW GUN OWNERSHIP AND RATE OF GUN HOMICIDES PER 100,000 POPULATION

COUNTRY	NIL	VERY LOW 0–25	LOW 26–50	HIGH 51–100	VERY HIGH 101–411
ARGENTINA		ownership			
		homicides			
BELARUS		ownership			
		homicides			
HUNGARY		ownership			
		homicides			
JAPAN		ownership			
		homicides			
MALAYSIA		ownership			
		homicides			
POLAND		ownership			
		homicides			
ROMANIA		ownership			
		homicides			
SINGAPORE		ownership			
		homicides			
SLOVAKIA		ownership			
		homicides			
TANZANIA		ownership			
		homicides			
UNITED KINGDOM		ownership			
		homicides			
BRAZIL		ownership			very high
		homicides			
JAMAICA		ownership			very high
		homicides			
PHILIPPINES		ownership		high	
		homicides			

Appendix 2

TABLE 2: HIGH OR VERY HIGH GUN OWNERSHIP AND RATE OF GUN HOMICIDES PER 100,000 POPULATION

COUNTRY	NIL	VERY LOW 0–25	LOW 26–50	HIGH 51–100	VERY HIGH 101–411
AUSTRALIA		ownership			
		homicides			
AUSTRIA		ownership	ownership		
		homicides			
CANADA		ownership	ownership		
		homicides			
FINLAND		ownership	ownership		
		homicides			
GERMANY		ownership	ownership		
		homicides			
NEW ZEALAND		ownership	ownership		
		homicides			
SPAIN		ownership	ownership		
		homicides			
SWEDEN		ownership	ownership		
		homicides			
SOUTH AFRICA		ownership	ownership	ownership	
		homicides	homicides	homicides	homicides
UNITED STATES		ownership	ownership	ownership	
		homicides	homicides	homicides	homicides

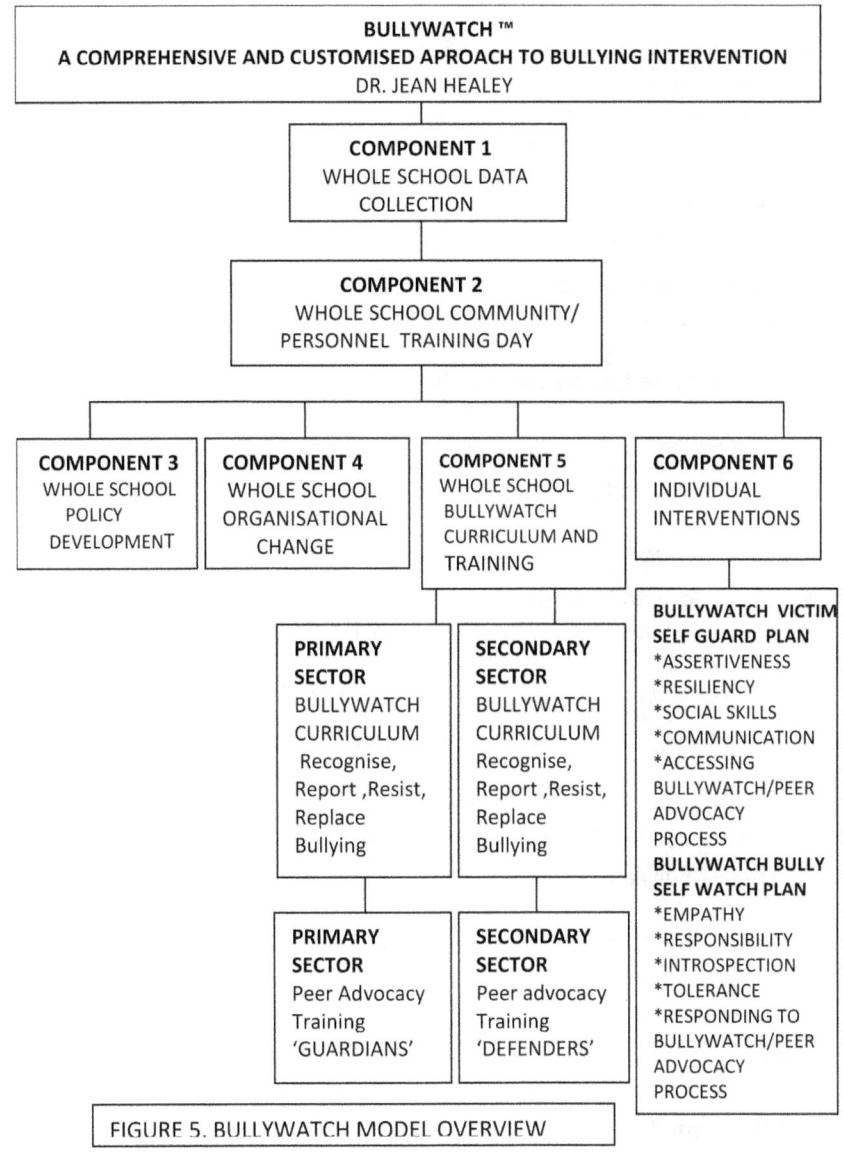

FIGURE 5. BULLYWATCH MODEL OVERVIEW

Permissions

The following journalists, individuals and organisations are gratefully acknowledged for giving permission for inclusions in the book. Their work has made a valuable contribution to this discussion of contemporary issues, and to maintaining vigilance in relation to childhood bullying.

1. Newspix / Newslimited, Peter Montague, *The Daily Telegraph* and these journalists for articles:
   - Bruce McDougall (page 21) 'Teen dies in fight club'
   - Gemma Jones (page 139-140), 'Hollywood the villain of Aussie school violence'
   - Kara Lawrence (page 3), Merrylands High School

2. *The Sunday Age* and John Elder for an article by John Elder and Anna Krien
   - 'The truth behind youth battles' Sunday Age 18/04/04 (page 4)

3. *The Sydney Morning Herald* and journalists for the articles :
   - Saffron Howden (page 6) 'High school bullying drove teen to suicide'
   - Alex McDonald (page 58) 'Bullying almost to Death'

4. *The Werribee Banner/Fairfax Ltd.* for an article by Margaret Burin (page 7)
   - 'Death highlights trauma of cyber-bullying'

5. *Sunday Star Times* /Auckland, New Zealand, Michael Donaldson, Editor, for an article by Susan Bramwell and Deidre Mussen November 2003, (page 8)
   - 'Boy text bullied to death'

6. *National Times* for an article by Stephanie Peatling 9/05/10 (page 96)
   - 'New bullying laws'

7. *The Courier-Mail,* for an article by Tuck Thompson and Greg Stolz 02/04/08 (page 80)
   - 'Violent youth gangs take control of streets'

8. Further acknowledgement is made for articles from the following web site: http://news.bbc.co.uk/2/hi/8361968.stm
    - *Inside Out* reporter Des Coleman for 'Scary Guy"(page 185)
    - 'Bebo bully victim in suicide bid' (page 165)
    - 'Girl bullies guilty of fall death' (page 108)

10. I have been unable to locate the original photographer of the photo shown on page 56, but have acknowledged the source. I would be pleased to hear from anyone who can identify the photographer in order that they can be acknowledged here. Their copyright is acknowledged here.

11. Acknowledgement and thanks are also due to Ms. Melea Lang for kind permission for her daughter Isabella Harvey to model for the front cover photo and several other photos included in the book. The work of Isabella was exceptional and her professional and personal demeanour much valued during the photo shoot.

12. The author is grateful to Sandra and Victoria for permission to include their story in the foreword of this book. Their courage and dignity is acknowledged with thanks.

www.ingramcontent.com/pod-product-compliance
Lightning Source LLC
Chambersburg PA
CBHW060339170426
43202CB00014B/2824